Rewired

DISTINGUISHED DISSERTATIONS IN CHRISTIAN THEOLOGY

Other titles in the series:

The Theology of the Cross in Historical Perspective
by Anna M. Madsen

Series Foreword

We are living in a vibrant season for academic Christian theology. After a hiatus of some decades, a real flowering of excellent systematic and moral theology has emerged. This situation calls for a series that showcases the contributions of newcomers to this ongoing and lively conversation. The journal *Word & World: Theology for Christian Ministry* and the academic society Christian Theological Research Fellowship (CTRF) are happy to cosponsor this series together with our publisher Pickwick Publications (an imprint of Wipf and Stock Publishers). Both the CTRF and *Word & World* are interested in excellence in academics but also in scholarship oriented toward Christ and the Church. The volumes in this series are distinguished for their combination of academic excellence with sensitivity to the primary context of Christian learning. We are happy to present the work of these young scholars to the wider world and are grateful to Luther Seminary for the support that helped make it possible.

Alan G. Padgett
Professor of Systematic Theology
Luther Seminary

Beth Felker Jones
Assistant Professor of Bible and Religion
Huntington University

www.ctrf.info
www.luthersem.edu/word&world

Rewired

Exploring Religious Conversion

Paul N. Markham

Pickwick *Publications*

An imprint of *Wipf and Stock Publishers*
199 West 8th Avenue • Eugene OR 97401

REWIRED
Exploring Religious Conversion

ISBN: 978-1-55635-294-2

Cataloging-in-Publication data:

Markham, Paul N.

Rewired : exploring religious conversion / Paul N. Markham.

Distinguished Dissertations in Christian Theology 2

xii + 244 p. ; 23 cm.

Includes bibliography

ISBN: 978-1-55635-294-2

1. Conversion—Christianity. 2. Wesley, John, 1703–1791—Contributions in doctrine of conversion. I. Title. II. Series.

BV 4916 .M37 2007

Contents

Foreword

IN 1891 THEOLOGIAN AUBREY Moore wrote that "Darwinism appeared, and, under the guise of a foe, did the work of a friend." Today many see neuroscience as a foe. Columnist David Brooks, writing about the mass killings at Virginia Tech, laments that the scientific study of human behavior, especially by neuroscientists, has "had the effect of reducing the scope of the human self. . . . [W]e are renegotiating what you might call the Morality Line, the spot where background forces stop and individual choice—and individual responsibility—begins."[1]

Paul Markham's study, promoting an account of religious conversion and moral responsibility entirely consistent with contemporary neuroscience, could not come at a better time. I was made aware of the importance of addressing the topic of human nature in the church by my Fuller Seminary colleague, neuropsychologist Warren Brown. Brown pointed out that while scientists in a number of disciplines assume a physicalist account of the person (we are physical organisms whose exceedingly complex neural systems, along with cultural development, give us our distinctive human capabilities), Christians tend to be dualists (we are composed of a physical body and a non-material, immortal soul). Since then I have lectured extensively on the acceptability and value of a physicalist Christian anthropology. As I've done so I've taken the opportunity to poll my audiences. I have found to my surprise that trichotomism (we are body, soul, and spirit) is at least as common a view as dualism, and these two theories together account for the views of most Christians. In an audience of 2,000 in Portland, Oregon, I discovered only one physicalist!

The message that contemporary Christians need to hear is that biblical scholars and church historians, over a century ago, began to question whether dualism is a biblical teaching. Rabbi Neil Gillman well represents current scholarly views of the Hebrew Scriptures: "Biblical anthropology knows nothing of this dualistic picture of the human person which claims that the human person is a composite of two entities, a material body and a spiritual or non-material soul. . . . The Bible . . . portrays each human as

---

1. David Brooks, "The Morality Line," *The New York Times*, April 19, 2007.

a single entity, clothed in clay-like flesh which is animated or vivified by a life-giving spark or impulse. . . ."

There has been controversy over New Testament teachings, but it is now only a minority of scholars who find a dualist anthropology in the texts. The best explanation for the continuing controversy comes from New Testament scholar James Dunn, who argues that the New Testament authors were not interested in the question of trichotomism, dualism, or physicalism. This being the case, they were able to use a variety of culturally available concepts of human nature to make points about the topics that they did take to be essential: primarily human relationships--to the community and, especially, to God. Body-soul dualism, then, came to be taught only later as Christianity adapted to and adopted Greek and Roman philosophy.

It is unfortunate that this (near) consensus among scholars has not been conveyed to the church at large. It leaves Christians unprepared to engage in conversation with the scientific world, and in particular unable to respond to authors such as Francis Crick, who claims in his book *The Astonishing Hypothesis: The Scientific Search for the Soul,* that to show that there is no soul is to contract religious belief.

Not only do Christians need to investigate a physicalist anthropology in order to dialogue with science. We need also to investigate its implications for our own lives. I argue that Christians have taken a long detour away from their true calling by focusing on saving souls for heaven. Returning to a biblical view of humans made from the dust of the ground can encourage us to return to a more authentic Christian witness. Theologians and biblical scholars have made it clear that Jesus' central message is the present and future kingdom of God: a new social order in which enemies are reconciled and the lowly are lifted up; a kingdom in which we shall participate fully as resurrected, glorified *bodies.* If this is the case, then neuroscience is indeed doing the work of a friend, by leading us Christians to re-evaluate and reject the predominant dualism of the past centuries.

Paul Markham offers here not only a valuable examination of physicalist anthropology, but also a major contribution to the task ahead, which is to re-examine church teaching and practice in its light. In his examination of theories of conversion and in his recommendations for evangelical practice in light of new understandings of human neurobiology, he addresses the very issues of character and moral responsibility that are now in the news. The science not only does not count against personal responsibility, it also does not rule God's action out of the picture. Rather, it helps us see how better to open ourselves to the transforming power of God.

Nancey Murphy
Professor of Christian Philosophy
Fuller Seminary
May, 2007

Acknowledgments

I EXTEND MANY THANKS TO Charlie Collier, Alan Padgett, Beth Felker Jones, and David Lose for their advice and assistance in the publication of this work. In addition, I express my appreciation to the following:

Robert Song and David Wilkinson for their friendship, guidance, and hospitality offered during my time at Durham University.

Nancey Murphy for her years of guidance and support. Her contribution to my development is immeasurable.

Warren S. Brown and Ann Loades for their time and constructive criticism.

Other prolific thinkers that have inspired me. These include: Joel B. Green, James D. G. Dunn, Bishop Tom Wright, Stanley Hauerwas, Brad Kallenberg, Randy L. Maddox, James McClendon, Robert John Russell, and John Howard Yoder.

My parents, Eddie and Suellen Markham. Their dedication to each other and to those around them has taught me how to love and give. I can only hope to be the kind of parent to my children that they have been to me.

My wife, Brandi Barnes Markham. She is an infinitely dedicated wife, friend, and gift for which I am forever grateful.

CHAPTER I

Approaching the Issues

For many of the churchly, the life of the spirit is reduced to a dull preoccupation with getting to heaven. At best, the world is no more than an embarrassment and a trial to the spirit which is otherwise radically separated from it. . . . As far as this sort of "religion" is concerned, the body is no more than the lustreless container of the soul, a mere "package" that will nevertheless light up in eternity, forever cool and shiny as a neon cross. This separation of the soul from the body and from the world is no disease of the fringe, no aberration, but a fracture that runs through the mentality of institutionalized religion like a geologic fault. And this rift in the mentality of religion continues to characterize the modern mind, no matter how secular or worldly it becomes. . . . And yet, what is the burden of the Bible if not a sense of the mutuality of influence, rising out of an essential unity, among soul and body and community and world?
—Wendell Berry[1]

THE PURPOSE OF THIS chapter is to present the issues that will be addressed throughout the whole of this work. I identify the main problem as being an incomplete view of Christian spirituality within the Western religious traditions, particularly in American evangelicalism that claims nearly forty percent of the population of the United States.[2] Owen C. Thomas says, "In the tradition of writing about the Christian life or

---

1. Berry, *Recollected Essays*, 283–84.

2. This statistic is provided by the Institute for the Study of American Evangelicals. See http://www.wheaton.edu/isae/defining_evangelicalism.html (accessed 14 June 2006). My analysis is primarily concerned with American evangelicalism for two reasons: first, the evangelical tradition in America has a substantial presence on the continent and with the dissemination of missionaries throughout the world, American evangelical ideologies are having a global impact; second, I am the product of an evangelical heritage. I speak from within the socio-historical tradition itself. In this sense, I am able to speak of the state of evangelical spirituality with more practical authority than I could of the state of spirituality in other religious traditions.

spirituality, commonly known as ascetical theology, down to the present burgeoning of this literature, a pervasive emphasis and focus has been on the inner or interior life as distinct from the outer, bodily, and communal life."[3]

This particular view of Christian spirituality has profound implications for how a tradition interprets and facilitates conversion, in both an individual and communal sense. It is this issue of *Christian conversion* that will be at the center of my investigation. I submit that an incomplete view of Christian spirituality has naturally led to an equally short-sighted notion of conversion. What is needed is a re-examination of conversion that is faithful to the long-standing beliefs and practices of the Christian faith, yet critical of ideologies that compromise Christian community orthopraxis.

The model of conversion that I will offer in this book will be presented in light of Wesleyan theology and a nonreductive physicalist view of human nature. John Wesley is often referred to as a *practical* theologian in that he was concerned not with the production of systematic theologies, but with the practice of theology in a transformative context. That is, Wesley was primarily concerned with the transformation of persons—the realisation of "holiness of life." As such, Wesley offers a vital *process-oriented* language that will be central throughout this work.

How one conceives human nature has an immense effect on issues concerning spirituality and conversion.[4] I argue for a *non*reductive physicalist view of human nature. Nonreductive physicalism is best viewed as a research programme that considers both scientific and metaphysical resources. In this way, a *theory* of nonreductive physicalism can inform an investigation of a particular phenomenon in a more complete way than any single data source (cognitive science for example).[5] Central to my argument is the relationship of the nonreductive physicalist view of human nature that I espouse and the process view of conversion that I argue for. I flatly claim that a nonreductive physicalist view of the human person *requires* a

3. Thomas, "Interiority," 41.

4. I recognize that "human nature" is a broad concept discussed by a number of disciplines (psychology, anthropology, theology, etc.); however, for the purpose of the present work, the term is meant to refer specifically to philosophical views dealing with the "substance" of humankind (a predicament usually addressed in philosophical anthropology). This concept is best captured by the question, "what are humans made of?" or "what are the constituent parts of the human species?" For a comprehensive resource on the overall theme of human nature, see Pojman, *Who are We?*

5. Data from cognitive science say nothing in and of themselves. It is only through philosophical analysis or other presuppositions that data can speak to a particular inquiry.

process view of conversion. Consequently, one of the goals of the present work will be to establish an operational description of conversion using both theology and science as vital resources; thus, throughout this work the terms "moral conversion," "moral transformation," and as I will argue, John Wesley's notion of "sanctification," can be used interchangeably.

In what follows, I will offer a brief analysis of the "problem" of Christian spirituality as I have proposed it. This will be followed by a discussion of the notion of conversion that proceeds from such a view of Christian spirituality.[6] In addition, I will cover some important presuppositions that must be considered through the length of this analysis.

Christian Spirituality in Context

The concept of "spirituality" is a generally elusive notion. Despite the difficulty of defining the term, it is a concept that permeates the whole of human culture. In an attempt to properly understand "spirituality," Brian J. Zinnbauer and colleagues performed a substantial analysis of the perceptual difference between "religiousness" and "spirituality." Their research points out that religion and spirituality are polarized by three main themes—"organized religion versus personal spirituality," "substantive religion versus functional spirituality," and "negative religiousness versus positive spirituality."[7]

While religion is concerned with groups and collective societal concerns, "the common perception is still that spirituality is primarily concerned with the life of the soul, the inner life, one's prayer life, one's spiritual life, as a separate compartment of the Christian life. The tendency to equate the spiritual life with the interior life is particularly prevalent in our own day."[8]

Regarding the perceptual dichotomy between religion and spirituality, Thomas comments that "Along with this honorific [spirituality]/pejorative [religion] distinction goes the assumption that whereas religion deals with the outer life, that is, institutions, traditions, practices, doctrines, and moral codes, spirituality treats the inner life, which thus tends to be individualized and privatized."[9] Thomas concludes that these common

---

6. To be clear, I do not claim to offer an exhaustive account of Christian spirituality, nor a complete chronicle of conversion within the Christian tradition; I only seek to establish the context in which I offer a nuanced model of conversion.

7. Zinnbauer et al., "Emerging Meanings," 889–919.

8. Downey, *Understanding Christian Spirituality*, 105.

9. Thomas, "Interiority," 42. Thomas sees this interior emphasis in spirituality as "mis-

assumptions have led to a damaging view of spirituality. He asserts that spirituality is a universally human trait—all people are spiritual.[10] In this sense, neither religion nor spirituality can claim primacy over any particular domain, inner or outer. In fact, Thomas claims that spirituality and religion are synonymous terms.[11]

Thomas's assessment highlights the state of Western spirituality with its heightened sense of the "self." One of the most salient features of selfhood in the West is the notion of "inwardness"; that is, we have the sense that mental states, emotions, feelings, etc. are things that dwell within us (or perhaps more particularly in our heads).[12] In his evaluation of the Western notion of selfhood, Robert Innes comments:

> We perceive ourselves as having inner depths. We talk of the possibility of expressing our inner selves. We commonly say that we have inner potentials and capacities that need to be developed. We may understand our conscious self to be merely the tip of an iceberg that conceals a vast personal or even cosmic unconscious. We readily distinguish between our "persona", or what people see of us

---

taken both philosophically, theologically, and ethically." He concludes that this situation needs to be "redressed not only on a more balanced view of the inner/outer relation but also to an emphasis on the outer as primary and as a major source of the inner" (42).

10. Thomas defines spirituality as "the sum of all the uniquely human capacities and functions . . . all understood as embodied." See Thomas, "Some Problems," 268. Extending from this assertion, I claim that "spirituality" is best understood as the innate human capacity to understand oneself in relation to the world as a whole—a world consisting of both material and transcendent concepts. Spirituality emerges within the context of relationships and is characterized by particular cultural-linguistic systems that an individual deems to be of ultimate concern. For more on spirituality as an inherently anthropological concept, see Schneiders, "Study," 3–12; and Chandler et al., "Counselling," 168–75.

11. See Thomas, "Some Problems," 270. I depart from Thomas on one point: while I do agree that religion and spirituality are much more intimately related than some recognize (for example see Ryrie, "What is Spirituality?," 204–13, where Ryrie equates "spirituality" with "Christian maturity"), I do argue that they are indeed not synonymous. While I agree that spirituality is an innate human characteristic, religion should be viewed as a variety of cultural-linguistic modes in which spirituality can be embodied.

12. Thomas describes "interiority" not as physically inner but "psychologically or spiritually inner such that the self or soul is inner and the facial expression and gesture are outer; such that the mind is inner and the brain is outer; and such that the will or intention is inner and the bodily action and speech are outer" (ibid., 57). Also, from the field of psychology, Jerome Bruner refers to our way of understanding this inner and outer distinction as a "preemptive metaphor" characterising the human person. See Bruner, *Toward a Theory of Instruction*.

on the outside, and our "real self" that lies hidden and protected on the inside.[13]

This sentiment echoes the well-known account of the self given by Charles Taylor. He states that

> In our language of self-understanding, the opposition "inside-outside" plays an important role. We think of our thoughts, ideas, or feelings as being 'within' us, while objects in the world which these mental states bear on are "without". . . . But strong as this partitioning of the world appears to us, as solid as this localization may seem, and anchored in the very nature of the human agent, it is in large part a feature of our world, *the world of modern, Western people*. The localization is not a universal one, which human beings recognize as a matter of course, as they do for instance that their heads are above their torsos. Rather it is a function of a historically limited mode of self-interpretation, one which has become dominant in the modern West and which may indeed spread thence to other parts of the globe, but which had a beginning in time and space and may have an end.[14]

In Taylor's account, the possibility of achieving an integrated sense of self involves the unification of our sources of moral significance. Historically, Plato initiated the dominant Western moral tradition where the possibility of unifying the self is dependent upon the achievement of rational self-mastery.[15] Taylor claims that people have traditionally derived their sense of self from a particular moral source (e.g. the Platonic *Good*).

In this sense, one achieves a unified sense of self (or becomes a "whole person") to the extent that they are truly oriented toward this ultimate source of value or "hypergood."[16] Taylor argues that the most influential "moral source" in the Western world is found in the Christian God as articulated in Augustinian theology.[17] Taylor states that

---

13. Innes, *Discourses of the Self*, 29.

14. Taylor, *Sources of the Self*, 111 (emphasis added). Taylor claims, "our *modern* notions of inner and outer are indeed strange and without precedent in other cultures and times" (114).

15. Plato's ideal gave privileged position to a state of self-recollection in which one's expressive powers are united under the rational contemplation of the *Good*.

16. See Taylor, *Sources of the Self*, 62–75.

17. Taylor argues that, on the particular issue of interiority, Augustine was heavily influenced by Plotinus. For the present purposes, I note this influence, but will not pursue it further. For an additional source see Turner, *The Darkness of God*, 75–79.

Augustine's turn to the self was a turn to radical reflexivity, and that is what made the language of inwardness irresistible. The inner light is the one which shines in our presence to ourselves; it is the one inseparable from our being creatures with a first-person standpoint. What differentiates it from the outer light is just what makes the image of inwardness so compelling, that it illuminates the space where I am present to myself. *It is hardly an exaggeration to say that it was Augustine who introduced the inwardness of radical reflexivity and bequeathed it to the Western tradition of thought.* The step was a fateful one, because we have certainly made a big thing of the first-person standpoint. The modern epistemological tradition from Descartes, and all that flowed from it in modern culture, has made this standpoint fundamental—*to the point of aberration*, one might think. It has gone as far as generating the view that there is a special domain of 'inner' objects available only from this standpoint; or the notion that the vantage point of the "I think" is somehow outside the world of things we experience.[18]

Augustine stands at the intersection between the ancient and medieval worlds. He is responsible for bequeathing a particular understanding of the self to the generations that followed him. Augustine's legacy is twofold—not only did he offer a decisive description of the soul's relation to God (the "Godward self"), but, as Taylor points out, he also is responsible for initiating the Western tradition of interiority or introspective spirituality.[19]

It is important to note that *the distinction between "inner" and "outer" is not equivalent to the distinction between soul and body.* That these have come to be understood as equivalent is a fact of historical origin. Augustine's notion that one has an "inside" and that one can enter into that "inner" space arose within the context of his reflection on the problem of the location of the soul.[20] The combination of Augustine's metaphor of entering one's self, together with the Neoplatonic emphasis on the care of the soul, has constituted a complex of ideas that has shaped the whole of Western spirituality.

18. Taylor, *Sources of the Self*, 131. Emphasis added.

19. For a helpful account of Augustine and the development of the notion of interior spirituality see Cary, *Augustine's Invention of the Inner Self*.

20. Teresa of Avila exemplifies Augustine's metaphor by stating that "we consider our soul to be like a castle made entirely out of a diamond or of very clear crystal, in which there are many rooms . . . some up above, others down below, others to the sides; and in the middle is the main dwelling place where the very secret exchanges between God and the soul take place." See Teresa of Avila, "Interior Castle," 283–84.

Augustine synthesized traditional Judeao-Christian faith and Neo-Platonic philosophy in light of his own experiences and religious convictions. The result was a remarkable emphasis on an inward notion of selfhood and the self's relation to God. In his *Tracts on the Gospel of John*, Augustine wrote

> Recognize in yourself something which I want to call within, within you. . . . Leave behind what lies outside, leave behind your clothing and your flesh. Descend into yourself; go to your secret place, your mind. . . . If you are far from yourself, how can you draw near to God? . . . for not in the body but in the mind has human being been made after the image of God. In his own likeness let us seek God; in his own image let us recognize the creator.[21]

In Augustine's interpretation, the mode of access to the "moral source" was understood to be from within the self.[22] As the above passage makes clear, the self or soul, as an immaterial and eternal entity, should pursue God which is immaterial and eternal. While Plato emphasized the eternal/transient dichotomy, Augustine focused on the inner/outer distinction where the eternal is linked with the inner and the transient with the outer.

This distinction continued in the practices of the Church. Spiritual teaching advised converts to flee from that which jeopardized union with the divine (sin) and focus instead on the cultivation of the soul's ascension to God. In their account of the history of moral theology, Daniel Harrington and James Keenan note that during the early medieval period

> moral theology was shaped predominately by a concern about the sins one should avoid, and not about the good to be pursued. Similarly, with emphasis on one's own moral state, the Christian's communal self-understanding was less important, and a long period of moral narcissism began, in which Christians became anxious not about the kingdom or the needs of the Church, but rather about the state of their individual souls.[23]

---

21. Augustine, *Tractatus in Joannis evangelium* (23.10), 29.

22. This shift in language initiated by Augustine differed from Plato's understanding of the pursuit of the "Good." Although Plato located moral sources in the realm of thought, he did not equate access to such as a turn inward. In contrast to Augustine, Plato held that becoming rational involved a turning from that which is transient to the "light" (allegory of the cave).

23. Harrington and Keenan, *Jesus and Virtue Ethics*, 3.

Fergus Kerr claims that this historical condition has an extended presence in contemporary Christian theology and spirituality. Kerr states that

> Spiritual writers in the last three centuries or so have driven many devout people into believing that the only real prayer is silent, worldless, "private". . . . It is amazing how often devout people think that liturgical worship is not really prayer unless they have been injecting special "meaning" to make the words work. The inclination is to say that participation consists in private goings-on inside the head. . . . There is . . . a central strain in modern Christian piety which puts all the emphasis on people's secret thoughts and hidden sins.[24]

This amounts to no less than an implicit (or explicit) dualism in Christian spirituality. Obvious dichotomies exist between body and soul, and between church/kingdom of God and world. For many within the Christian tradition the goal of the church has been "to rescue souls from bodies, rescue the church from the world, and transport its passengers safely to the heavenly realms."[25]

This dichotomy is obvious on several levels of analysis. The area of missiology takes seriously how people groups are engaged for the sake of Christian mission. In his critique of Western Christian spirituality, Bryant L. Myers comments that

> As the foundational paradigm shift of the Enlightenment has worked itself out in Western culture, one of its most enduring features has been the assumption that we can consider the physical and spiritual realms as separate and distinct from one another. On the one hand, there is the spiritual or supernatural world where God lives and acts, along with other cosmic Gods like Allah. This is the world of religion. On the other hand, there is the real world: the material world where we hear, see, feel, touch, and smell. . . . This framework of separated areas of life is also deeply embedded in the Western part of the Christian church, in its theology, and in the daily life of its people.[26]

---

24. Kerr, *Theology After Wittgenstein*, 50.

25. Stassen and Gushee, *Kingdom Ethics*, 115. Stassen and Gushee offer a helpful analysis of the negative impact that such "spirituality" has on the practice of Christian ethics. They baldly claim that "To the extent that Christians adopt any kind of body/soul, earth/heaven dualism we simply do not understand the message of Scripture—or of Jesus" (28–29).

26. Myers, *Walking with the Poor*, 5.

Bryant's notion of *transformational development* takes seriously the holistic nature of human beings and realizes that transformation is no more about the changing condition of one's "soul" than it is about the changing of one's "mind." Transformation is a thoroughly holistic process that cannot be understood as occurring in any way apart from physical embodiment.

The dualistic interpretation of spirituality discussed above has far-reaching implications regarding Christian community orthopraxis. I claim that an important example can be seen in the understanding of conversion that pervades much of evangelical thought in America.

Conversion as an Interior Experience

The view of spirituality discussed above has had a tremendous impact on how Christians conceive conversion, particularly within American evangelicalism. For many evangelicals, conversion is primarily presumed to occur instantaneously as God responds to prayerful petition. Conversion is then understood as receiving Jesus Christ as one's *personal* Lord and Savior and is subsequently characterized as a "personal relationship with God."[27] Conversion in this context is considered to be a change that occurs within the soul—hence the popular phrase "salvation of the soul."

In a sobering appraisal of North American evangelical Christianity, Mark D. Baker notes that evangelicals tend to read the Bible through an individualistic and spiritualized lens.[28] This reading places the salvation of the soul at the center of the Christian faith. Such an understanding causes many evangelicals to interpret all aspects of Christian life in relation to this central idea. Baker comments that

> Rather than seeing their individual salvation as part of a larger theme, like the kingdom of God, people attempt to understand

27. Richards, *Born to Grow*, 11.

28. This *individualism* is best described by Dennis Hollinger as "a view of reality in which the individual is the most basic entity and the defining principle of all existence. It is an atomistic conception of reality in which a collective has no existence apart from its constituent parts. . . . The social whole is a composite of separate individuals." See Hollinger, *Individualism and Social Ethics*, 16–17. Sociologist Stephen Hart observes that the United States is "probably the most individualistic nation the world has ever known. Our individualism is not only a set of value preferences sacralizing individual freedom, but also a cognitive framework blinding us to the supra-individual aspect of human life." See Hart, "Privatization," 325. Roy F. Baumeister has produced an insightful historical analysis concerning the evolving notion of "self" marked by a strong sense of individualism. Baumeister sees this self-contained individualism as *the* spiritual problem or our time. See Baumeister, "How the Self Became a Problem," 163–76.

the kingdom of God as a subcategory of individual salvation. They might only equate the kingdom of God with heaven or as something within the individual Christian. What cannot be brought into line with the central theme of future individual salvation is left as optional or secondary in the Christian life. As long as this lens is in place, much of the biblical holistic gospel will either be spiritualized, rejected or considered an appendix to the gospel.[29]

The issue is not that individualism produces a society of social hermits. On the contrary, communities do form, but these are communities where the individual is primary to the group. Theologian C. Norman Kraus observes that in individualistic societies "Community is seen as a contractual association of independent individuals. . . .The group [becomes] a collection of individuals created *by* individuals *for* their own individual advantages."[30] This condition creates a Christian culture that views the church as a community offering care for individual souls rather than serving the role of the visible kingdom of God in the world.

Ronald J. Sider has issued a number of sharp critiques against American evangelicals regarding their participation in social justice concerns. Sider states

I am convinced that at the heart of our problem is a one-sided, unbiblical, reductionist understanding of the gospel and salvation. Too many evangelicals in too many ways give the impression that the really important part of the gospel is forgiveness of sins. If we just repeat the formula and say we want Jesus to forgive our sins, we are Christians. . . . Salvation becomes, not a life-transforming experience that reorients every corner of life, but a one-way ticket to heaven.[31]

In a helpful analysis of American evangelicalism, James Davison Hunter notes the increasing methodization and standardization of spirituality within the evangelical tradition. Although Protestantism in the

---

29. Baker, *Religious No More*, 57. Evangelical historian, Nathan Hatch shows the connection between American revivalism in the eighteenth and nineteenth centuries and the emergence of American individualism. Hatch notes that many early American evangelical leaders saw religion as "a matter between God and individuals." See Hatch, "Democratization," 112.

30. Kraus, *Community of the Spirit*, 32.

31. Sider, *The Scandal of the Evangelical Conscience*, 57–58. Furthermore, Sider criticizes the evangelical tendency to think of persons primarily as individual souls, thus many evangelicals describe evangelism as "saving souls." See pp. 69–73.

eighteenth and nineteenth centuries did display certain propensities for the rationalization of spirituality, Hunter notes that

> What is different about contemporary American Evangelicalism is the intensification of this propensity to unprecedented proportions. This intensification comes about as an adaptation to modern rationality. Thus one may note the increasing tendency to translate the specifically religious components of the Evangelical world view, previously understood to be plain, self-evident, and without need of elaboration, into rigorously standardized prescriptions.[32]

In this way, the spiritual aspects of evangelical life are interpreted in terms of "guidelines" or "laws." The means by which one enters the Christian faith can be systematized in this fashion. In *How To Be Born Again*, Billy Graham offers the following "Four Steps to Peace with God":

> First, you must recognize what God did: that He loved you so much He gave His Son to die on the cross. Second, you must repent for your sins. It's not enough to be sorry; repentance is that turnabout from sin that is emphasized. Third, you must receive Jesus Christ as Savior and Lord. This means that you cease trying to save yourself and accept Christ without reservation. Fourth, you must confess Christ publicly. *This confession is a sign that you have been converted.*[33]

A similar methodological presentation can be seen in the writing of Bill Bright. Bright claims that "just as there are physical laws that govern the material universe, so are there spiritual laws which govern your relationship with God."[34] Conversion then occurs through acknowledging the validity of the *Four Spiritual Laws*[35] and then by responding to specific

32. Hunter, *American Evangelicalism*, 74–75.

33. Graham, *How To Be Born Again*, 167–68. Italics added to emphasize the past tense "have been converted." This is an important feature of this notion of conversion—it is an instantaneous event that can be connected to a single moment in time. The case can be made that the fourth step is Graham's way of insuring that conversion is not a solely an *interior* experience. The point that I wish to emphasize here is that the coming forward in the mass revivals, etc. is a way to publicly express that conversion has already occurred. The public proclamation (external) is simply a witness to the completed conversion moment (internal).

34. See Bright, *Four Spiritual Laws*, introduction text.

35. Law One—"God loves you, and offers a wonderful plan for your life." Law Two—"Man is sinful and separated from God. Therefore, he cannot know and experience God's love and plan for his life." Law Three—"Jesus Christ is God's only provision for man's sin. Through him you can know and experience God's love and plan for your life." Law Four—"We must individually receive Jesus Christ as Savior and Lord; then we can know

instructions on how to "receive Jesus Christ as Savior and Lord." This instruction, also known as the *Sinner's Prayer*, is presented by Graham as follows:

> Lord Jesus, I need you. Thank You for dying on the cross for my sins. I open the door of my life and receive You as my Savior and Lord. Thank You for forgiving my sins and giving me eternal life. Take control of the throne of my life. Make me the kind of person You want me to be.[36]

One need not go further than Graham and Bright to uncover the widespread popularity of these teachings regarding Christian conversion. Graham has led hundreds of thousands of individuals to this conversion experience as he has preached to over 200 million people in 185 countries. He has written twenty-four books, many of which have been translated into thirty-eight languages. He has been awarded numerous honors and has served as advisor to several U.S. presidents.

In a TIME magazine article, Harold Bloom writes that Graham "is the recognized leader of what continues to call itself American evangelical Protestantism, and his life and activities have sustained the self-respect of that vast entity. If there is an indigenous American religion—and I think there is, quite distinct from European Protestantism—then Graham remains its prime emblem."[37]

In similar fashion, Bill Bright has been enormously influential through his role as founder of the world's largest Christian ministry—Campus Crusade for Christ. This organisation is active in 191 countries through a staff of 26,000 full-time employees and more than 225,000 trained volunteers. Bright's *Four Spiritual Laws* has been written in over 200 languages and distributed to more than 2.5 billion people. Likewise, his *Jesus Film* has become the most widely viewed (5.1 billion) and translated (786 languages) film in history.[38]

This systematization of the gospel message and subsequent presentation of conversion creates a "packaged" spirituality that ultimately allows for ease of appropriation. Hunter asserts that this methodical presentation of the conversion experience produces effects with parallels in market economics. Hunter states that

---

and experience God's love and plan for our lives." Ibid.

36. Graham, "How To Be Born Again," 287.

37. Bloom, "Billy Graham," 3.

38. See http://billbright.ccci.org/public/ (accessed on 30 May 2006).

In the rationalized economy, mass production allows for widespread distribution and consumption while maintaining a high degree of quality control over the product. Likewise the reduction of the gospel to its distilled essence and the methodization of the conversion process make widespread distribution of the gospel possible, while maintaining a cognitive uniformity in substantive quality of the message and an experiential uniformity in functional quality of the process.[39]

Beyond the popular evangelical literature, there are substantial works of systematic theology that reinforce the ideas presented above. As a case study, I offer the *Systematic Theology* of Louis Berkhof.[40] For the purpose of the present work, I will focus on Berkhof's theological interpretation of conversion.[41] Berkhof's soteriology is rooted in an *ordo salutis* (order of salvation). This logical sequence is the means through which God administers salvation to each individual convert.[42]

Conversion, which lies in the middle of Berkhof's *ordo salutis*, precedes *regeneration*[43] as the first act of the regenerate soul in accordance with its newly acquired holy disposition. Berkhof offers the following two-fold definition of conversion:

> Active conversion is that act of God whereby He causes the regenerated sinner, in his conscious life, to turn to Him in repentance and faith. . . . Passive conversion is the resulting conscious act of

---

39. Hunter, *American Evangelicalism*, 83–84. This sentiment is echoed by Philip Lee. Lee notes that for many evangelicals, conversion is a (necessary) technique for salvation. Here, the history of Israel as well as the life and ministry of Jesus is spiritualized beyond recognition and important only insofar as these concepts can be employed to bring sinners to repentance. See Philip Lee, *Against the Protestant Gnostics*, 109.

40. Berkhof, *Systematic Theology*. I choose this particular work due its widespread use in evangelical seminaries as well as its general popularity within theologically conservative circles (e.g. the text is in fourth edition and has been printed in five languages).

41. This appears in part four of Berkhof's volume. My critique of Berkhof's interpretation of conversion is based on an analysis offered by Brad Kallenberg. See Kallenberg, "Conversion Converted," 335–64.

42. The complete order is calling, regeneration, conversion, faith, justification, sanctification, perseverance, and glorification. See Berkhof, *Systematic Theology*, 415–16. It will become increasingly obvious that I reject Berkhof's separation of "conversion" from "sanctification."

43. *Regeneration* is understood to be the change in an individual soul's basic disposition resulting from the implantation of new life through the indwelling Holy Spirit. ibid., 415.

the regenerate sinner whereby he, through the grace of God, turns to God in repentance and faith.[44]

Kallenberg claims that Berkhof's formulation of conversion is deficient in three ways.[45] It suffers from: (1) *metaphysical reductionism*, (2) *linguistic reductionism*, and (3) *epistemological absolutism*.[46]

Metaphysical reductionism appears in Berkhof's account as he conceives of the whole as nothing but the some of its parts—the Church is *nothing but* the sum of the members that make it up. Subsequently, Berkhof views conversion as a limited transaction between God and the individual, thus downplaying the role of community in the conversion process. In this sense, "true conversion" is characterized by a private experience with God and the Christian community (Church) becomes, at best, a collection of individuals that have a shared experience—"the individual is treated as the real center of action and the community is treated as nothing more than the sum of its individual members."[47] The weakness of this view is its failure to recognize the formative or "causal" powers of the community.

The second reductionist feature of Berkhof's account is linguistic in nature. Berkhof adopts a propositionalism that disregards the transformative power of language itself. Following Calvin, Berkhof appears to understand the regenerate individual in intellectualist terms. In this view, moral progress is attained by knowing and understanding God's truths. The strong cognitive element that appears in Berkhof's account emphasizes the representational function of the biblical propositions while compromising their performative function.

In short, for Berkhof, true saving faith cannot operate apart from knowing the content of biblical propositions—"the knowledge of faith consists in a positive recognition of the truth, in which man accepts as true whatsoever God says in His Word."[48] Much like the metaphysical reduction discussed above, Berkhof's linguistic reductionism fails for what it leaves out. A preoccupation with propositional content fails to recognize language as a social fact within itself. In this sense, language has the causal power to shape experience. This is a point that should not be taken lightly.

---

44. Ibid., 483.

45. These deficiencies are closely connected with Berkhof's presuppositions regarding modern philosophy.

46. Kallenberg, "Conversion Converted," 338.

47. Ibid., 339.

48. Berkhof, *Systematic Theology*, 503.

Edward Sapir comments that "the fact of the matter is that the 'real world' is to a large extent unconsciously built up on the language habits of the group. . . . We see and hear and otherwise experience very largely as we do because the language habits of our community predispose certain choices of interpretation."[49] As I will discuss in chapter four, conversion amounts to no less than the acquisition of a new conceptual language.

The final deficiency in Berkhof's account concerns his epistemological absolutism. For Berkhof, faith and certainty of knowledge are directly proportional to one another. He claims that "faith carries its own certainty with it. . . . It is a certainty that is unwavering and indestructible."[50] Subsequently, Berkhof's view of conversion is based on what he conceives to be a "correct" interpretation of Scripture—the sole court of appeal concerning doctrinal matters.[51]

Faith derives its certainty from the existence of God; however, knowledge of God is mediated through Scripture, thus the Bible becomes the ultimate foundation for certainty. Berkhof asserts that

> The doctrine of conversion is, of course, like all other doctrines, based upon Scripture and should be accepted on that ground. Since conversion is a conscious experience in the lives of many, the testimony of experience can be added to that of the Word of God, but this testimony, however valuable it may be, does not add to the certainty of the doctrine taught in the Word of God.[52]

The obvious weakness of Berkhof's foundationalist view of certainty is that no such universal and timeless expression of the doctrine of conversion exists. He ignores the historical consciousness that lies behind doctrinal formulation, thus exposing the thoroughly modern (Enlightenment) philosophical presuppositions that undergird his position.

There are those that oppose this understanding of Christian conversion. Lesslie Newbigin is a harsh critic of dualistic and individualistic characterizations of Christian life. Newbigin asserts that

---

49. Quoted in Bowie et al., *Twenty Questions*, 274.

50. Berkhof, *Systematic Theology*, 504.

51. This same notion is reflected in popular evangelical literature. Miles Stanford states that above all "true faith must be based solely upon scriptural facts. . . . Unless our faith is established on facts, it is no more than conjecture, superstition, speculation or presumption. Once we begin to reckon (count) on facts, our Father begins to build us up in the faith." See Stanford, *Principles of Spiritual Growth*, 7.

52. Berkhof, *Systematic Theology*, 482.

The hope set before us in the gospel is fundamentally corporate, not individualistic. . . . This purely individualistic conception of the Kingdom robs human history as a whole of its meaning. According to this view, the significance of life in this world is exhaustively defined as the training of individual souls for heaven. Thus there can be no connected purpose running through history as a whole, but only a series of disconnected purposes for each individual life. History, on this view, would have no goal, no *telos*.[53]

The model of conversion that I offer is intended to reflect Newbigin's sentiment and to avoid the short-comings pointed out above. I claim that the spirituality espoused by many contemporary evangelicals renders a theologically and scientifically faulty concept of conversion. I reject the notion that conversion is an isolated affair of the individual "inner self"; rather, I maintain that conversion is a significant social reorientation commensurate with a transformation of identity.

As I pointed out earlier, an "inner" and "outer" distinction is not the same as distinguishing between soul and body. It is feasible that one could be a body-soul dualist and avoid an excessively inward-oriented spirituality. Furthermore, it is also possible for one with a physicalist anthropology to ignore the responsibilities of "Kingdom work" by retreating to solitude, self-examination and contemplation. The salient point here is that a nonreductive physicalism along with the eschatological hope of "new creation" leads more *naturally* to a Christian worldview marked by concern for the physical world and its transformation than does a dualist anthropology.

The type of conversion that I seek to describe should not be understood as "salvation of the soul," but as the holistic process of socio-moral transformation of a person within the context of a Christian community.[54] Conversion, in this sense, is not simply about a "correct" system of beliefs, but *necessarily* involves a transformation in socio-moral attitude and

53. Newbigin, *Signs Amid the Rubble*, 24. Newbigin understands that, as a social philosophy, individualism stresses personal morality over social ethics and views individual transformation as the key to social change (mission). It is a position that he is bound to reject. For more see Hollinger, *Individualism and Social Ethics*, 44.

54. The multi-dimensional character of conversion was recognized by Catholic Theologian Bernard Lonergan. He spoke of the intellectual, moral, and religious dimensions of the conversion process. See Lonergan, *Method in Theology*. Lonergan's concept of conversion has been expanded by a number of scholars. For example Donald L. Gelpi adds *affective* and *socio-political* conversion to Lonergan's triad. See Gelpi, *Conversion Experience*. See also the addition of *somatic conversion* in Sperry, *Transforming Self and Community*. The point of noting these is to emphasize the critical holistic understanding of conversion that I wish to espouse in this work.

behavior. The intimate connection between this claim and John Wesley's understanding of sanctification will become apparent throughout this work.[55]

As with any intellectual endeavor, there are a number of scientific, philosophical, and theological presuppositions that underlie my basic thesis. While I argue many of these at length in later chapters, I will point out two important positions at the outset that will inform my further investigation. These concern *moral theory* and *theological method*.

Moral Theory

Because my view of conversion is intrinsically and inextricably tied to moral transformation, I deem it necessary to say a few words regarding moral theory. All versions of moral theory claim to speak to what an agent ought to do; however, there is less agreement regarding the substance of these moral "oughts" and the subsequent moral psychologies that are required for effective reasoning and behavior. Within the modern Western tradition there are two predominate moral theories—*utilitarianism* and *deontology*. In addition to these, *virtue theory*, having roots in ancient Greek thought, has risen to popularity in contemporary studies.

Utilitarianism, classically advanced by the British philosopher John Stuart Mill,[56] suggests that in the case of moral judgment one should take the action (or follow the rule) that maximizes pleasure and minimizes pain for the largest number of people. A popular form of this moral theory is known as "rule utilitarianism." Here, the moral evaluation is based on the "rule" rather than a particular act.[57]

To make the appropriate moral judgment, utilitarianism requires that a moral agent is capable of recognizing and computing salient utility functions. The utilitarian would then be moved to act on such judgments by the cultivation of "feelings" that are identified with "happiness" (whether they be altruistic in nature or involve mere self-concern). So, for the most part, a utilitarian moral psychology is constituted by cognitive mechanisms dedicating to learning what actions or rules bring about a state of happiness.

---

55. Due to its historical and doctrinal evolution, the term "sanctification" has come to refer to a variety of processes and/or events. In what follows, I will argue for the process-oriented understanding of sanctification while formally rejecting the view of "crisis event."

56. See Mill, *Utilitarianism*.

57. For more see Hooker, *Ideal Code*.

Deontology, as emphasized in the work of Immanuel Kant,[58] focuses less on the consequences of an action and more on the maxim of the action itself, that is, the intent-based principle that arises through a rational process of deliberation.[59] Kant argued that moral action is based on a standard of rationality which he called the "categorical imperative"[60]—moral acts are rational and immoral acts violate the categorical imperative and are thereby irrational.

A Kantian moral psychology will focus on the individual's ability to "reason" about the demands of the categorical imperative and act accordingly. Kant insisted that one be moved to perform his or her "duty" by the demands of duty alone; thus, there is a premium placed on the rational deliberative process. Here, the influence of emotions or "animal nature" is seen in a negative light and to work against true moral behavior.

Virtue theory has ancient historical roots including the work of the Greek philosophers Plato and Aristotle.[61] This approach deemphasizes rules, consequences, etc. and shifts the focus to the "character" of the moral agent. So, the issue is not primarily whether or not one follows the correct rule; rather, the salient feature of virtue ethics is whether the moral agent is expressing good character, or virtues.[62] William C. Spohn points out five key features of a virtue-based moral theory.[63]

1. Moral evaluation focuses on the agent's character; actions are important because they display the agent's values and commitments.

2. Good character produces practical moral judgments based on beliefs, experience, and sensitivity more than on (or instead of) rules and principles.

---

58. See Kant, *Groundwork*.

59. For a helpful collection of essays on deontological ethics see Darwall, *Deontology*.

60. Essentially, the categorical imperative requires that an individual act only on maxims that he or she would want to become a universal law.

61. It is interesting to note that D. Stephen Long has claimed that Wesley's public theology is best understood as "moral theology" stemming from the virtue tradition, particularly the work of Thomas Aquinas. For more see Long, *John Wesley's Moral Theology*.

62. Some challenge the strict dichotomy between Virtue and Kantian (deontological) ethics, claiming that Kantian ethics is able to promote and sustain the same sort of character as virtue theory. For example see O'Connor, "Are Virtue Ethics," 238–52. O'Connor's argument suffers from one central weakness—his supporting material for virtue theory denies the role of emotion in ethical formation and decision-making. Such a denial is not only unnecessary, but ignores a central component of the moral life; thus, there may indeed be a greater divide between virtue and Kantian ethics than he proposes.

63. Spohn, "Return of Virtue Ethics," 61.

3. A moral psychology gives an account of how virtues and vices develop.

4. A theory of human fulfilment describes the goal towards which virtues lead and/or in which the virtues are components.

5. Increasingly, attention is paid to the cultural shaping of virtues and what relation, if any, exists between specific historical manifestations of virtues and more universal human traits.

The moral psychology implied in virtue theory is intrinsically connected to the moral "nature" of the agent. The virtuous person is not primarily concerned with superior moral reasoning, but with becoming a particular type of person whose attitudes and behavior flow from a particular holistic disposition. That is, the moral psychology required by virtue theory is a whole brain-body affair that involves the emotions and a serious consideration of the social context within which a person is situated.

The importance of social context cannot be overstated. Regarding the social dimension of moral theory, Alasdair MacIntyre claims that

> A moral philosophy . . . characteristically presupposes a sociology. For every moral philosophy offers explicitly or implicitly at least a partial conceptual analysis of the relationship of an agent to his or her reasons, motives, intentions and actions, and in so doing generally presupposes some claim that these concepts are embodied or at least can be in the real social world. . . . Thus it would generally be a decisive refutation of a moral philosophy to show that moral agency on its own account of the matter could never be socially embodied; and it also follows that we have not yet fully understood the claims of any moral philosophy until we have spelled out what its social embodiment would be.[64]

MacIntyre argues for a virtue ethic that takes seriously the social dimension of the moral life. Going forward I will consider virtue theory to be the most viable of the moral theories discussed above. Not only is this position philosophically defensible, I claim that a virtue-based moral theory provides the best understanding of moral formation *and* transformation.

Theological Method

At the heart of my research is a conviction that for a phenomenon to be thoroughly understood, multiple levels of explanation must be considered. The greater the number of aspects from which a phenomenon is explained,

---

64. MacIntyre, *After Virtue*, 23.

the better our understanding will be of the event in question. Such a conviction necessarily recruits insights from both theology and science. I am persuaded that such an integrated approach is not only possible, but also beneficial.[65]

This persuasion is not new to theological methodology. There are a number of scholars who have offered theological methods that take seriously the multidimensional nature of theological analysis. In an effort to describe Methodist contributions to a theory of divine providence, David Wilkinson reminds readers of the distinctively Wesleyan approach to theological inquiry—the so-called *Wesleyan Quadrilateral* that consists of scripture, reason, tradition and experience.[66]

Wilkinson points out that too often philosophers and theologians develop doctrine in epistemic isolation. In contrast, he emphasizes the importance of human experience, not least of which regards the insights of reason in terms of modern scientific discovery. In the case of understanding God's activity in the world, Wilkinson claims that "Chaos and quantum theory must be taken seriously. . . . They remind us also that any model of providence must reflect the varied and complex nature of the universe."[67]

Also from with the Wesleyan tradition, Warren S. Brown offers a theological method that he refers to as the "resonance model."[68] Brown's primary concern is developing a model that allows for the constructive relationship between science and theology. Brown asserts that a helpful way of thinking about the relation between theology and the sciences is to consider an auditory/acoustic metaphor involving the property of resonance. Here resonance refers to "the amplification or enrichment of sound when two or more auditory signals vibrate together synchronously or harmonically."[69]

Using the Wesleyan Quadrilateral, Brown splits reason into "rationality" and "science," thus yielding the domains of scripture, tradition,

65. Despite the opinion depicting science and theology as adversaries, I claim that this disjuncture is far from insurmountable and in most cases excessively overstated. Both science and theology are in the business of making claims about the world and as such they necessarily share the common goal of describing reality. For a helpful historical overview of the relationship between science and religion see Ferngren, *Science and Religion*. For a popular work on the interaction of science and theological issues see Barbour, *When Science Meets Religion*.

66. Wilkinson, "The Activity of God," 148–50.

67. Ibid., 149.

68. Brown, "Resonance," 110–20.

69. Ibid., 113.

experience, rationality and science. The resonance model presents the arbitration of differences between these domains as a process of finding "maximal resonance" between the data contributed by each source. Brown states that

> To seek resonance is not to look for different domains to say the same thing, nor is it allowing one field to trump another. Rather, it is presumed that if a conclusion is true within one domain, it should have some form of resonance with other domains. . . . thus, the most reliable knowledge and understanding is to be found somewhere in the resonant field where information from different domains intersect.[70]

The type of approaches offered by Wilkinson and Brown exemplify the need for a theological method that considers multiple sources of investigation. I submit that Nancey Murphy has offered one of the most original and well-articulated approaches in contemporary theology. Murphy's theological method will serve as a guiding resource for the whole of my research project. In what follows, I will offer a brief description of this method.

Murphy's theological method incorporates insights from philosophy of science, philosophy of religion, ethics, metaethics, biblical studies, and various scientific disciplines.[71] Murphy works from a self-proclaimed *postmodern*[72] position and therefore challenges many of the presuppositions found in both liberal and fundamentalist branches of theological thought.[73]

Murphy claims that theology has yet to recover from the philosophical treatises of David Hume.[74] In fact, Hume's work has led to a great divide separating modern from pre-modern theism. Murphy claims that

70. Ibid., 114.

71. For Murphy's most extensive analysis of theological methodology see Murphy, *Theology in the Age of Scientific Reasoning*.

72. The type of "postmodernity" espoused by Murphy is *Anglo-American* in nature. She is careful to distance herself from the strong deconstructionism found in the likes Jean-François Lyotard and Michel Foucault. For more see Murphy, *Anglo-American Postmodernity*.

73. See Murphy, *Beyond Liberalism & Fundamentalism*.

74. Hume's work regarding religion took the form of an assault on any attempt to formulate a unified theory of theological knowledge claims. He provided logical arguments against revelation and the occurrence of miracles. In addition, Hume argued against the notion of divine creation and design.

> The failure of theism to withstand the application of the new probable reasoning seems to give theologians a choice between two positions. Some accept Hume's critique as final and seek some other "vindication" for religion and theology outside the cognitive domain. Others ignore the crisis created by the epistemological changes that ushered in modernity, and go on about their business as though Hume had never written.[75]

Murphy claims that those who ignore Hume's work "pay the price of becoming intellectually isolated from and irrelevant to the host culture."[76] Among those who accept Hume's criticism as final must either (a) "find some other vindication for theology (moral, aesthetic, existential), with the consequence that theology loses its cognitive content and becomes uninteresting"; or (b) "redefine terms so that theology has its own form of 'rationality,' with the consequence that theology becomes unintelligible to those who operate with the standard epistemology."[77]

This first response is exemplified by Immanuel Kant and later by Friedrich Schleiermacher. Kant by-passed objections to the cognitive certainty of religious faith by relegating Christian truth to the moral or ethical sphere (the realm of "practical reason"). In an effort to further insulate religion from rational criticism, Friedrich Schleiermacher built on Kant's work by removing religious thought from science and placed it in the realm of "feeling." Schleiermacher states that

> Only by keeping quite outside the range of both science and of practice can [religion] maintain its proper sphere and character. Only when piety takes its place alongside of science and practice, as a necessary, an indispensable third, as their natural counterpart, not less in worth and splendour than either, will the common field be altogether occupied and human nature on the side complete.[78]

Both of these epistemological tactics, even if implicitly, conceded to Hume's argument and thus removed religious concerns from the domain of rational consideration.

75. Murphy, *Theology in the Age of Scientific Reasoning*, 12.

76. Ibid., 12.

77. Ibid., 14. The term "standard epistemology" is to be equated with *modern* epistemology in so far as it refers to the determination of one's beliefs according to the weight of "internal" (relating to the character of the event itself apart from the witness's personal characteristics) evidence.

78. Schleiermacher, *On Religion*, 36. Schleiermacher's argument avoided the reduction of religion to morality and thus avoided the rejection of theism on behalf of many of those that found Kant's arguments insufficient.

The second response is found in the work of Karl Barth. Barth claimed that divine revelation is the sole source of any knowledge of God that human beings may possess. Theology, then, is an attempt to seek partial knowledge of what we already believe to be the case—this is what is meant by *fides quaerens intellectum* (faith seeking understanding). Although this move insulated Barth from Hume's criticisms, he abandoned apologetics altogether, thus requiring that one begin with an authoritative view of "God's word" before a legitimate rational theological inquiry can commence.

Murphy offers a third alternative—"a new possibility for rational support of theism using the resources of postfoundationalist (postmodern) epistemology."[79] This alternative has similarities to a theological approach suggested by Wolfhart Pannenberg;[80] however, Murphy's proposal differs in its basic theory of scientific methodology. Murphy notes contributions from Karl Popper[81] and Thomas Kuhn;[82] however, the most important figure in her view of scientific methodology is Imre Lakatos.

Lakatos proposed that scientific rationality requires the specification of a criterion for choice between competing "research programmes."[83] These research programmes consist of a set of theories and a body of data. The central theory or "hard core" represents the primary concern of the research programme itself. The auxiliary hypotheses constitute the supporting evidence by allowing data to be related to the central theory. These auxiliary hypotheses form a "protective belt" around the hard core and are modified whenever potentially falsifying data are discovered.

A research programme is best understood as a series of complex theories whose "hard core" remains the same while the auxiliary hypotheses are modified or replaced in order to account for problematic data. Lakatos argued that the history of science is best viewed in terms of competing

79. Ibid., 13. Murphy stresses the use of *postmodern* epistemology over against "modern" epistemologies due to the failure of the latter to resolve conflicts regarding foundationalism, representationalism in philosophy of language, and metaphysical reductionism (ibid., 199–208).

80. See Pannenberg, *Theology and the Philosophy of Science*. Pannenberg claims that it is the theologian's responsibility to test the Christian tradition's concept of God against everything that is known today about the course of history and judge whether the tradition's understanding is the best available account.

81. See primarily Popper, *Logic of Scientific Discovery*.

82. See Kuhn, *Structure of Scientific Revolutions*.

83. See Lakatos, *Methodology of Scientific Research Programmes*, especially section one "Falsification and the Methodology of Scientific Research Programmes," 8–101.

research programmes, some of which are "progressive" and others that are "degenerating."

A degenerating research programme is one whose central theory is preserved only by *ad hoc* modifications of the "protective belt." Lakatos referred to these manoeuvres as "mere face-saving devices" or "linguistic tricks." In contrast, Lakatos was greatly concerned with the justification of progressive programmes. A programme is said to progressive when the following conditions are met:[84]

1. each new version of the theory (core plus its auxiliaries) preserves the unrefuted content of its predecessor;

2. each has excess empirical content over its predecessor; that is, it predicts some novel, hitherto unexpected facts; and

3. some of these predicted facts are corroborated.

When the first two of these conditions are met, the theory is said to be "theoretically progressive." When all three are met it is "empirically progressive" as well. Murphy notes that

> A research program is *degenerating* when the change from one version to the next accounts at most for the one anomaly (or set of anomalies) for which the change was made, but does not allow for the prediction and discovery of any novel facts. The choice of a theory thus becomes a choice between two or more competing series of theories, and chooses the more *progressive* of the programs. Consequently, the choice depends on the program's relative power to increase scientific knowledge.[85]

Murphy argues that the scientific method presented by Lakatos is a viable candidate for finding a way through the theological dilemma created by Hume. This third alternative is a middle way between attempts offered by Kant and Schleiermacher on one hand and Barth on the other.

Murphy claims that in order to avoid the pitfalls fashioned by Hume, theology must, if it can, "substantiate its knowledge claims in the court of probable reasoning. . . . Consequently the appropriate response to Hume's arguments is to show that theology measures up to the best available *theory* of scientific method."[86] Thus, Murphy demonstrates how theologi-

---

84. Ibid., 31–46.

85. Murphy, *Theology in the Age of Scientific Reasoning*, 60. Emphasis added.

86. Ibid., 88. Emphasis added. This claim resonates with Pannenberg's observation that it is now *philosophy of science* that provides the definitive account of the canons of probable reasoning. See *Theology and Philosophy of Science*.

cal arguments can be presented and tested in the same manner as Lakatos suggested for theories in science. That is, first one establishes a "hard core" that will serve as the central thesis of the research programme. Second, one appends auxiliary hypotheses that demonstrate the programme to be progressive rather than degenerating.[87]

It is important to note that these auxiliary hypotheses include data from multiple sources. For Murphy, these sources include, but are not limited to: historical theology, epistemological theories, research from various branches of science (psychology, evolutionary biology, cognitive science, etc.), ethics, biblical studies, and various types of "experience." All of these sources constitute "data" that can be applied toward doctrinal formulation. Thus, doctrines are heuristic (problem solving) devices that stem from the shared experiences of the Christian religious tradition.[88]

Murphy's view of theological methodology serves as a guiding resource for my analytical approach to conversion. I will consider data from multiple sources—theological, philosophical, and scientific.

Evaluating a "Doctrine" of Christian Conversion

Offering a new paradigm of Christian conversion amounts to no less than suggesting a new "doctrine" of conversion. The methodology outlined in the previous section, together with some critical insights from Alasdair MacIntyre, provide a context in which I will speak of "doctrines" of conversion and how they may been seen as competing "research programmes" in the Lakatosian sense. To fully expand this idea would move beyond the scope of the present work; however, I offer this brief section in order to demonstrate how these resources provide the methodological and epistemological space to address my overall concerns.

I must begin by establishing why it is desirable to offer a new doctrine (or "theory" as I will refer to it below) of conversion. The very concept of a theory is more complex than it may first appear. Following Lakatos, it must be understood that the evaluation of a particular theory, in reality, consists of the appraisal of a series of interrelated theories—this is the basis of his concept of a "research programme."

---

87. For examples see Murphy, *Theology in the Age of Scientific Reasoning*, 88–129. See also Murphy, "Theology and Science within a Lakatosian Program," 629–42.

88. Likewise, doctrines have as supporting data the biblical texts, theological analysis, natural and social sciences, and a host of shared experiences within the Christian community itself.

To be clear, when evaluating a particular theory, one is in fact appraising a history, for the set of beliefs that the theory represents stand in various complex relationships to each other over the course of time. In this case, a theory is never a static structure, but continually grows and develops. MacIntyre offers the example of the development of the kinetic theory of gases.

> If we read the scientific textbooks for any period we shall find presented an entirely ahistorical account of the theory. But if we read all the successive textbooks we shall learn not only that the kinetic theory of 1857 was not quite that of 1845 and that the kinetic theory of 1901 is neither that of 1857 nor that of 1965. Yet at each stage the theory bears the marks of its previous history, of a series of encounters with confirming or anomalous evidence, with other theories, with metaphysical points of view, and so on.[89]

Thus, the kinetic theory not merely possesses, but *is* a history. To evaluate this history involves consideration of how it has fared in a large variety of encounters. Therefore, "to evaluate a theory, just as to evaluate a series of theories, one of Lakatos's research programs, is precisely to write that history, that narrative of defeats and victories."[90]

Lakatos recognized this in his paper on the "History of Science and Its Rational Reconstructions." Here he claimed that theories are to be assessed by the extent to which they satisfy historiographical criteria. That is, the *best* theory is that one which can supply the most complete rational reconstruction of the history that has brought the theory to its current form.[91] This rational reconstruction then enables us to understand precisely why a competing theory must be modified and why. It does so by introducing new standards for evaluation and recasts the developing narrative that constitutes the continuous reconstruction.

So then, this reconstruction must be viewed in the context of a historical continuum. Kuhn provides a practical example of how this occurs in the natural sciences. He notes that "in some important respects, though by no means at all, Einstein's general theory of relativity is closer to Aristotle's mechanics than either of them is to Newton's."[92] Therefore, Kuhn surmises that the superiority of Einstein to Newton is to be found in "puzzle solving" rather in an approach to a true ontology.

---

89. MacIntyre, "Epistemological Crises," 154.
90. Ibid., 154.
91. See Lakatos, "History of Science," 91–135.
92. Kuhn, *Structure of Scientific Revolutions*, 206–7.

Kuhn's point is that Aristotelian mechanics could never have led directly to special relativity—the Aristotelian paradigm will not yield the questions to which special relativity is the answer. Therefore, a history that moved from Aristotelianism directly to relativistic physics is not an imaginable history.

The American evangelical tradition has rendered a particular doctrine or "theory" of conversion that stands open to critique in the same way as the various scientific theories mentioned above. In essence, I am offering a competing theory of conversion with the presupposition that it is only from the standpoint of a newly evolved theory that one can characterize the inadequacy of the prior. Considering the discovery of new forms of data (which are constitutive of the nonreductive physicalism for which I argue), it is only from the standpoint of the new theory that the continuities of the relevant narrative history (conversion in the evangelical tradition) can be re-established.

In the context of Murphy's theological methodology, tradition, reason, and revolution need not be counterposed. If traditions can be conceived of as the bearers of reason, then certain periods of revolution are needed for their continuance. Therefore, in MacIntyre's words, "Every tradition is always in danger of lapsing into incoherence and when a tradition does lapse it can only be recovered by a revolutionary reconstitution."[93]

While I am not prepared to claim that the whole of American evangelicalism has fallen into incoherency, I do believe that the doctrine (theory) of conversion which is simply taken for granted among countless evangelicals has strayed from its traditional roots, as exemplified in Wesley. This, taken together with the new scientific discoveries presented in this book, exacerbates the need to evaluate the current model of conversion and offer a competing theory.[94]

Summary

The purpose of this chapter has been to present the context in which I seek to offer a new model of Christian conversion. I began by claiming that the

93. MacIntyre, "Epistemological Crises," 146.

94. A key way in which this claim can be developed (in relation to future research building upon my current project) is to evaluate the American evangelical theory of conversion that I am critiquing in this work in light of the "results" that it has produced—i.e., how the evangelical churches in America compare to Jesus' image of the Kingdom of God. Without substantial empirical investigation it is impossible to speak to this with any authority; however, I submit that the type of "conversion" that I criticize, marked by its highly interiorized and individualized character, would be found lacking.

idea of "spirituality" seems to defy definition.[95] The version of spirituality that I criticize is primarily Western and particularly indigenous to North America. I have claimed that the state of Christian spirituality in American evangelicalism is characterized by a dualistic and ultimately interior form of expression. Spirituality, understood in this way, subsequently leads to a doctrine of conversion characterized by the rhetoric of "saving souls."

I have suggested that this condition needs to be corrected. Conversion is only peripherally about the adoption of a particular belief or "meaning-making" system. Rather, I claim that Christian conversion is primarily concerned with socio-moral transformation—that is a transformation in moral attitude and behavior that is ultimately expressed in a social context.[96]

I also suggested that the way forward is to formulate a new "doctrine" of conversion in light of Wesleyan theology and a nonreductive physicalist view of human nature. In order to accomplish this goal, I have listed two presuppositions that will inform the investigation further—a *virtue*-based moral theory and a theological method best represented in the work of Nancey Murphy. In addition, I suggested that forming this new model or "theory" of conversion makes it possible to properly reflect on the doctrine of conversion predominant in American evangelical circles.

Chapter two will present the relevant work of John Wesley. Wesley's work, as a *practical* theologian, possesses an inherent "telos" which, in his own terms, is best understood as "new creation." At the center of Wesley's "way of salvation" is a distinctive *affectional moral psychology*. Here the emphasis is placed on the acquisition of holy tempers; that is, the heart of religion, for Wesley, is the transformation of those inclinations in human nature that serve as motivators for moral attitude and behavior. This insight, together with Wesley's concept of "sanctification" will provide a critical theological language for the observed socio-moral change that I call *conversion*.

---

95. Philip Sheldrake has dedicated a significant amount of academic energy toward articulating the notion of spirituality. He describes spirituality as "one of those subjects whose meaning everyone claims to know until they have to define it." Despite this, one must struggle to articulate it for "if it has no conceptual limits, effectively it means nothing." See Sheldrake, "What Is Spirituality?," 21.

96. To be clear, I reject the understanding of belief as mere mental assent. In the present context "belief" can be understood to be equivalent to the term "conviction" as defined by James McClendon and James Smith. Here a conviction "means a persistent belief such that if X (a person or community) has a conviction, it will not easily be relinquished and it cannot be relinquished without making X a significantly different person (or community) than before." See McClendon and Smith, *Convictions*, 5.

In chapter three, I argue that a proper view of human nature is critical to any cogent description of conversion. I claim that both dualism and reductive materialism are undesirable on philosophical and theological grounds. Instead, I offer a third alternative, *nonreductive physicalism*, as a viable theory of human nature. Such a theory avoids the problems of ontological substance dualism while preserving the causal efficacy of "higher" order capacities necessary for a proper theological anthropology. The theory also describes how humans possess the capacity for relatedness without positing the existence of an ontologically distinct immaterial entity representing the true "self." In addition, the final section of chapter three will include a discussion of conversion and sanctification as process or event. Here, I offer a corrective based on the nonreductive physicalist view of human nature.

The purpose of chapter four is to present a new conceptual model of Christian conversion that synthesizes the contributions from Wesley's theology and practices in light of nonreductive physicalism. This discussion necessarily involves scientific insights, including contributions from neuroscience and various branches of cognitive science.

I define Christian conversion as a process involving normal human biological capacities. It is characterized by a change in socio-moral attitude and behavior, and is best understood as the acquisition of virtues intrinsic to Christian faith. Such acquisitions are facilitated through social interaction and participation in practices inherent to the Christian community. Furthermore, the conversion process should be viewed as the co-operant result of Divine grace and human participation. I spend the remainder of chapter four justifying this definition.

Finally, in chapter five I will claim that the model of conversion presented here necessitates a theology of corporate conversion. Without seeking to offer systematic methods, I present an example of a "conversion community" that constitutes the type of space required for Christian conversion to occur. This final chapter is intended to highlight the practical implications of the overall project.

CHAPTER 2

Theological Insights
Beginning with the End

How small a part of this great work of God is man able to understand! But it is
our duty to contemplate what he has wrought, and to understand as much of it
as we are able.
—John Wesley[1]

THESE WORDS SPOKEN BY the eighteenth-century theologian, John
Wesley, are brief, but provide an example of his thinking and approach to questions about God, humanity, and the cosmos. The intent
of this chapter is to provide theological insights that contribute to my
ultimate goal of offering a practical understanding of Christian religious
conversion. My central claim is that the theology of John Wesley provides
a view of creation that possesses an inherent *telos*—aim, purpose, or ultimate end. Wesley's telic exposition is characterized by the redemption of
the whole of creation through the process of *new creation*. At the center of
this redemption, lies the notion of the salvation of humankind.

Wesley's "way of salvation" places particular emphasis on the acquisition of "holy tempers," this is to say that the heart of religion for Wesley
was the transformation of those inclinations in human nature that serve
as motivators for moral attitude and behavior. Throughout this chapter, I
will demonstrate how Wesley's notions of the "way of salvation," and his
concept of *sanctification* in particular, provides a useful language for my
approach to the phenomenon of conversion. In fact, I claim that Wesley's
mature view of salvation (characterized by *sanctification*) is equivalent to
my concept of Christian conversion.

I have chosen to begin this theological investigation with Wesley
because of his distinctive approach to theological issues. I argue that

---

1. Sermon 56, "God's Approbation of His Works," in Baker, *Works*, 2:387. Further
references from this edition will be designated as "*BE*." This designation will be followed
by the respective volume and page number (vol:page).

Wesley is best viewed as a *practical* theologian.[2] By this, I mean that he was concerned with the embodiment of theological principles. He prioritized issues of theological importance not according to their adherence to theological dogma, but to their ability to transform the lives of people. This distinctive feature is one that I wish to share with Wesley in my effort to describe Christian conversion.

In addition, Wesley's articulation of salvation is vital to my effort to provide a theological language for moral transformation in a Christian context. It is important to note that I do not intend to offer an exhaustive summary of Wesley's theology, rather I will summarize the overall tone of his work and focus on those aspects that offer greater clarity to my specified goal. I admire Wesley's willingness to engage in theological struggles, and like him, I too am dedicated to articulating a theological discourse that impacts religious life in a practical way.

John Wesley as a Practical Theologian

Some may consider it unusual to speak of Wesley as a theologian (or at least a serious one). After all, he did not produce any lengthy theological treatises or put forth any substantial works of systematic theology. He did, however, leave behind a bounty of sermons, letters, hymns, and journal entries written for the purpose of practical instruction. Wesley understood theology to be intrinsically related to the process of Christian living and mission. As a result, his writing dealt less with philosophical systematics and more with practical engagement. This is what is meant by Wesley's "practical" theology—theology for the purpose of transforming life both in a personal and social sense.

Wesley was keen on the challenge of interpreting life in light of theology and vice versa. His focus on an "experimental divinity" epitomized the goal of religion—the expression of true living faith. Robert E. Cushman notes Wesley's tendency to present doctrine as being intricately bound to Christian life. He states, "Wesley is saying that the character of a Methodist is (or should be) exhibitive of the individual's Christian doctrine; and, conversely, that essential doctrine is (or should be) constitutive of the Christian life."[3] Cushman's observation is fitting in that it identifies Wesley's emphasis on the interdependence of doctrine and the pragmatic aspects of life.

---

2. Here, the term "practical" denotes an object's use that extends beyond the theoretical and is manifested in action and purpose.

3. Cushman, *Experimental Divinity*, 63.

Wesley's work has been called into question by a number of scholars both within and without the Methodist tradition.[4] Much of this can be attributed to the fact that the most significant of Wesley's theological contributions come from his sermons that were written within the context of his audience. As Wesley's audience changed so did his emphasis on various theological concerns. In addition, his writing reflects his own personal maturation process by demonstrating his evolving theological struggles. This is why contemporary Wesleyan scholars will refer to Wesley's "early position" on a particular issue or appeal to the "mature Wesley" for insight into a specific theological concept. This lack of consistency throughout his career and the fact that Wesley was not systematic in the arrangement of his doctrines "does not warrant the assumption that he was inconsistent or contradictory in his theological opinions."[5] Many contemporary Wesleyan scholars have recognized this issue and have attempted to piece together a systematic theology from Wesley's writing.[6] Despite these worthy attempts, I propose a different approach.

Moving forward I will espouse the view offered by Randy L. Maddox concerning Wesley's approach to theology as a practical discipline.[7] Here Maddox is clear to distinguish between contemporary theology as an academic enterprise and the pre-university model of Wesley's day. In this model,

> The quintessential practitioner of theology was not the detached academic theologian; it was the pastor/theologian who was actively shepherding Christian disciples in the world. Likewise, the defining task of "real" theologians was neither developing an elaborate system of Christian truth-claims nor defending these claims to their "cultured despisers;" it was nurturing and shaping the worldview that frames the temperament and practice of believers' lives in the world. Finally, the primary (or first order) literary forms of "real"

---

4. For example, E. P. Thompson criticized Wesley's Methodism as a system of thought calling it a "ritualized form of psychic masturbation." See Thompson, *Making of the English Working Class*, 368. Also Paul Johnson criticized Wesley's form of Christian thought to be totally devoid of intellectual content. See *History of Christianity*, 365. Even some within the Methodist tradition question Wesley as a "real" theologian. For example, see Davies, *History of the Methodist Church*, 147.

5. Cannon, *Theology of John Wesley*, 7–8. For more on the consistency of Wesley's theological positions see Heitzenrater, *Elusive Mr. Wesley*, 28; Tuttle, *John Wesley*, 10; Outler, *John Wesley*, 27.

6. For example, see Oden, *John Wesley's Scriptural Christianity*; Coppedge, *John Wesley in Theological Debate*, and "How Wesleyans Do Theology," 267–89.

7. Maddox, "John Wesley—Practical Theologian?," 122–47.

theological activity were not systematic theologies or apologetics; they were carefully-crafted liturgies, catechisms, hymns, sermons, and the like. Judged on such terms, Wesley's voluminous writings emerge as serious theological activity indeed![8]

Given this understanding, the focal point of theological activity is rooted in the life of the Christian community. Likewise, the measure of such a practical theological method relies not on its establishing systematic doctrine, but on its ability to clearly define the nature and purpose of its own existence.

I begin with this dimension of Wesley's life for the purpose of demonstrating his priority on a theology that "works." A theological concept or doctrine would have been of little use to Wesley if it did not act to further the purpose of God in the world. If human beings were not moved or transformed for the glory of God, then it would have been little more than casual advice or a passing opinion. This sense of "purpose" rooted in Christian community was a prominent feature of Wesley's theology and is the topic to which we will now turn our attention.

Wesley and the New Creation

So if anyone is in Christ, there is a new creation: everything old has passed away; see, everything has become new!—2 Cor 5:17

For I am about to create new heavens and a new earth; the former things shall not be remembered or come to mind.—Isa 65:17

I consider that the sufferings of this present time are not worth comparing with the glory about to be revealed to us. For the creation waits with eager longing for the revealing of the children of God; for the creation was subjected to futility, not of its own will but by the will of the one who subjected it, in hope that the creation itself will be set free from its bondage to decay and will obtain the freedom of the glory of the children of God. We know that the whole creation has been groaning in labor pains until now; and not only the creation, but we ourselves, who have the first fruits of the Spirit, groan inwardly while we wait for adoption, the redemption of our bodies.—Rom 8:18–23[9]

8. Maddox, "Reading Wesley as a Theologian," 12. This work resonates with the earlier work of Albert Outler. See Outler, "Towards a Re-appraisal," 5–14.

9. These Scripture references are taken from the New Revised Standard Version.

Wesley was unquestionably a man of the Bible. It was from Scripture that his foundational concepts about God and humankind were formulated. A tension existed in Wesley's life between what he read in Scripture and what he observed both in his own life and in the lives of the Methodists. While never ceasing to uphold the authority of Scripture, he ever sought ways to both make sense of his own religious experiences and to effectively present his theological insights in an accessible way to those to whom he ministered.

It can be demonstrated that despite the lack of a grand volume of systematic theology, Wesley's work possessed an inherent trajectory.[10] This is to say that a survey of his life and writing provides a path to understand both the passion of his theological analysis and the goals to which it led.

Unabashedly, Wesley claims, "Ye know that the great end of religion is to renew our hearts in the image of God."[11] Indeed, for Wesley this was the heart of Christianity. This renewal is the "axial theme of Wesley's soteriology" according to Wesleyan scholar, Albert Outler.[12] This concept may not seem novel on the surface; however, it is this claim that first sets Wesley apart from his contemporaries. He is convinced that we can derive God's purpose from the original creation. Wesley's ability to weave together scriptural passages into a narrative was key in his theological position on the divine purpose in creation. Citing verses from both the Old and New Testaments, Wesley declares:

> Suppose now the fullness of time to be come, and the prophecies to be accomplished—what a prospect is this! . . . Here is no din of arms, no "confused noise," no "garments rolled in blood." . . . no country or city divided against itself, and tearing out its own bowels. . . . Here is no oppression to "make (even) the wise man mad," no extortion to "grind the face of the poor"; no robbery or wrong; no rapine or injustice; for all are "content with such things as they possess." Thus "righteousness and peace have kissed each other"; they have "taken root and filled the land"; righteousness flourishing out of the earth, and "peace looking down from heaven."[13]

Biblical passages such as these led Wesley to believe that God had indeed created the world with purpose and this divine intent was active and pro-

10. The term "trajectory" is borrowed from Maddox, "Nurturing the New Creation," 21–52; and Collins, "Reconfiguration of Power," 164–84.

11. Sermon 44, *Original Sin, BE* (2:185).

12. Outler, *Bicentennial Edition of the Works of John Wesley* (2:185).

13. Sermon 4, *Scriptural Christianity, BE* (1:170–71). Scripture references: Isa 9:5; Eccl 7:7; Isa 3:15; Heb 13:5; Ps 85:10; Ps 80:9, 14.

gressing. Likewise, Wesley understood creation to illustrate a harmony that bore witness to God's plan.

> Such was the state of the creation, according to the scanty ideas which we can now form concerning it, when its great Author, surveying the whole system at one view, pronounced it "very good." . . . There was "a golden chain" (to use the expression of Plato) "let down from the throne of God"—an exactly connected series of beings, from the highest to the lowest; from dead earth, through fossils, vegetables, animals, to man, created in the image of God, and designed to know, to love, and enjoy his Creator to all eternity.[14]

After a period of profound growth, Wesley came to express the notion that God is redeeming the world through the process of *new creation*.[15] The whole of this belief can be summed up into the notion that God has a purpose for the world and a means to see this purpose to fruition.[16] In this sense, Wesley's notion of new creation can be understood as a *grand narrative*.[17] Wesleyan scholar Joel B. Green places new creation within the grand narrative of God's salvation of the world. Green relates new creation with

---

14. Sermon 56, *God's Approbation of His Works*, BE (2:395–97).

15. It is obvious that from Wesley's early sermons that he found the greatest promise in life not to be a present reality, but a hope in that which comes after death. E.g., "we all agree in calling life a burden . . . [and that] death is not only a haven, but an entrance into a far more desirable country." Sermon 133, *Death and Deliverance*, BE (4:208). Wesley's mature position was dramatically different in that it placed the hope of salvation in the context of a present reality.

16. New Testament scholar, Greg Beale has argued that the notion of new creation should be seen as the controlling conception for all of eschatology and the core around which all major theological ideas in the New Testament revolve. See Beale, "The Eschatological Conception," 11–52.

17. I realize that my introduction of the term "grand narrative" opens the door to philosophical criticism. It is important to note here that I define "grand narrative" as a global concept or historical story by which humans order their personal narratives at both the individual and communal level. The term was first introduced into philosophical analysis by Jean-Francois Lyotard in *The Postmodern Condition: A Report on Knowledge*. Despite Lyotard's claim that, "the ideas of Western civilization issuing from the ancient, Christian and modern traditions are bankrupt" (*Postmodern Fables*, 235), I will continue to argue for the appropriateness of viewing Christianity and more specifically salvation as a "grand narrative." For additional supporting work see Browning, *Lyotard and the End of Grand Narratives*; Taber, "Gospel as Authentic Meta-Narrative Source," 182–94; Westphal, "Postmodernism," 6–10; Sutherland, "Providence," 171–85. Perhaps the most often read source on narrative and theology is Hauerwas and Jones, *Why Narrative?* For more on salvation as Biblical grand narrative see Wright, *Challenge of Jesus*. Here Wright expounds on the "Kingdom of God" and its connection to the Scriptural theme of redemption.

the life of the Church—as the "Body of Christ" the Church is carrying on Jesus' mission by existing as the visible Kingdom of God in the world.[18]

Wesley's view of new creation possessed elements or dimensions that were intimately connected to his concerns to articulate a meaningful soteriology and eschatology. I follow Maddox in identifying three salient dimensions of Wesley's view of new creation—the *spiritual* dimension, the *socioeconomic* dimension, and finally the *cosmic dimension*.[19]

Wesley's concern for the socioeconomic dimension of new creation led him to produce tracts like *Thoughts on the Present Scarcity of Provisions* (1773) and *Thoughts upon Slavery* (1774). Contemporary Wesleyan scholarship has produced a number of significant works articulating Wesley's theological perspectives as they apply to socioeconomic concerns.[20] In addition, the later years of Wesley's life brought an emphasis on the cosmic dimension of new creation. His strong affirmations of both a new heaven and a *new earth* were highlighted by inclusion of animals and the physical world within the scope of new creation.[21]

Wesley's preoccupation with these two dimensions of new creation fuelled his concerns for the third aspect that centered on spiritual renewal. This dimension was marked by Wesley's insistence that its primary feature was the regeneration of humanity in the image of God.

The Nature of Humankind—
Wesley's Theological Anthropology

Wesley's overall theology revolved around the dynamics of the God-human relationship. His utmost concern was to both understand and articulate the relationship of the creator God to divine creation, particularly humankind. As the result of this effort, Wesley developed a distinctive theological

18. See Green, *Beginning with Jesus*, 151–62.

19. Maddox, "Nurturing the New Creation," 21–52.

20. For a helpful example see Jennings, *Good News to the Poor*.

21. For example, Wesley assumed that, along with humans, animals suffered from the effects of sin; therefore, they will also participate in God's healing work. Wesley claimed that "the whole brute creation will undoubtedly be restored, not only to the vigour, strength, and swiftness which they had at their creation, but to a far higher degree of each than they ever enjoyed. . . . In the new earth, as well as in the new heavens, there will be nothing to give pain, but everything that the wisdom and goodness of God can create to give happiness. As a recompence for what they once suffered, while under the 'bondage of corruption,' when God has 'renewed the face of the earth,' and their corruptible body has put on incorruption, they shall enjoy happiness suited to their state, without alloy, without interruption, and without end." See Sermon 60, *The General Deliverance, BE* (2:437–50).

anthropology. At its core, this refers to his efforts to express an understanding of human nature that would describe both the essence of humanity and the ways in which we can relate to God.[22] In expounding on this matter, three distinct features emerge in regards to Wesley's theological anthropology. They are his: *relational* anthropology, *holistic* anthropology, and his emphasis on an inherent *affectional moral psychology*.[23]

Before I address each of these features in detail, I will speak to the general theological climate that surrounded Wesley as he sought to work through these important issues. The contrasting ways in which the Eastern and Western Christian traditions approached the issues of human nature played a large part in Wesley's maturing views. The Western tradition typically assumed that humans were created in a state of perfection. Despite God's original will that they stay in this perfect condition, they nevertheless sinned and "fell" from this created state.

They (Adam and Eve) were able to bring about this consequence due to a critical aspect of their creation—the ability for self-determination. Thus, the Fall brought devastating effects, primarily the loss of self-determination (henceforth humanity is no longer free not to sin). This condition of sin being transmitted through all of humanity is known as Original Sin. The West saw this fallen condition as the "natural" state of humankind. In short, the Western view of human nature is based on the Fall and humanity's inability to recover from this fallen state apart from the intervention of God.

In contrast to this view, the Eastern tradition presents human nature in a significantly different perspective. Generally speaking, Christianity of the East and West differ in their assessments of original "guilt." Following Augustine, the Western tradition held that all inherit the guilt of the original sin of Adam and Eve. The Eastern tradition differs on this point. George Cronk states that,

> We are born into a world conditioned by Adam's sin and by the accumulated sins of others; we are involved in and influenced by that world; and our lives are often shaped by the ongoing consequences of human sinfulness. But we are guilty of, and therefore morally and spiritually responsible for our own actual sins, and not the sins of others. The tendency to sin is "original" (or "congenital") in that it is a natural consequence of being born into a fallen world. In

22. Inherent to this exposition of human nature are issues concerning the Fall, the problem of sin, and how it is that humans are to overcome the sinful human condition.

23. These three aspects are introduced by Randy L. Maddox. See Maddox, *Responsible Grace*.

this restricted sense, we may be "born sinful," but we are not "born guilty." The Orthodox Church has always repudiated the doctrine of "original guilt" that is, the view that all men share not only the consequences of but also the guilt for the sin of Adam and Eve.[24]

In this view, humanity was created in a state of innocence, but not in a state of completeness.[25] God created humans with a dynamic nature capable of growing in intimacy with the divine creator. Herein rests the Eastern meaning of the "image" and "likeness" of God. These terms referred to both the potential and progressive realization of intimate life in the Divine creator. This realization is also referred to as "deification" in Eastern Orthodoxy and is made possible by participation in the community of God. Maddox notes that such was neither inevitable nor automatic, but it, "necessarily included the aspect of human freedom, *though it centred in the larger human capacity for communion with God.*"[26]

Although the East and West agreed that the cause of the Fall was rooted in disobedience, they disagreed on the results of it. The most prominent theological differences are the notions of inherent guilt and the total depravity of grace. On the first point, those in the Eastern tradition did not believe that Adam's sin cast inherent guilt upon every human being to come after him.[27] From this perspective, humans are not born with inherent sin; we learn sin and ultimately come to imitate it throughout the course of our lives.[28]

As to the second issue, although the Eastern theologians did believe that the Fall prevented human beings from assuming the image of God on our own merit, it did not, however, leave humanity without access to grace. Most fundamentally, this means that human beings inherently possess the capacity (and responsibility) to respond to God's grace.[29] The ultimate end of this theological view was that Eastern Christianity based its theological anthropology on creation rather than the Fall. The emphasis

24. Cronk, *Message of the Bible*, 45.

25. This idea is traced from the second-century theologian Theophiles and further from Gregory of Nyssa. See Chrestou, *Partakers of God.*

26. Maddox, *Responsible Grace*, 66. Emphasis added.

27. For more see Meyendorff, *Byzantine Theology*, 145.

28. For more see Clendenin, *Eastern Orthodox Christianity*, 132–33.

29. It is important to note that Wesley did not embrace this notion in its entirety. While he did believe that humans could respond to God, it was not through an inherent capacity, but rather through God's graceful restoration of our human faculties. I will discuss this further in the proceeding section.

was on the hope in and ability of humanity to respond to God's love and purpose in the world.

On the surface, Wesley's work appears to fit well within the boundaries of reformation thought. For instance, Wesley's exegetical method reflected that of the Protestant reformers who claimed that the Bible was the sole authority in matters of faith and practice.[30] In fact, Wesley was greatly influenced by the work of Augustine. Much of Wesley's understanding regarding grace can be traced back to Augustine's concept of *gratia praeveniens*.[31]

Despite Wesley's place as a theologian of the West, a close examination of his work also reveals theological particularities characteristic of the Eastern tradition.[32] The Eastern Fathers seemed to have greatly influenced Wesley's understanding of soteriology. The Eastern tradition's view of salvation as having an explicit *therapeutic nature* appealed to Wesley as he sought to articulate his mature view of salvation. In this sense, renewal or salvation was as much about being well and healing from sin as it was a juridical declaration of forgiveness.[33] One cannot overstate the importance

30. For an analysis of Wesley's exegetical method see Martin, "John Wesley's Exegetical Orientation," 104–38.

31. By claiming that God's grace was active in *all* persons, Augustine was able to conceive of the virtue and wisdom found in pagan culture as the activity of the one true God. This idea has obvious resonance with Wesley's notion of Prevenient Grace. For more on Augustine's influence on Wesley's theological thought see Horton-Parker, "John Wesley," 1–22.

32. Maddox stresses the point that Wesley would most likely not have made a conscious distinction between these theological doctrines of the East and West. He would have dealt with this practically by struggling to affirm the faith of the early church while considering the Protestant notion of justification by faith which hinged on a Western conceptualisation of the Fall and Original Sin. *Responsible Grace*, 286. Maddox further speculates that a likely source of Wesley's connection to Eastern thought was the work of the Egyptian, Macarius. For more see Lee, "Experiencing the Spirit," 197–212, 245–48, and Snyder, "John Wesley," 55–60. For more on Eastern Patristic tradition see Christensen, "Theosis," 71–94; Merritt, "Dialogue," 92–116; Spidlik, *Spirituality of the Christian East*; Saldanha, *Divine Pedagogy*.

33. For example, see Wesley's sermons, *A Farther Appeal to Men of Reason and Religion*, *BE* (11:106); *A Plain Account of Genuine Christianity*, *BE* (10:38); *The Witness of Our Spirit*, *BE* (1:304); *Original Sin*, *BE* (2:185). To be clear, Wesley did speak about humanity being created in a state of perfection. See Sermon 141, *The Image of God*, *BE* (4:293) and Sermon 60, *The General Deliverance*, *BE* (2:439) for examples. However, it is clear that whatever the original state of humanity might have been, Wesley placed a strong emphasis on the dynamic nature of *present* spiritual development. Maddox points out that Wesley apparently did not realize that there was an alternate developmental view of original human nature in the earlier Christian tradition. *Responsible Grace*, 67.

of soteriology in Wesley's theology—for Wesley, the Bible was an essentially soteriological book.[34]

My purpose in providing this brief sketch is to point out that much of what is seen as distinctive in Wesley's theological views is derived from his particular intermingling of Eastern and Western theological ideologies. Supporting this view, H. S. Horton-Parker states that Wesley's great legacy is his "synthesis of Western and Eastern theologies, in which his answer to the question of the tension between faith and works was *energoumene di agapes* [faith filled with the energy of love]."[35] This "synthesis" joins the Western emphasis upon justification with the Eastern concept of *theosis*.[36] With these points in mind, I will proceed to address the three features that emerge from Wesley's theological anthropology.

Wesley's Relational Anthropology

Working from within the Wesleyan tradition, New Testament scholar, Joel B. Green notes that a scriptural portrayal of human nature emphasizes "the construction of the self as ineluctably nested in social relationships and, then, the importance of relational interdependence for human life and identity."[37] It is from both scripture and the doctrines of the Church that Wesley would have derived his understanding of the relational nature of God.

Within orthodox Christianity, God is spoken of as Trinity—three *persons* in one.[38] The very concept of "personhood" denotes the capacity for relationship. The Latin rendering of Yahweh is *Adsum* connotes, "I shall be with you as who I am." This title exemplifies God's covenantal relation-

34. George Lyons characterizes Wesley's hermeneutic as "soteriocentric" in nature. Lyons claims that Wesley "studied the Bible with one overriding question in mind: What is the way to heaven." See Lyons, "Hermeneutical Bases for Theology," 67.

35. Horton-Parker, "John Wesley," 11.

36. *Theosis* means "deification," "divinization," or "making divine." See McKim, *Westminster Dictionary of Theological Terms*, 282. In the Eastern Orthodox tradition, Theosis "is a vision of human potential for perfection, anticipated in ancient Greece, witnessed to in both the Old and New Testaments, and developed by Patristic Christian theologians of the first five centuries after Christ." See Christensen, "Theosis and Sanctification," 71. This synthesis led to Wesley's distinctive articulation of sanctification.

37. Green, *Salvation*, 23.

38. For more on the Trinity and the concepts of personhood and relationality see Grenz, *Social God and the Relational Self*; Gunton, *Triune Creator* and *Promise of Trinitarian Theology*; Torrance, *Christian Doctrine of God*; Moltmann, *Trinity and the Kingdom*; Lacugna, *God For Us*, and "The Relational God," 647–63; Schwobel and Gunton, *Persons Divine and Human*.

ship with Israel. Within the Christian tradition, Jesus is the culmination of God's relationship with humanity. Indeed, he is "Emmanuel"—*God with us.*

Likewise, according to the Christian understanding of creation (both Eastern and Western), God, who is characterized by this deep relational nature chose to create humankind in God's own image thus possessing a similar relational capacity and subsequent need for community. Just as God is conceived as relational in divine essence, humankind is subsequently characterized by this relationality.

It is important to clearly understand what Wesley meant when he spoke of human nature being cast in the *image* of God. Unlike many others of his day, Wesley saw the image as rooted in relationship rather than something that humans inherently possess.[39] These ideals were characteristic in the work of the Eastern Fathers and influenced Wesley in his way of thinking about the image. In this sense, humanity is meant to *reflect* or *mirror* the image of God to the world.[40]

Furthermore, it is important to note that God's image did not refer to the "nature" of God per se, but rather to the "actions" of God in the world. In this way of understanding the image, Wesley would have been much more sympathetic to speaking of *love* being the image of God in humanity rather than reason or conscience. The *act* of love spoke more about the nature of God than intellectual processes.

Theodore Runyon, in his work on Wesley's concept of the new creation, states the following:

> The image of God as Wesley understands it might best be described as a vocation or calling to which human beings are called, the fulfilment of which constitutes their true destiny. Because it is not innate, the image can be distorted, or forfeited or betrayed. *It resides not so much in the creature as in the way the creature lives out his or her relation to the Creator,* using whatever gifts and capacities have been received to be in communion with its source and to reflect that source in the world.[41]

Here Runyon stresses Wesley's belief that humans are created with a calling to reflect the image of God in the world. In other words, people do not inherently reflect the image of God in and of themselves; instead they

---

39. For example, Deists saw the "image of God" as the ability to exercise reason.

40. For more on the Eastern Fathers and their influence on Wesley's theological ideals see Meyendorff, *Study of Gregory Palamas,* 120.

41. Runyon, *New Creation,* 13–14. Emphasis added.

come to reflect that image in the world by being in proper *relationship* with God and the whole of creation. As stated above, Wesley viewed this calling to become the image of God as a central element in the purpose or "telos" of the new creation.

Like much of the principal doctrines of the Eastern tradition, Wesley adhered to this notion of human relationality as indispensable in his overall theological anthropology.[42] In speaking of the original state of humankind, Wesley says:

> Above all, (which was his highest excellence, far more valuable than all the rest put together,) he was a creature capable of God; capable of knowing, loving, and obeying his Creator. And, in fact, he did know God, did unfeignedly love and uniformly obey him. This was the supreme perfection of man; (as it is of all intelligent beings;) the continually seeing, and loving, and obeying the Father of the spirits of all flesh. From this right state and right use of all his faculties, his happiness naturally flowed.[43]

These words from Wesley demonstrate his notion that humankind reflects the glory of God in a relational sense and it is this relational integrity that he strove to see restored in the new creation.

It is in the fulfilment of relational or communal life that we reach our full potential as human beings.[44] The ultimate example of Christian community is the Church—those people who exist in a particular relationship with God and each other. For Wesley, those that are in proper relationship with the Creator have been connected with the telic narrative of God in new creation, and as a result, their personal narratives now coexist, all the while culminating toward being the "body of Christ" in the world.[45] At the center of this Christian community is to be found participation with God and divine purpose in new creation.[46]

---

42. This point is fundamental to Wesley's articulation of justification and sanctification. For more on relationality in the Eastern tradition see Zizioulas, *Being as Communion*.

43. Sermon 60, *The Great Deliverance*, BE (2:439).

44. For supporting material on the social nature of personhood see McFayden, *Call to Personhood*.

45. I argue that this strong metaphor offered by Paul (1 Cor 12:27, Eph 1:22–23; Col 1:18) serves an incredibly helpful role in understanding the mission of the Church and the end to which the community of God should strive.

46. This participation is marked by knowing, loving, obeying, and enjoying God eternally. *An Earnest Appeal to Men of Reason and Religion*, BE (11:62).

Wesley's Holistic Anthropology

A further dimension of Wesley's theological anthropology dealt with the dichotomy between the physical and spiritual aspect of humanity. There were several traditional interpretations of this issue in Wesley's day. In the Greek philosophical tradition, it was common to speak of the body and soul as completely separate entities resulting in both a metaphysical and ethical dualism. Some of Wesley's writing reflects this point of view. Note that in his sermon on *The Good Steward* he claims:

> [God] hath entrusted us with our souls, our bodies, our goods, and whatever other talents we have received: But in order to impress this weighty truth on our hearts, it will be needful to come to particulars. And, first, God has entrusted us with our soul, an immortal spirit, made in the image of God; together with all the powers and faculties thereof, understanding, imagination, memory, will, and a train of affections, either included in it or closely dependent upon it, —love and hatred, joy and sorrow, respecting present good and evil; desire and aversion, hope and fear, respecting that which is to come. . . . Secondly, [God] entrusted us with our bodies (those exquisitely wrought machines, so fearfully and wonderfully made,) with all the powers and members thereof. He has entrusted us with the organs of sense; of sight, hearing, and the rest: But none of these are given us as our own, to be employed according to our own will. None of these are lent us in such a sense as to leave us at liberty to use them as we please for a season. No: We have received them on these very terms, that, as long as they abide with us, we should employ them all in that very manner, and no other, which he appoints.[47]

In contrast to the Greek philosophical view of the body and soul, Green notes that the scriptural witness operates under "the assumption that a person *is* one's behavior—that is, that one's deepest commitments are unavoidably exhibited in one's practices—so that attention focuses on 'embodied life,' disallowing the possibility that the 'real' person might be relegated to one's interior life."[48] This "embodied" view of human nature depicted in scripture would have also influenced Wesley's thoughts on human nature.

Although it is obvious from his writing that he existed in this tension, he did speak of the human person in much more holistic terms than many of his contemporaries. It is safe to say that Wesley considered human be-

47. Sermon 52, *The Good Steward*, BE (2:284).
48. Green, *Salvation*, 23.

ings to be embodied souls or spirits, but he was careful to place emphasis on the particularly "embodied" dimension of this view. This position can be seen in his notes on 1 Thess 5:23:

> And may the God of peace sanctify you—By the peace he works in you, which is a great means of sanctification. *Wholly*—The word signifies wholly and perfectly; every part and all that concerns you; all that is of or about you. *And may the whole of you, the spirit and the soul and the body*—Just before he said you; now he denominates them from their spiritual state. The spirit—Gal. vi, 8; wishing that it may be preserved whole and entire: then from their natural state, the soul and the body; (*for these two make up the whole nature of man*, Matt. X, 28;) wishing it may be preserved blameless till the coming of Christ.[49]

Wesley continues this theme in a sermon from 2 Cor 4:7 by acknowledging the embodied existence of the human person. Wesley saw that "the soul, during its vital union with the body, cannot exert any of its operations, any otherwise than in union with the body."[50]

Wesley took further issue with any belief that separated a "spiritual life" from a life to be lived in the physical world.

> Many eminent men have spoken thus: Have advised us "to cease from all outward actions"; wholly to withdraw from the world; to leave the body behind us; to abstract ourselves from all sensible things—to have no concern at all about outward religion, but to "work all virtues in the will," as the far more excellent way, more perfective of the soul, as well as more acceptable to God.[51]

These words, spoken by Wesley, reflect a common attitude toward religious expression during his day. Just as Wesley espoused the fundamentally social and embodied nature of Christianity, I too argue for this position.

Green's charge that Scripture makes the critical assumption that "a person *is* one's behavior" is an interesting and important claim.[52] This line

49. From *John Wesley's Notes on the Bible*, 1 Thess 5:23. Emphasis added.

50. Sermon 129, *Heavenly Treasures in Earthen Vessels, BE* (4:165).

51. Sermon 24, *Sermon on the Mount IV, BE* (1:532). This passage from Wesley's sermon directly addresses the words of his former mentor, William Law. As a part of the Moravian tradition, Law's advice had a quietistic and individualistic tone. This position held by Law represents the antithesis of my argument regarding the embodied nature of humanity and religious expression.

52. I am careful here point out that Green's claim does not represent "behaviorism" in the classical sense; rather, it points toward issues of virtue and character which are intrinsically bound to an individual's moral life.

of thinking is rich in the field of virtue theory. As mentioned in the previous chapter, this literature emphasizes the notion of embodiment and its place in human nature. As a mode of moral philosophy, virtue theory provides a distinct place for the dimension of human passions or affections.[53] In the following section, I will discuss at length the importance that Wesley placed on the affections.

My point in stressing this dimension of Wesley's holistic anthropology is to show that although Wesley used the language of "body and soul," he did not assume that the purpose of renewal could be separated from the life lived in the body. Not only do we exist as embodied persons now, but we will be "re-embodied" at the resurrection. This sentiment can be observed in his sermon, *What is Man?* (1872). Here he claims that "in my present state of existence, I undoubtedly consist both of soul and body: And so I shall again, after the resurrection, to all eternity."[54] To Wesley, the great renewal in the image of God, to which humanity was called, involved the soul and body in a holistic sense.[55]

Wesley's Affectional Moral Psychology

Thus far, I have argued that Wesley can be considered a *practical* theologian in the sense that he was interested in a theological discourse that led to actual transformation. He was not concerned with theology for theology's sake, but rather advocated active religious experience in the lives of the people that he ministered to. We have seen that Wesley's notion of *new creation* reflected God's ultimate "telos" in the world—the renewal of creation in the image of God.

I have presented the first two salient features of Wesley's theological anthropology—*relational* and *holistic* anthropologies. The time has now come to present the third aspect of Wesley's theological anthropology—his *affectional moral psychology*. This aspect of Wesley's thought reflects perhaps the most distinctive feature of his theology. His moral psychology is particularly prominent in his articulation of the "way of salvation." In addition, Wesley's understanding of moral psychology is a critical aspect of my endeavor to describe religious conversion.

53. For a wonderful example see Harak, *Virtuous Passions*.

54. Sermon 116, *What is Man, BE* (4:23).

55. This dimension of theological anthropology is critical to the current project. The following chapter is dedicated to working out a viable view of human nature in detail. Suffice to say for now, that Wesley is not considered a strong "dualist" in this dimension of his theological anthropology.

I will begin this section by explaining what exactly is meant by "moral psychology." On the surface, such a discussion would seem to be a terrible anachronism; after all, psychology is a rather modern method of scientific investigation. I am using the term "moral psychology" to refer to the fundamental assumptions concerning human moral attitude and behavior.[56] Such a psychology seeks to answer questions like: Are we truly free to make moral choices? If we answer in the affirmative, then what is it that hinders us from choosing the good? If such a reason can be identified, then what type of "therapy" can be enacted that would allow us to choose differently? It should be clear at this juncture that these inquires would have been of great concern to Wesley. In what follows, I intend to show his evolution of thought and experience that led him to propose answers to these questions. The application of which has come to be known as Wesley's *affectional moral psychology*.[57]

Philosophical inquiries regarding the moral life are ancient and naturally extend into the realm of Christian history. The initial generation of Christians did not appear to engage in an extended interaction with the philosophical dialogues of their Greek-Roman context; however, as time passed, an explicit interaction developed between Christians and the prominent moral psychologies of the time. While there is evidence of some interaction with Gnostic ideals, Clement of Alexandria's strong endorsement of self-determinism seemed to be a more commonly held idea.[58]

Clement's form of self-determination was primarily informed by Plato's emphasis on habitual rational control of the passions.[59] This model of moral psychology stresses the human ability to reason as the primary mode of self-determination. Here, reason maintains a polar relationship with human passion or emotions. Thus, it follows that the most significant obstacle to rational moral life is the interference that occurs in emotional reaction. So to be a truly moral person was to bring the emotional aspect of human life under subjection to the rational self. Likewise, we can in-

56. For a helpful resource regarding the ancient practice of psychology see Stevenson, *Ten Theories of Human Nature*. Stevenson claims that ancient psychology could be considered the "study of the soul" and as such was synonymous with many religious concerns.

57. For a further discussion of Wesley's affectional moral psychology see Clapper, "Orthokardia," 49–66.

58. Aune, "Mastery of the Passions," 125–58.

59. "Self-determinism" refers to the mediating strategy that acknowledges the significant influence of motivating dynamics on human attitude and behavior, but allows for some degree of autonomy for a person's will to serve as the final arbitrator of moral action.

crease in our aptitude to maintain such rational control through a process of habituation.

An opposition arose to Plato's moral psychology. The voice of St. Augustine brought a new perspective to understanding the moral life. Augustine's determination to live a moral life according to rational control failed and left him searching for a means to live the proper Christian life. His failure to gain habituated rational control over his passions led him to draw two conclusions: (1) the attempts to live the moral life by exhibiting rational control over the passions placed far too much emphasis on the human element and not enough on the possibility of divine intervention; and (2) that reason is more the slave of the passions than a master to rule over them.

These conclusions led to the development of Augustine's moral psychology[60] which remains one of the most prominent examples of deterministic thought in Christian spirituality.[61] He argued that the whole of human moral choice is dependent upon pre-existing affections. As a result of the Fall, humans are born with corrupt affections that can only give rise to negative moral choice. The answer to this dilemma rests in the ability of God to renew these inherent affections through the process of regeneration. It is only through this action of God that right moral attitude and behavior can proceed.

It followed that Augustine would emphasize the state of total depravity in humankind—humanity is helpless to choose the good without the regenerative power of God. For Augustine, then, any belief in self-determination stood in direct opposition to the notion of salvation by grace.

So then, we see a definite tension between the views of the moral life that were presented by both Plato and Augustine. The prior tradition emphasized rational control over the passions or affections while the latter viewed the will as being doomed to serve them. It is in this tension between the moral psychologies articulated by Plato and Augustine that Wesley found himself. A brief examination of Wesley's biography will prove helpful going forward.

John Wesley was born on 17 June 1703 to the Reverend Samuel Wesley and Susanna (Annesley) Wesley. Both of Wesley's parents were

60. For an analysis of Augustine's moral psychology see Wetzel, *Augustine and the Limits of Virtue*.

61. "Determinism" here refers to the assumption that motivating dynamics (passions, emotions, etc.) exhaustively account for human choice and action. The result is that the will eventually falls victim to these motivating dynamics.

ambitiously involved in the movement against the Puritan resistance and supported the prominence of the Anglican Church.[62] Due to Samuel's extended travels, the domestic duties were primarily assumed by Susanna. This included the rearing of John and his brothers. We have a fairly good picture of the type of discipline that Susanna exercised in the home. John and his brothers were taught "to fear the rod, and to cry softly, by which means they escaped abundance of correction which they might otherwise have had."[63]

Wesley's childhood was characterized by Susanna's firm dedication to raise her children as well-fitted Christians. In her eyes, such a "well-fitted" Christian life can only be achieved through the subjugation of the natural inclinations of the developing will. A letter from Susanna regarding her educational beliefs and practices makes the point well.

> As self-will is the root of all sin and misery, so whatever cherishes this in children insures their after-wretchedness and irreligion; whatever checks and mortifies it promotes their future happiness and piety. This is still more evident if we further consider that religion is nothing else than the doing the will of God and not our own: that the one grand impediment to our temporal and eternal happiness being this self-will, no indulgencies of it can be trivial, no denial unprofitable. Heaven or hell depends on this alone. So that the parent who studies to subdue it in his child works together with God in renewing and saving a soul. The parent who indulges it does the devil's work, makes religion impracticable, salvation unattainable; and does all that in him lies to damn his child, soul, and body forever.[64]

It is clear from this excerpt that Wesley was nurtured under the habituated rational control model of moral psychology. Indeed Platonic moral psychology was widely accepted in eighteenth century Anglicanism.[65] This vein of thought can be seen in Wesley's early sermons. A clear example is offered in his sermon on *The Wisdom of Winning Souls*.

> When due care has been used to strengthen his understanding, then tis time to use the other great means of winning souls, namely, the regulating of his affections. Indeed without doing this the

62. For a helpful biography see Rack, *Reasonable Enthusiast*, 45–60. See also Collins, *John Wesley*.

63. Wallace, *Susanna Wesley*, 369.

64. Wesley copied this letter from Susanna into his journal. The entry can be found in Wesley, *Works of John Wesley*, 389.

65. For support of this point see Lovin, "Physics of True Virtue," 264–72.

other can't be done thoroughly—he that would well enlighten the head must cleanse the heart. Otherwise the disorder of the will again disorders the understanding.[66]

Susanna's influence rings clear in Wesley's early position on the moral life. This position, however, would soon change. Many Wesleyan scholars consider Wesley's experience at Aldersgate in 1738 to mark a significant transformation in his theology. While not diminishing the significance of this event in Wesley's life, I suggest that much of the change that he underwent was due to the "expectation" set by the occurrences leading up to Aldersgate.

I propose two primary factors that served as catalysts in the transition of Wesley's stance on the moral life—(1) his exposure to Augustinian tradition via his encounter with the English Moravians; and (2) his embrace of empiricism within eighteenth-century British philosophy. Augustine's appeal to divine intervention in order to overcome the obstacles in moral life was appealing to Wesley. In addition, his spiritual struggle was heightened by Augustine's insistence that rational conviction alone could not effectuate moral action. This made sense of Wesley's personal struggles and he was able to see the value of Augustine's position on the issue. However, Wesley was troubled by Augustine's claim that God infuses irresistible dispositions through the act of regeneration. Wesley found his way out of this theological quagmire by appealing to the rise of empiricist thought in British philosophy.

From the seventeenth century, philosophy offered two routes for how we understand the acquisition of knowledge—rationalism and empiricism.[67] The basis of rationalism rests on the notion that there are certain innate ideas that are accessible to humans through the process of rational thought. In contrast, empiricists claim that truth is experienced receptively by the human intellect, *not pre-existent within it*. I argue that Wesley identified himself with the empiricists over the rationalists.[68] Although the case

---

66. Sermon 142, *The Wisdom of Winning Souls*, BE (4:313).

67. For an extensive investigation of rationalism and empiricism see Descartes, *Selected Philosophical Writings*; Hume, *Inquiry Concerning Human Understanding*; Leibniz, *New Essays on Human Understanding*; Locke, *Essay on Human Understanding*. For a user friendly introduction to epistemological theories see Aune, *Rationalism, Empiricism, and Pragmatism*. The classic articulation of the debate between rationalists and empiricists is articulated by Thomas Reid. For a recent reprint of his work see Brookes, *Thomas Reid*.

68. For a discussion on Wesley's epistemological concerns see Brantley, *Locke, Wesley, and the Method of English Romanticism*; Dreyer, "Faith and Experience," 12–30; Wood, "Wesley's Epistemology," 48–59; and Noro, "Wesley's Theological Epistemology," 59–76.

can be made that Wesley did exhibit some tendencies toward rationalist thinking, he did consciously espouse the alternate view. Perhaps, the most poignant example of this is found in Wesley's sermon *On the Discoveries of Faith*. Here Wesley states:

> For many ages it has been allowed by sensible men, *Nihil est in intellectu quod non fuit prius in sensu*: That is, "There is nothing in the understanding which was not first perceived by some of the senses." All the knowledge which we naturally have is originally derived from our senses. And therefore those who want any sense cannot have the least knowledge or idea of the objects of that sense; as they that never had sight have not the least knowledge or conception of light or colours. Some indeed have of late years endeavoured to prove that we have innate ideas, not derived from any of the senses, but coeval with the understanding. But this point has been now thoroughly discussed by men of the most eminent sense and learning. And it is agreed by all impartial persons that, although some things are so plain and obvious that we can very hardly avoid knowing them as soon as we come to the use of our understanding, yet the knowledge even of these is not innate, but derived from some of our senses.[69]

Here Wesley is plainly rebuking the rationalist approach to knowledge. He was much more receptive of the Empiricist's methodology. Wesley spoke favorably of John Locke's work on human understanding. There was, however, a point of divide between Wesley and Locke.[70] Wesley's strongest point of divergence from the Lockean school of thought concerned how empiricists addressed the issue of knowledge of God. Most empiricists of Wesley's time strictly attributed knowledge of God to that of external experience or to inferences from Scripture.[71] Wesley was reluctant to adopt this view because he held to the notion that knowledge could come directly from God.

69. Sermon 117, *On the Discoveries of Faith*, BE (4:29). Emphasis added. This phrase, "Nihil est in intellectu quod non fuit prius in sensu" is quoted again by Wesley in his sermon on *Walking by Sight and Walking by Faith*, Sermon 119, BE (4:51).

70. Among these Maddox notes that Wesley "disputed Locke's distinction between primary qualities (really in external objects) and secondary qualities (only in the mind). . . . He also rejected Locke's suggestion that abstract classifications like 'species' are products of reasoning rather than derived from experience. . . . For Wesley, reason abstracts from experience what is truly there!" Maddox, *Responsible Grace*, 262, note 6.

71. For a classic example see Browne, *Procedure, Extent, and Limits of Human Understanding*. Also see Wesley's discussion of Browne's work in *Survey of the Wisdom of God in Creation or A Compendium of Natural Philosophy in Two Volumes*, BE (5:153).

While adhering to the empiricist inclination that knowledge comes through the senses, Wesley allowed for *direct* knowledge through what he called the *spiritual senses*. He employed the presence of the spiritual senses most often when discussing the New Birth. Wesley held that it was through the New Birth that spiritual senses where activated by way of the prevenient grace of God. When speaking of the person in the pangs of New Birth, he says:

> It is true he may have some faint dawnings of life, some small beginnings of spiritual motion; but as yet he has no spiritual senses capable of discerning spiritual objects; consequently, he "discerneth not the things of the Spirit of God; he cannot know them, because they are spiritually discerned." . . . But when he is born of God, born of the Spirit, how is the manner of his existence changed! His whole soul is now sensible of God, and he can say, by sure experience, "Thou art about my bed, and about my path;" I feel thee in all my ways: "Thou besettest me behind and before, and layest thy hand upon me." . . . And by this new kind of spiritual respiration, spiritual life is not only sustained, but increased day by day, together with spiritual strength, and motion, and sensation; all the senses of the soul being now awake, and capable of discerning spiritual good and evil.[72]

Empiricist philosophy played a crucial role in forming Wesley's moral psychology because it ultimately led to the insistence that humans are motivated to action only as we are experientially affected. So, practically speaking, the rationally persuasive thought of a moral act such as loving others cannot itself move us to do so. It is rather in the experience of being loved ourselves that we are in turn able to express love toward others. According to the empiricists, the reason for this is that the "will" is neither a cipher for intellectual convictions nor a repository of volitional spontaneity, it is rather a "set of responsive holistic 'affections' that must be engaged in order to incite us to action."[73]

Wesley's adoption of empiricist thought together with the events leading up to and including his Aldersgate experience paved the way to what would become his mature affectional moral psychology. To articulate this view is it necessary to place the conversation within the bounds of Wesley's primary concern as a theologian—the fulfilment of new creation through God's great renewal. So then, what *exactly* in human nature needs

---

72. Sermon 19, *The Great Privilege of Those That Are Born of God*, BE (1:433).
73. Maddox, "Reconnecting the Means to the End," 34.

to be renewed? What does this have to do with the previous discussion of moral psychology?

To answer these questions, we must return again to Wesley's theological anthropology. Recall that regarding the creation of humankind he says,

> Man was created in the image of God: Because he is not mere matter, a clod of earth, a lump of clay, without sense or understanding; but a spirit like his Creator, a being endued not only with sense and *understanding*, but also with a *will* exerting itself in various affections. To crown all the rest, he was endued with *liberty*; a power of directing his own affections and actions; a capacity of determining himself, or of choosing good or evil. Indeed, had not man been endued with this, all the rest would have been of no use: Had he not been a free as well as an intelligent being, his understanding would have been as incapable of holiness, or any kind of virtue, as a tree or a block of marble.[74]

This emphasis on *understanding, will,* and *liberty* is critical in Wesley's description of moral psychology and the greater end of renewal in the image of God. Here, "understanding" refers to the *capacity* for humankind to exhibit reason, and participate within the created order. Wesley's concept of the *will* is an important one that is worthy of closer inspection. What did Wesley mean when he spoke of the will? In his understanding, "will" does not refer to the rational actions that we might assign to it in a contemporary context. To Wesley, the will was equated with the terms *affections* and *tempers*.

An affection is a "transitory feeling state" such as love or desire (because we *feel* these toward another).[75] A temper is a "habituated affection, or said differently, an enduring disposition to perceive/feel/think/act in a consistent manner (e.g., to *be* a loving person)."[76] These affections (or tempers as they become primary motivators) are "the indispensable motivating inclinations behind human action."[77] While possessing the capability of

74. Sermon 57, *On the Fall of Man, BE* (2:400–401). Emphasis added.

75. Strawn and Brown, "Wesleyan Holiness," 121.

76. Ibid, 121.

77. Maddox, "Reconnecting the Means to the End," 33. Also, it should be noted that a parallel could be drawn between the present use of the term "inclinations" and Michael Polanyi's "tacit knowledge." Polanyi began from the premise that humans somehow "know more than we can tell." See Polanyi, *Tacit Dimension*, 4. Polanyi considers tacit knowledge to be the framework for moral acts and judgment. It is interesting that the construction of such a framework is contingent on practice. He asserts that "true knowledge lies in

provoking human action, the affections also have a crucial receptive dimension as well. This is to say that the affections are not *self-causative*, but are awakened and thrive in response to the experience of external reality. For Wesley the primary experience of reality was to be found in God's love toward us.

> It is in consequence of our knowing God loves us, that we love him, and love our neighbour as ourselves. Gratitude towards our Creator cannot but produce benevolence to our fellow creatures. The love of Christ constrains us, not only to be harmless, to do no ill to our neighbour, but to be useful, to be "zealous of good works;" "as we have time, to do good unto all men;" and to be patterns to all of true, genuine morality; of justice, mercy, and truth. This is religion, and this is happiness; the happiness for which we were made. This begins when we begin to know God, by the teaching of his own Spirit. As soon as the Father of spirits reveals his Son in our hearts, and the Son reveals his Father, the love of God is shed abroad in our hearts; then, and not till then, we are happy.[78]

For Wesley, the tempers were at the heart of human *motivation* and it was the goal of salvation to transform the unholy tempers within humankind to holy tempers characterized by the love of God and creation. When speaking of the temper of love, Wesley states:

> Let *love* not visit you as a transient guest, but be the constant ruling temper of your soul. See that your heart be filled at all times and on all occasions with real, undissembled benevolence; not to those only that love *you*, but to every soul of man. Let it pant in your heart; let it sparkle in your eyes, let it shine on all your actions. Whenever you open your lips, let it be with love; and let there be in your tongue the law of kindness. Your word will then distill as the rain, and as the dew upon the tender herb. Be not straitened or limited in your affection, but let it embrace every child of man.[79]

This poetic explanation of the place of love in the life of the Christian is a quintessential example of Wesley's practical theology. To be "saved" for Wesley was to have a transformed life *marked by transformed attitudes and behaviors* and such was possible only through the renewal of the tempers.

---

our ability to use it. . . . It is not by looking at things, but by dwelling in them, that we understand their joint meaning" (ibid., 17–18).

78. Sermon 120, *The Unity of the Divine Being*, BE (4:67). This theme permeates Wesley's latter works.

79. Sermon 100, *On Pleasing All Men*, BE (3:422).

Wesley stated that "true religion, in the very essence of it, is nothing short of holy tempers."[80]

This grounding of moral attitude and behavior within the affections shares obvious similarities with Augustine. Recall that for Augustine, the renewal of the passions or affections coincides with divine regeneration. These newly infused holy affections then take on the same irresistible nature that characterized the prior unholy passions. Wesley considered the notion of "irresistible" passions to be problematic and thereby included the concept of *liberty* in his moral psychology. He carefully distinguished "liberty" from "will," by specifying that while the "will" reflected our various inclinations to act; "liberty" is our limited autonomous capacity to refuse to enact a particular inclination.

Having expounded on the three primary features of Wesley's theological anthropology—his *relational* anthropology, his *holistic* anthropology, and finally his *affectional moral psychology*, I will now discuss how these points relate to Wesley's understanding of salvation at large.

Wesley's Way of Salvation

> What is salvation? The salvation which is here spoken of is not what is frequently understood by that word, the going to heaven, eternal happiness. It is not the soul's going to paradise, termed by our Lord, "Abraham's bosom." It is not a blessing which lies on the other side of death; or, as we usually speak, in the other world. The very words of the text itself put this beyond all question: "Ye *are saved*." It is not something at a distance: it is a present thing; a blessing which, through the free mercy of God, ye are now in possession of. Nay, the words may be rendered, and that with equal propriety, "Ye *have been* saved": so that the salvation which is here spoken of might be extended to the entire work of God, from the first dawning of grace in the soul, till it is consummated in glory.[81]

The previous discussion of Wesley's theological anthropology has provided us with the critical context to develop his view of salvation. As seen from Wesley's affectional moral psychology, the relation between sin and salvation is based in human nature and as such requires not only "pardon," but "healing"—*the whole of Wesley's soteriology revolves about this notion.*[82]

---

80. Sermon 91, *On Charity,* BE (3:306).

81. Sermon 43, *The Scripture Way of Salvation,* BE (2:156).

82. For examples of this theme in Wesley's work see Sermon 101, *The Trouble and*

Maddox comments that, "Wesley understood human salvation in its fullest sense to include deliverance (1) immediately from the *penalty* of sin, (2) progressively from the *plague* of sin, and (3) eschatologically from the very *presence* of sin and its effects."[83] It is obvious from a survey of Wesley's writing that he primarily focused on the second point—how is it that humans are to heal from the present reality and effects of sin?[84]

As mentioned above, many of Wesley's theological ideas were the result of a synthesis between the Eastern and Western traditions. One of the most critical of these ideas involved Wesley's notion of sin. It is important to note that Wesley stressed the notion of *inbeing sin* over "original sin." Here, the emphasis is more on relational depravity than the transmission of Adam's sin to future generations.[85] Maddox notes that "the most basic cause of our present infirmity for Wesley was not some "thing" that we inherit, but the distortion of our nature resulting from being born into this world already separated from the empowering Divine Presence. *Deprived* of this essential relationship, our various faculties inevitably become *debilitated*, leaving us morally *depraved*."[86]

When Wesley dealt with this notion of depravity or inbeing sin, he was seeking the source of sin, not a way to classify individual sin*s*. Wesley's affectional moral psychology is again relevant here, because it is from the corrupted affections or tempers that sinful actions flow—getting Wesley closer to the *root* of sinful behavior. Inbeing sin can then be understood as the corruption of these basic human motivations. Recall that from Wesley's theological anthropology, the human faculties of *understanding, will,* and *liberty* are critical aspects of human nature. In the presence of inbeing sin, our understanding is obscured, our will is hampered by corrupt affections and tempers, and our liberty is lost.[87] It is from this depravity that our actual (individual) sins emerge.

Rest of Good Men, BE (3:533) and Sermon 69, *The Imperfection of Human Knowledge, BE* (2:581).

83. Maddox, *Responsible Grace*, 143.

84. It is important to note that although I am suggesting that this was Wesley's primary concern, he stressed that salvation proper is concerned with the intertwining of all three of these points. None was more important than the other in that the "working out" of salvation was a thorough process involving all three.

85. For more on Wesley's notion of "inbeing sin," see Bryant, "John Wesley's Doctrine of Sin."

86. Maddox, *Responsible Grace*, 81.

87. For Wesley's words on the effects of inbeing sin see, Sermon 141, *The Image of God, BE* (4:298); Sermon 146, *The One Thing Needful, BE* (4:354); Sermon 44, *Original Sin, BE* (2:177); Sermon 40, *Christian Perfection, BE* (2:118–119), Sermon 34, *The Original,*

In this sense, *total* depravity does not refer to the worse possible moral condition that a human can assume; rather, it refers to the scope in which sin affects human capacities. Inbeing sin pervades every human faculty, thus leaving us unable to save ourselves apart from the healing offered through God's grace. Thus, we see the prominence of a therapeutic view of salvation in Wesley. Indeed, what is needed is not "forgiveness" alone, but the *healing* of our corrupt affections and tempers. Wesley notes that the proper nature of religion is "*therapeia psyches,* God's method of *healing a soul* which is thus diseased. Hereby the great Physician of souls applies medicines to heal this sickness; to restore human nature, totally corrupted in all its faculties."[88]

Wesley was careful to point out that his concept of salvation as healing was not restricted to the internal or spiritual life. He insisted that true salvation involved not only inner renewal, but outward transformation marked by moral righteousness.

> By salvation I mean, not barely (according to the vulgar notion) deliverance from hell, or going to heaven, but a present deliverance from sin, a restoration of the soul to its primitive health, its original purity; a recovery of the divine nature; the renewal of our souls after the image of God in righteousness and true holiness, in justice, mercy, and truth. This implies all holy and heavenly tempers, and by consequence all holiness of *conversation.*"[89]

This holistic view of salvation balances the inner holiness of our affections and tempers with the renewal of our actions that are marked by relationship with God and others. In addition, Wesley was careful to strike a balance between his presentation of grace as bringing both *pardon* and *power*, and he did so within the greater context of his understanding of salvation as God's healing of inbeing sin.

> By "the grace of God" is sometimes to be understood that free love, that unmerited mercy, by which I a sinner, through the merits of Christ, am now reconciled to God. But in this place it rather means that *power* of God the Holy Ghost, which "worketh in us both to will and to do of his good pleasure." As soon as ever the grace of God in the former sense, his *pardoning* love, is manifested

---

Nature, Properties, and Use of the Law, BE (2:7).

88. Sermon 44, *Original Sin, BE* (2:184). Emphasis added.

89. *A Farther Appeal to Men of Reason and Religion, BE* (11:106). I have italicized "conversation" in order to emphasize its reference to the whole of human conduct, not just spoken words.

to our souls, the grace of God in the latter sense, the *power* of his
Spirit, takes place therein. And now we can perform, through God,
what to man was impossible. Now we can order our conversation
aright . . . [and achieve] holiness, a recovery of the image of God,
a renewal of soul "after his likeness."[90]

Given Wesley's view of salvation as healing, we can now turn to a more detailed account of his way of salvation. I am careful here to stress "way" over
the term "order." This tendency to speak about the "order of salvation" or
ordo salutis was evident in both Lutheran and Reformed scholasticism.
The primary feature of this view was the depiction of salvation as God's
progressive sequence of works operative within the human soul. This notion would have been familiar to Wesley through theologians like William
Perkins.[91]

A number of contemporary Wesleyan scholars have noted that
the gradual dynamics inherent in Wesley's concept of salvation is better
described as a *way* rather than successive steps—thus *via salutis*.[92] This suggestion seems appropriate given that Wesley himself used the term often in
his various writings.[93] Wesley's sermons tended to emphasize the unfolding
of God's grace in human life rather than abrupt transitions in an order of
salvation. For Wesley (particularly in his mature view), salvation was more
a gradual journey into the depths of God's grace.

This is an indispensable aspect of Wesley's theology. God's grace is
at work at all points along the course of one's life; thus; Wesley's idea of
atonement was closely linked to participation in Christ. As a result of
this theological position, Wesley had great resonance with the Catholic
tradition of his day. Wesley's notion of sanctifying grace resonated with a
Catholic understanding of sanctification. In Catholic thought, sanctification progresses in the life of a Christian by the increase of justice received
through the grace of Christ. Grace, understood in this fashion, is co-operant in nature and precedes, accompanies, and follows "good works."[94]

90. Sermon 12, *The Witness of Our Own Spirit*, BE (1:309–10). Emphasis added.

91. See Perkins, *Golden Chain*. For a helpful discussion on the Reformed view of the
order of salvation see Kuyper, *Work of the Holy Spirit*.

92. For two such examples see Heitzenrater, *Mirror and Memory*, 109; and Runyon,
"What is Methodism's Theological Contribution Today?," 11.

93. For example, "The *Way* to the Kingdom," "The Scripture *Way* of Salvation" and
"The More Excellent *Way*."

94. This position was discussed during the Council of Trent's session on Justification.
See Schroeder, *Canons and Decrees of the Council of Trent*. Also for a more recent discussion
of the similarities between Wesley and the Catholic tradition see Del Colle, "John Wesley's

There are obvious similarities here between the Catholic position and Wesley's understanding of sanctification and prevenient grace.[95]

Furthermore, this view emphasizes Wesley's conviction that salvation is a dynamic relationship characterized by *responsible* grace—"Wesley was convinced that, while we *can* not attain holiness (and wholeness) apart from God's grace, God *will* not effect holiness apart from our responsive participation."[96] There is a significant departure between Wesley and the Protestant Reformers (mainly Luther and Calvin) on this point. Wesley saw justification as the doorway to life in Christ. He was most concerned with holiness, thus; Wesley taught sanctification (becoming holy) as distinct from justification and as being processive in nature. In regards to the tension between Wesley and the Reformers, Ralph Del Colle states that

> As the Reformers would have it, we are always reappropriating the gift of justification even as Christ is formed in us through a life of faith and obedience, which can properly be termed sanctification. For Wesley, once we are justified, we enter a new stage, sanctification, still dependent though upon grace received through faith. We can fall from this stage (as opposed to Calvin) but nevertheless the focus is upon the reigning and indwelling Christ and not exclusively on the continual actualisation of justification.[97]

Wesley stressed the need for continued growth in grace. Wesley's comments during a 1770 conference with his preachers make this clear.

> Does not talking, without proper caution, of a justified or sanctified state, tend to mislead [people]; almost naturally leading them to trust in what was done in one moment? Whereas we are every moment pleasing or displeasing to God, according to our works; according to the whole of our present inward tempers and outward behaviour.[98]

So for Wesley, salvation was not a series of ascending steps leading a person to God; rather, salvation was a growing relationship with God characterized by intertwining facets. Salvation was not a pinnacle from which there was no return, but a term designating a journey leading to peace

---

Doctrine of Grace," 172–89.

95. See Wesley's sermon on *Circumcision of the Heart*, Sermon 17 *BE* (1:403).

96. Maddox, *Responsible Grace*, 148.

97. Del Colle, "John Wesley's Doctrine of Grace," 183. My only criticism of Del Colle is his use of the term "stage." It seems much more appropriate to speak of "dimensions" of grace in Wesley's work.

98. Point 77, *BE* (8:338).

and renewed relationship with God. In addition, this journey was to be understood as a *gradual process*.[99] Wesley considered it normative for all of God's providential acts to be gradual in nature; thus, he referred to the "gradual process of the work of God in the soul."[100]

In what follows, I will summarize the "intertwining facets" that characterize Wesley's mature view of salvation. Again, I emphasize that, for Wesley, salvation is based on God's grace. Furthermore, he stressed the co-operant nature of grace; that is, it is the intimate relationship between God's grace *and* human action that brings transformation. So, as I move forward it is important to understand that while Wesley's view of salvation involved definite *works of grace*, appropriately understood, these works are to be viewed as degrees of the same divine action, rather than separate works in and of themselves.

To be clear, one cannot overemphasize the place of grace in Wesley's theology. In fact, his distinctive view of "prevenient grace" made for a way between Plato and Augustine. Plato held that humankind is free to make a choice for "good" whenever one is ruled by his or her rational faculties. In contrast, Augustine held that Adam's sin left humanity unable to freely choose the good. A person must turn to God where this ability is infused through a work of God. It is important to notice that a central aim of the Reformation was to return to Augustine's position, which according to the reformers, had gradually declined in the Catholic Church. The reformers maintained that the Catholic Church had fallen into a state of "Semi-Pelagianism."[101]

There is an obvious resonance between this position of "Semi-Pelagianism" and Wesley's articulation of prevenient grace.[102] Wesley held that God's grace preceded any choice, thus making morally "good" actions possible. This is explicit in Wesley's discussion of salvation at large. I will begin this analysis with a discussion of Wesley's view of *regeneration*.

99. For examples see *A Farther Appeal to Men of Reason and Religion*, *BE* (11:107) and Sermon 85, *On Working Out Our Own Salvation*, *BE* (3:203–4).

100. *Hymns and Sacred Poems*, *BE* (14:326).

101. The term "Semi-Pelagianism" is meant to denote the belief that the Fall *weakened* humanities will, but did not *destroy* it. In addition, humankind's nature is diseased, but not depraved; thus, humanity can cooperate with God's grace or reject it.

102. Wesley, on occasion, referred to Pelagius as a "wise and holy man" (letter to Alexander Coates, 7 July 1761. See Telford, *Letters of the Rev. John Wesley*, 158.

Regeneration

Wesley's departure from the Reformed notion of *ordo salutis* is obvious in his exposition of *regeneration*. The Reformed Scholastics equated regeneration with the New Birth—God's instantaneous and irresistible work in the life of sinners. Here God transformed humans, who are incapable of good works, into "new creatures" now able to operate in the realm of repentance and faith. The essential feature of this Reformed view was that regeneration or the New Birth must take place before humans can respond to God.

Wesley's view of regeneration was quite different. This is mostly due to his understanding of salvation as a "way" as opposed to an "order." To Wesley, regeneration meant "being inwardly changed by the almighty operation of the Spirit of God; changed from sin to holiness; [and being] renewed in the image of him who created us."[103] This description, which places emphasis on therapeutic and holistic transformation, resonates with Wesley's understanding of salvation at large.

Wesley was careful (particularly following his Aldersgate experience) to differentiate between the New Birth and sanctification—the former referred to the renewal of the human faculties that accompanied the restored pardoning grace of God, while the latter designated the gradual restoration of our moral nature made possible by the New Birth. So in this sense, the New Birth was the beginning of sanctification.[104] To Wesley, regeneration was not to be strictly equated with either the New Birth or sanctification proper, rather; it was to be understood to describe the whole experience of salvation—New Birth and sanctification were seen as increasing degrees of a larger reality.

This aspect of "increasing degrees" is central to Wesley's mature view of salvation. As noted above, this should not be understood as an "order" or ascending steps in the salvation experience, but should rather be characterized by its relational features. Thus, regeneration is "the crucial facet of God's prevenient empowering realized in intensifying degrees throughout human salvation as a whole."[105] In this context, Wesley spoke of the various works of grace that act to transform human lives and thus play a role in the greater experience of regeneration.

103. *Doctrine of Original Sin*, BE (9:308).

104. For examples of Wesley's view of the New Birth as the beginning of the process of sanctification proper see Sermon 43, *The Scripture Way of Salvation*, BE (2:158); Sermon 45, *The New Birth*, BE (2:198); Sermon 107, *On God's Vineyard*, BE (3:506–7); and *The Doctrine of Original Sin*, BE (9:310).

105. Maddox, *Responsible Grace*, 160.

Within Wesley's greater theme of regeneration, he spoke of individual "works of grace." Again, these are not to be seen as a sequential order through which one must pass, but multidimensional facets portraying the same work of God in human lives. Wesley saw grace as being manifested in three ways: "in our creation, in God's forgiveness, and in our transformation and re-creation."[106] It is because of love, the divine essence of grace, that God created the world and humankind, and it is this same grace that works within us to forgive and transform. Grace is intimately intertwined with Wesley's notion of salvation; thus, he speaks of grace as *prevenient*, *justifying*, and *sanctifying*.

Prevenient Grace

In Wesley's *Collection of Forms of Prayers*, he prayed:

> O that we may all receive of [Christ's] fullness, grace upon grace; grace to pardon our sins, and subdue our iniquities; to justify our persons and to sanctify our souls; and to complete that holy change, that renewal of our hearts, whereby we may be transformed into that blessed image wherein thou didst create us.[107]

This grace acts upon humanity in a variety of ways, some of which are subtle and unconscious to us. Grace can operate in a "prevenient" way turning us toward God and the fullness of life offered in that response. This notion of *prevenient grace* is a key Wesleyan distinctive and one that merits our understanding.

In many ways, the development of Wesley's notion of prevenient grace was in response to the tension that he experienced in articulating the notion of *total depravity*. This tension existed between the Eastern understanding of depravity which held that God had restored an inherent capacity within human nature allowing us to respond to God's grace and the Western reformed notion of total depravity which seemed to lead to the Calvinist doctrine of Predestination.

Seeing inherent problems in both of these traditions, Wesley sought for a way to affirm that all avenues to restoration, including our earliest inclinations toward God, were dependent upon grace. In this sense, prevenient grace is meant to affirm that *every* act of human virtue, from the

---

106. Runyon, *The New Creation*, 26.

107. John Wesley, "A Collection of Forms of Prayers, 'Prayers for Families,'" in Jackson, *Works of the Rev. John Wesley*.

earliest expressions of faith through increasing degrees of sanctification, are to be seen as grounded in the prior empowering of the grace of God.

In addition to this general sense of prevenient grace, Prevenient Grace (proper) refers to the action of God that "comes before" justification. It is this grace that moves us toward God and directs us to seek the Divine will. In his sermon entitled *On Working Out Our Own Salvation*, Wesley says:

> First. God worketh in you; therefore you *can* work: Otherwise it would be impossible. If he did not work it would be impossible for you to work out your own salvation. . . . Seeing all men are by nature not only sick, but "dead in trespasses and sins," it is not possible for them to do anything well till God raises them from the dead. It was impossible for Lazarus to come forth, till the Lord had given him life. And it is equally impossible for us to *come* out of our sins, yea, or to make the least motion toward it, till He who hath all power in heaven and earth calls our dead souls into life.
>
> Yet this is no excuse for those who continue in sin, and lay the blame upon their Maker, by saying, "It is God only that must quicken us; for we cannot quicken our own souls." For allowing that all the souls of men are dead in sin by *nature*, this excuses none, seeing there is no man that is in a state of mere nature; there is no man, unless he has quenched the Spirit, that is wholly void of the grace of God. No man living is entirely destitute of what is vulgarly called *natural conscience*. But this is not natural: It is more properly termed *preventing grace*. Every man has a greater or less measure of this, which waiteth not for the call of man. Every one has, sooner or later, good desires; although the generality of men stifle them before they can strike deep root, or produce any considerable fruit. Everyone has some measure of that light, some faint glimmering ray, which, sooner or later, more or less, enlightens every man that cometh into the world.[108]

This passage stresses two important aspects of Prevenient Grace—(1) God's grace "precedes" any act of goodness that humans may perform, and (2) there is no human being beyond the reach of Prevenient Grace—thus stressing the universal availability of God's grace.[109] For Wesley, God had granted to humanity the ability to respond to divine grace and pursue further renewal. The prevenient grace of God is the first stage in the renewal process.

---

108. Sermon 85, *On Working Out Our Own Salvation*, BE (3:206–7).

109. For more on the universal availability of grace see Sermon 110, *Free Grace*, BE (3:544–59).

> Salvation begins with what is usually termed (and very properly) *preventing grace*; including the first wish to please God, the first dawn of light concerning his will, and the first slight transient conviction of having sinned against him. All these imply some tendency toward life; some degree of salvation; the beginning of a deliverance from a blind, unfeeling heart, quite insensible of God and the things of God.[110]

So then, according to Wesley, prevenient grace can be seen as God's initial move toward a restored relationship with humanity. This move is expressed in three ways: (1) God removes inherited guilt by virtue of Christ, thus addressing the notion of *total* depravity—God had not restored in humans an inherent ability to respond, rather God was continually extending prevenient grace to humanity in order to free them from the guilt of original sin (hence Wesley's emphasis on "inbeing sin" over "original sin"); (2) God brings a partial healing of the debilitated human capacities of understanding, will, and liberty—such a partial healing allows us the ability to sense and respond to God; and (3) God extends further opportunities to "grow in grace" through specific overtures to individuals. Because of the nature of grace, these overtures can either be embraced, leading to further growth in grace, or rejected.

Prevenient grace, in its general sense, is then understood as that *continual* extension of God's grace to all of humanity. Any human moral action is to be seen as flowing from this expression of God's grace. Prevenient Grace (proper) was commonly used by Wesley to designate that specific form of grace that preceded *justification*—an equally interesting dimension of Wesley's soteriology.

Justifying Grace

Wesley seemed to substitute lengthy explanations of justification for one simple word—forgiveness.

> Justification is another word for pardon. It is the forgiveness of all our sins; and, what is necessarily implied therein, our acceptance with God. The price whereby this hath been procured for us (commonly termed "the meritorious cause of our justification"), is the blood and righteousness of Christ; or, to express it a little more clearly, all that Christ hath done and suffered for us, till He "poured out His soul for the transgressors."[111]

110. Sermon 85, *On Working Out Our Own Salvation, BE* (3:203–4).
111. Sermon 43, *The Scripture Way of Salvation, BE* (2:157).

As discussed earlier, Wesley's understanding of justification differed from the Protestant reformers (particularly Luther and Calvin).[112] For the purposes of this chapter, it is sufficient to say that Wesley understood justification to be that act of forgiveness that opens the door to *participation* with the divine purpose.

In Wesley's view of justification, with pardon came power. This power gives humanity the ability to participate actively in the process of reflecting the image of God. Runyon states that

> *Justification* is how God, to use a computer term, *realigns* humanity, restoring us to the relationship for which we were created. For Wesley, this realignment is made possible through God's forgiveness and love manifested toward us in Christ, cutting through the vicious circle of our self-induced alienation and estrangement and setting up a new relationship based on God's reconciling mercy. . . . Justification begins the process of restoring the image of God in us, for our lives are realigned for a purpose: not only to receive from God but to share what we have received with others.[113]

Although, justification can be considered an independent theological category in itself, it should not, as Wesley emphasized, be separated from the salvation narrative at large. We are forgiven, but this forgiveness is the beginning of a process leading to renewal in the image of God.[114]

Wesley's emphasis on the connection between pardon and participation ushers in another feature within his way of salvation—the relationship between justification and *sanctification*. Wesley was careful to point out that salvation was not for forgiveness (justification) alone, but for the continuing renewal of our moral lives by the grace of God.[115] This continued renewal was characterized by the gradual therapeutic transformation of God's grace. Perhaps this characterisation is the most appropriate way to speak of God's sanctifying grace.

112. For more on Wesley's distinctive articulation of justification see Outler, *Place of Wesley in the Christian Tradition*; "John Wesley as Theologian"; and *John Wesley*.

113. Runyon, *New Creation*, 42.

114. Wesley also used the language of *adoption* in reference to the restored participation in God. This idea fit within the theme of justification as pardon for the purpose of participation. For more see Sermon 1, *Salvation by Faith*, BE (1:121–23); and Sermon 4, *Scriptural Christianity*, BE (1:161).

115. See Sermon 5, *Justification by Faith*, BE (1:187); Sermon 43, *The Scripture Way of Salvation*, BE (2:158); and Sermon 85, *On Working Out Our Own Salvation*, BE (3:204).

Sanctifying Grace

As I formally introduce the topic of *sanctification*, it is important to reemphasize that, for Wesley, the works of grace that I have mentioned above are not indicative of steps in an order, but represent intertwining dimensions of God's grace.[116] In this way, salvation *by* grace is a continual growth *in* grace. This explains the recurrent themes in Wesley's handling of the various works of grace. This is no less true for sanctification, in that for Wesley, it was to be understood as greater degrees of prevenient grace in the life of a person—salvation was from "grace to grace."

The connection between pardon, participation, and truly reflecting the image of God reaches its full expression in sanctification. After prevenient grace has worked in a person's life, Wesley goes on to say that

> we experience the proper Christian salvation; whereby, through grace, we "are saved by faith;" consisting of those two grand branches, justification *and* sanctification. By justification we are saved from the guilt of sin, and restored to the favour of God; *by sanctification we are saved from the power and root of sin, and restored to the image of God.* All experience, as well as Scripture, shows this salvation to be both instantaneous *and* gradual. It begins the moment we are justified, in the holy, humble, gentle, patient love of God and man. It gradually increases from that moment, as "a grain of mustard-seed, which, at first, is the least of all seeds," but afterwards puts forth large branches, and becomes a great tree; till, in another instant, the heart is cleansed, from all sin, and filled with pure love to God and man. But even that love increases more and more, till we "grow up in all things into him that is our head;" till we attain "the measure of the stature of the fullness of Christ."[117]

116. This point becomes increasingly important in the following chapter where I formally argue against any position that considers sanctification a crisis-type stage in the conversion process. This style of thinking is found in the nineteenth-century holiness movement.

117. Sermon 85, *On Working Out Our Own Salvation*, BE (3:206). Emphasis added. Wesley's reference to "another *instant*" where the heart is cleansed from "*all* sin" is in direct reference to his notion of Christian perfection. His stance on this doctrine fluctuated throughout the course of his life. For the purposes of the present work, I will acknowledge it as a part of Wesley's theological view of sanctification, but will not expound upon it. For more on Wesley and Christian Perfection see Sangster, *Path to Perfection*; W. Stanley Johnson, "Christian Perfection," 50–60; Cubie, "Perfection" 22–37; Walters, "Concept of Attainment," 12–29; Cannon, "John Wesley's Doctrine of Sanctification," 91–95; Harrison, "Wesley," 396–405; and Wood, *Christian Perfection*.

This passage brings to light two points that I wish to stress. First "proper salvation" to Wesley does not consist of justification alone. It is because of justification that we can begin a *process* of sanctification. Given this view, it cannot be assumed that the purpose of salvation in the Christian life is to be forgiven alone. Just as God created in the beginning with purpose, so "New Creation" bears this same sense of purpose. God forgives humanity for the prospect of becoming something greater. This greater image is constituted by renewed relationships with the divine creator and the rest of creation.

Second, and perhaps the most pertinent point, sanctification should indeed be considered a process.[118] It is through this process that healing occurs in all aspects of human life. The practical approach that Wesley took in his theology made this evident. Time and again he witnessed people confess Jesus as Lord and experienced what he considered "justification by faith," but the ills so deeply embedded in the human experience healed only in the passing of time and with great attention.[119]

This is again obvious as Wesley stresses that justification is, "only the threshold of sanctification, the first entrance upon it. And as, in the natural birth, a man is born at once, and then *grows* larger and stronger *by degrees*; so in the spiritual birth, a man is born at once, and then *gradually* increases in spiritual stature and strength. The new birth, therefore, is the first point of sanctification, which may increase more and more unto the perfect day."[120]

Runyon describes sanctification as, "increasing holiness, that is, life made more and more healthy and whole by this communion with God and others."[121] It is this *goal* of health and communion with God and others that is the true mark of sanctification, as well as, the true embodiment of new creation—the *telos* to which humanity is called.

The end of this transformation is the reflection of God's own character or "holiness." Considering insights from Wesley's relational anthropology, just as self-identity cannot be formed outside of a social context, so

118. In fact, on several occasions, Wesley offered a view of the Christian life that was synonymous with natural human maturation from infancy through adulthood. For examples see Sermon 40, *Christian Perfection, BE* (2:105); Sermon 13, *On Sin in Believers, BE* (1:332–33); Sermon 83, *On Patience, BE* (3:175); Sermon 107, *On God's Vineyard, BE* (3:507); and Wesley's notes on the New Testament *1Cor. 2:6*, and *Col. 4:12*.

119. Evidence of Wesley's concern regarding this issue is seen in his emphasis on the Methodist "class" and "band" meetings. For more see Henderson, *John Wesley's Class Meeting*.

120. Sermon 108, *On God's Vineyard, BE* (3:507). Emphasis added.

121. Runyon, *New Creation*, 82.

"holiness" cannot exist apart from social relationships, hence Wesley's proclamation that he "knows of no religion but social; no holiness but social holiness."[122]

Theodore Runyon states that, "the social nature of holiness is not only written into the origins of the faith relationship but also into the ongoing direction of it as well."[123] The classic description of holiness is put forward by Wesley in his sermon on the *Great Privilege of Those that are Born of God.* Here Wesley states that holiness

> immediately and necessarily implies the continual inspiration of God's Holy Spirit; God's breathing into the soul, and the soul's breathing back what it first receives from God; a continual action of God upon the soul, and a re-action of the soul upon God; an unceasing presence of God, the loving, pardoning God, manifested to the heart, and perceived by faith; and an unceasing return of love, praise, and prayer, offering up all the thoughts of our hearts, all the words of our tongues, all the works of our hands, all our body, soul, and spirit, to be a holy sacrifice, acceptable unto God in Christ Jesus.[124]

In its essence, holiness is social, embodied, all-encompassing, and the great vocation to which humanity is called.

So what does Wesley's way of salvation have to do with my greater goal of offering an explanation of Christian conversion? In fact, Wesley's view of salvation provides an impeccable theological language for understanding the conversion phenomenon. In the following section, I will discuss in detail the relevance of the previous discussion to my overall project.

Conversion as Moral Transformation

There is an important relationship between Wesley's affectional moral psychology and his understanding of sanctification. Recall that Wesley placed a premium on the renewal of the tempers as the primary motivator for restored holy life—that is, the restored capacity for moral behavior. He recognized that a transition from corrupt to holy action did not occur naturally; rather, such action must be motivated by holy tempers. Thus, Wesley designated the recovery of holy tempers as the essential goal of religion.[125]

122. John Wesley, preface to *Hymns and Sacred Poems* (1739).

123. Runyon, "Holiness," 83.

124. *BE* (1:442).

125. Wesley wrote, "We conclude from the whole . . . that true religion, in the very

For Wesley, sanctification could be summed up as growth in the love of God, both in experience and expression.

> From the moment we are justified, till we give up our spirits to God, love is the fulfilling of the law; of the whole evangelical law, which took place of the Adamic law, when the first promise of "the seed of the woman" was made. *Love is the sum of Christian sanctification*; it is the one *kind* of holiness.[126]

Wesley saw love as the central temper through which all action hinged—"from the true love of God [and others] directly flows every Christian grace, every holy and happy temper. And from these spring uniform holiness of conversation."[127] So then, Wesley could summarize God's purpose in sanctification to be a desire for love to become the "constant ruling temper of [our] soul."[128]

This important connection between sanctification and the renewal of the tempers should be obvious. Maddox stresses that "Wesley's holy tempers would not simply be infused by God's sanctifying grace in instantaneous completeness; they would be developing realities, strengthened and shaped by our *responsible* participation in the empowering *grace* of God."[129] In this way, the gradual renewal of the tempers can be understood as the core of sanctification.

Although Wesley did not use the term "conversion," he was quite interested in human change or moral transformation. So, for the purposes of the present discussion conversion can be conceived as "moral transformation." The term "moral" is intended to designate social attitudes and behaviors. In this sense, morality is understood as right, good, or virtuous conduct. In its most basic sense, transformation refers to *change*. This change can occur in a variety of ways involving any number of life dimensions. Moral transformation, when spoken of in a religious context, should be concerned with *significant* life change. Changes of this nature involve substantial personal and social reorientation. They are not casual, but refer to transformation in a human life or community that acts to significantly alter the way that one views his or herself in the broader context of the world around him or her.

---

essence of it, is nothing short of holy tempers." Sermon 91, *On Charity*, BE (3:306).

126. Sermon 83, *On Patience*, BE (3:174–75). Emphasis added.

127. From *A Letter to the Rev. Mr. Baily of Cork*, BE, (9:309). Note that "conversation" refers to the whole of human life in all of its expressions.

128. Sermon 100, *On Pleasing All Men*, BE (3:422).

129. Maddox, *Responsible Grace*, 179.

In addition to the magnitude of the change, moral transformation (conversion) should also be understood as a process penetrating every aspect of an individual's life. According to Lewis Rambo, conversion should be understood as a "total transformation of the person by the power of God," and is "radically striking at the very root of the human predicament."[130] This understanding of conversion as moral transformation presents itself as a concern in which Wesley would have expressed considerable interest. Likewise, it resonates with the previous discussion of Wesley's way of salvation, particularly his articulation of sanctification. Furthermore, *I suggest that the process of conversion is equivalent to Wesley's concept of sanctification in so far as they are both concerned with the same end.* Both are process oriented and both entail a significant reorientation of our basic human system of motivation (tempers) and are marked by their intimate connection to observable change.

As discussed in the opening chapter, it is typical for the central rhetoric of conversion, in an American evangelical context, to deal with interior change. I find such a change to be suspect if not accompanied by a transformation in attitude and behavior. At the heart of the Christian faith is an inherent relationality; thus, the process of "becoming" a Christian is in many ways a growth in understanding how to relate in a particularly Christian way. This includes how we relate to God, others, and the world at large—learning to relate in this way is the key feature of conversion.[131]

I stand in agreement with Wesley that humans are inherently social creatures whose ultimate end is to achieve and be shaped by healthy (holy) relationships. In as much as this is true, morality should be concerned with the whole of the human experience, not *just* the internal state of the human heart in salvation.

With conversion understood in this way, it becomes central to the Christian faith as a way of relating to God and to the world. In moving forward, I do so with the understanding that conversion can be likened to Wesley's concept of sanctification, and as such can be understood as the process of "becoming Christian," that is, becoming a person that relates in a particularly Christian way.

As stressed repeatedly in this chapter, Wesley saw the potential for such a change to be completely dependent on the grace of God. The possibility of conversion exists only through this grace and it is by the *means of grace* that the change occurs. By the "means of grace," Wesley meant the

130. Rambo, *Understanding Religious Conversion*, xii.

131. Note how Wesley's emphasis on the relational component of his theological anthropology bears relevance to this point.

"*outward* signs, words, or actions, ordained of God, and appointed for this end, to be the ordinary channels whereby he might convey to men, preventing, justifying or sanctifying grace."[132]

Wesley insisted that "the whole value of the means depends on their actual subservience to the end of religion; that, consequently, all these means, when separate from the end, are less than nothing and vanity; that if they do not actually conduce to the knowledge and love of God, they are not acceptable in his sight."[133] Again we see Wesley's emphasis on the great end of religion and all that serves that end. Henry Knight argues that, "the means of grace form an interrelated context within which the Christian life is lived and through which relationships with God and one's neighbour are maintained."[134]

I do not wish to offer an in-depth description of Wesley's view of the means of grace; however, I do want to use this point to emphasize that Wesley considered a multitude of ways in which God could express divine, transformative love to humankind. In this sense, there are countless events that can be seen as "means of grace." This point is relevant to my project and one that I will return to in chapter four.

In summary, Wesley's description of the *way of salvation* is critical to a theological understanding of Christian conversion. His soteriology is based on the features of his theological anthropology that I have mentioned above—that is his, *relational* anthropology, *holistic* anthropology, and his *affectional moral psychology*. All of these features have a particular relevance to Christian conversion. Wesley was primarily concerned with the transformation of the affections or tempers; because, when this transformation occurred, it gave way to holy action—moral attitude and behavior. This transformation of the basic motivators of human action is the critical feature of conversion at large.

Summary: Moving Forward

Recall that I began this chapter with an appeal to view Wesley as a *practical* theologian. By this, I mean that Wesley was much less concerned about formulating intricate volumes of systematic doctrine than he was about passionately articulating a theology that both described and propagated transformation in human lives. I began with this point for a reason. I suggest that this theological approach predisposed Wesley to deal with issues

132. Sermon 16, *The Means of Grace, BE* (5:187). Emphasis added.

133. Ibid, *BE* (5:188).

134. Knight, *Presence of God in the Christian Life,* 2.

in a way that is particularly helpful to my overall goal of re-examining the view of conversion dominant among American evangelicals.

Wesley was uniquely positioned within the Western reformed tradition while having a connection with the theological ideas of the East. This connection influenced much of Wesley's thinking, particularly his ideas regarding the Fall, Original Sin, and the various dimensions of salvation.

Wesley's emphasis on *purpose* in the New Creation is of critical importance. Through original creation, God brought the world into being with a sense of purpose and likewise God has set forth in *New Creation* this same divine intention. For Wesley, this is the renewal of creation in the image of God—this "telos" is non-negotiable in understanding salvation at large. Furthermore, it is the community of God's people that act as the agent of God's renewal in the world.

The various features of Wesley's theological anthropology informed his soteriology in a fundamental fashion. His emphasis on human beings as relational and holistic in nature played a key role in the formation of his affectional moral psychology which subsequently led to his mature *way* of salvation.

Wesley considered the heart of salvation to be the "transformation of holy tempers." Keen as he was to the practical aspect of religious experience, Wesley observed that the forgiveness found in justification only opened the door to this renewal. It is through *sanctification* that this transformation is realized and the person reflects the image of God through a *process* of renewal that centers upon the human relationship to God and the whole of creation.

My central aim for this chapter has been to establish a theological language for conversion understood as moral transformation. I have done this by suggesting that Wesley's process of sanctification is equivalent to my notion of Christian religious conversion. This is true in as much as the ultimate goal of both are the transformation of attitudes and behaviors. In the Wesleyan paradigm, salvation proper necessarily includes moral transformation.

Recognizing that one's view of human nature has a dramatic impact on his or her notion of conversion, the following chapter will be dedicated to providing a cogent description of human nature. I will return to Wesley in chapter four where I will offer an integrated model of conversion based on the theological analysis provided in this chapter together with the scientific and philosophical research covered in the next.

CHAPTER 3

Searching for the Soul
A Case for Nonreductive Physicalism

Men go out and gaze in astonishment at high mountains, the huge waves of the sea, the broad reaches of rivers, the ocean that encircles the world, or the stars in their courses. But they pay no attention to themselves. . . . Oh Lord I am working hard in this field and the field of my labours is my own self. I'm not now investigating the tracts of the heavens or measuring the distance of the stars or trying to discover how the earth hangs in space. I am investigating myself, my memory, my mind. . . . What then am I my God? What is my nature?

—Saint Augustine[1]

T HE SEARCH TO UNDERSTAND our nature as human beings is an age-old venture. Philosophers and theologians alike have struggled with questions of ultimate reality, purpose, meaning, and consciousness. Such issues are at home in the area of theological investigation, after all, the practical essence of Christianity is understanding who we are as human beings, identifying our relationship to God and the world around us, and then deciding how we are to live in such a world.

This chapter is dedicated to addressing the particular question of human nature or theological anthropology—what are human beings?[2] Of what do we consist—body and soul; body, soul, and spirit; or maybe just a body? These are intricate questions whose answers will determine not only our basic philosophies of human life, but also our core theological perspectives such as how we are to relate to God, the world, each other, and ourselves.

---

1. Augustine, *Confessions*, Book X, Chapter VIII.
2. Recall from the introduction, the term "human nature" is meant to refer to philosophical discussions concerning the "substance" of humankind. That is, are humans "made up of" material substance only or a combination of material and immaterial substance?

The long history of this debate has led to two widely held alternatives—(1) ontological substance dualism and (2) reductive materialism. The first position holds that human beings essentially consist of two distinct substances, material and immaterial. The material substance, or body, is animated by a second distinct immaterial substance, the soul or spirit. The second option, reductive materialism, can be summed up in the statement that human beings in all of our complexities are "nothing but" the sum of our neural activity—that is, any sense that we have of free will is in essence illusory.[3]

My central claim in this chapter is that both dualist and reductive materialist views of human nature are undesirable on philosophical and theological grounds. I offer a third alternative, nonreductive physicalism (NrP), as a viable theory of human nature. Such a theory avoids the problems inherent in ontological substance dualism while preserving the causal efficacy of "higher order" capacities necessary for a proper theological anthropology. This is an idea that extends well into the literature of philosophy of mind. For example, philosophers such as Donald Davidson and John Searle argue for the causal efficacy of an emergent aspect of complex systems.[4]

This nonreductive physicalist approach to human nature provides a critical first step in resolving the issues that I outlined in chapter one of this book. In addition, this view, together with the insights from Wesleyan theology discussed in the previous chapter, supplies the critical elements necessary to propose an alternate view of religious conversion.

It is worth noting at the outset of this chapter that I am not insinuating that the issue of reduction vs. nonreduction is settled. It is still very much an open debate.[5] My purposes here are not to offer a comprehensive

3. This "nothing buttery" terminology has been used by Malcolm Jeeves in his work concerning psychological science and Christian belief. See Jeeves, *Human Nature at the Millennium* and Jeeves and Berry, *Science, Life, and Christian Belief.* The term originated with neuroscientist and Christian author Donald MacKay. MacKay states, "according to this [reductive materialist] view, only where physical explanation was impossible could any other account be taken seriously in its own right. Otherwise, the whole thing could be explained away as 'nothing but' the mindless motion of molecules." See MacKay, *Human Science and Human Dignity*, 27.

4. See D. Davidson, "Mental Events," 79–101; and Searle, *Rediscovery of the Mind.* Searle recognizes "causally emergent system features" that "have to be explained in terms of the causal interactions among the elements" (111). Searle then explicates the notion of *radical* emergence as the emergent property having its own causal powers which cannot be explained by the causal interactions of the parts of the system.

5. Jaegwon Kim offers perhaps the most widely read critique of nonreductive physicalism. See Kim, "Can Supervenience," 19–26; "Non-Reductivist's Troubles," 189–210; and

discussion of the reductionist argument, but rather to show how reductionism fails in a critical case—the case of "top-down causation."

I aim to support my central thesis by first discussing the historical context that has led to the current popular views of human nature. Then I will provide a cogent account of NrP that will address two major conceptual hurdles—overcoming dualism *and* reductive materialism. Through the process, I intend to stress that from a theological perspective neither of these views of human nature is desirable. While most within the Christian tradition would gladly reject reductive materialism, I will also argue that is theologically reasonable to renounce dualism. Finally, the closing section in this chapter will deal with issues related to the nature of conversion. In essence, I will suggest that a nonreductive physicalist view of the human person necessitates a process-oriented concept of conversion. By the same logic, I will reject the notion of crisis sanctification or "second blessing" on the basis that this phenomenon must adhere to process as well.

Human Nature in Historical Context

The issue of human nature, as originating in Greek philosophy, has come to rest in the quest to define the make-up of the human person. This quest manifests itself as questions regarding our constituent parts—are humans made of body and soul? body, soul, and spirit? or simply a body? The first of these options, body and soul, is commonly referred to as dualism or dichotomism. The second view, a claim that humans are made of three different substances, is called trichotomism.[6] Finally the view holding that human beings are composed of essentially one physical substance is known as monism.[7]

As pointed out in chapter one of this work, many Christians consider body-soul dualism to be an absolute essential element of Christian teaching. A natural tension arises between this belief (which amounts to no less than a worldview) and the ever burgeoning scientific data that points to

---

"Myth of Nonreductive Physicalism," 265–84. Kim argues that mental properties will be reducible to physical properties unless some type of "downward causation" is applied. He holds that all forms of downward causation necessarily suggest an ontological status for the mental and thus becomes dualism.

6. The trichotomist view has very little support in either philosophical or theological circles. The most popular proponent of this view is Watchman Nee. See Nee *Release of the Spirit*.

7. There are various types of monism. The literature will most often speak of some form of *physicalism* or *materialism*.

the notion that humans are physical creatures with no inner soul or self to serve as the "ghost in the machine."[8]

It is critical to understand that one cannot use the Bible as a definitive source for the existence of the soul as the ontological, immaterial essence of the human person. In fact, the Bible is silent on this issue of theological anthropology. New Testament scholar, James D. G. Dunn argues that questions put to the Bible regarding the constituent parts of the human person are foreign to biblical thought.

Dunn distinguishes between a *partitive* and an *aspective* understanding of the human person—the biblical text is concerned with the latter. From this point of view, one can only speak of the whole person in a relational context. So what appears in the biblical text to refer to an ontologically distinct part—the body, soul or spirit—is meant to designate the whole person conceived from a certain angle. Dunn asserts that biblical anthropology is concerned about relationships—to God and creation.[9]

Such radically differing views certainly did not spring up in any quick fashion; rather, there is a long and complex history that has led us to the views of human nature that we have today. In what follows, I will offer a rather brief history of theories of human nature as they have evolved both as a philosophical thesis and a theological concept. I will begin this exploration in ancient Greek philosophy.

It would be incorrect to assume any single view of human nature within the ancient Greco-Roman world.[10] In fact, the nature of matter it-

8. The term "ghost in the machine" is borrowed from Gilbert Ryle's classic work *Concept of Mind*. Ryle offers a critique of the notion that the mind or soul is distinct from the body. He argues that the traditional (Cartesian) approach to the relation of mind and body represents a basic "category-mistake."

9. See Dunn, *Theology of the Apostle Paul*, 51ff. Theologian Neil Gillman echoes this position by asserting that although the ancient Jews had a clear sense that the person somehow continued to "be" after burial, "this should in no way be interpreted to refer to the continued existence, after death, of a human 'soul'; there is no notion of this kind of entity, independent of the body, in the Bible." See Gillman, *Death of Death*, 69. Gillman's work in particular does a fine job of tracking the historical emergence of the concept of body-soul duality in the Jewish faith. Louis P. Pojman supports the notion that this Jewish belief carried over to the writers of the New Testament. Pojman states that "The idea of a separate soul does not appear in the Bible, though one might read the idea into some passages. . . . In the New Testament, believers in Christ are promised eternal life (Jn. 3:16); however, it is not the eternal life of a soul but of a glorified, resurrected body (1Cor. 15:35f)." See Pojman, *Who Are We?*, 5–6.

10. For support of this claim as well as a helpful discussion of the impact of Greek thought on human nature in a Biblical context see Green, "Bodies," 149–73. In addition, it is worth noting that some Biblical scholars tend to make a sharp distinction between the "holistic" account of human nature as interpreted from the Hebrew Scriptures and the

self was a contentious issue in ancient philosophy. For many ancient Greek philosophers, reality was conceived as existing in a hierarchy of beings that exhibited varying degrees of material existence.[11] Such a hierarchy would have at its base level inanimate objects, and from there, plants, animals, human beings, and finally various descriptions of divinities would extend upward. An important conflict arose as to where in the hierarchy the existence of the "soul" would arise. Plato and Aristotle are noted as the two most influential contributors to the development of hierarchical ontology.

Plato's account is indeed dualistic in nature—he described the human person as an immortal soul imprisoned within a mortal body.[12] Plato's tripartite notion of the soul consisted of an impulsive element (that corresponded to the lowest class in society), an element that corresponding to the solider-police (*thumos*, which may be translated "spirit"), and finally, reason, which was considered the highest element and associated with the ruling class.

Plato is well-known for his use of *Forms*. By this, he meant that ideas or concepts have real existence and are likewise eternal. He used the logic of forms to suggest that the rational part of the soul pre-exists the existence of the physical body that possesses it—thus arises the root of the immortal soul.

Aristotle also used the language of Forms; however, he applied the concept in a different manner. For Aristotle the soul was not a separate entity that pre-existed the body, but was rather conceived of as a *life principle*. In this manner of speaking, plants and animals possess souls just as humans (albeit these were thought of as nutritive or sensitive souls which

---

supposed dualism of Greek views. This is a complex issue that tends to be oversimplified. For an analysis emphasising a sharp contrast see Cullmann, "Immortality," 9–53. For a more moderate and recent analysis see Wright, *Resurrection of the Son of God*.

11. For a classic work on Plato's hierarchy of being see Lovejoy, *The Great Chain of Being*. For a recent discussion see Pojman, *Who are We?*, see especially chapters 3 and 4 regarding Plato's and Aristotle's theory of human nature.

12. For instance, in the *Phaedo* Plato writes: "The soul whose inseparable attitude is life will never admit of life's opposite, death. Thus the soul is shown to be immortal, and since immortal, indestructible. . . . Do we believe there is such a thing as death? To be sure. And is this anything but the separation of the soul and body? And being dead is the attainment of this separation, when the soul exists in herself and separate from the body, and the body is parted from the soul. That is death. . . . Death is merely the separation of the soul and body." See Plato, *Essential Plato*, 600. Again in Book X, Part 11 of *Republic*, Plato claims that the soul of man is immortal and imperishable. See Plato, *Republic*, X.11 (Jewett, 440).

gave them the capacity to react, reproduce, etc.). The capacity for rationality was reserved for humans alone.

Aristotle's well-known analogy demonstrating the relation of the soul to the body is: if the eye were a complete animal, sight would be its soul.[13] In this sense, Aristotle ascribed to all living organisms a *Psuche* or the *Form* of a living, natural body.[14] The phrase "to have a *psuche* (or soul)", in an Aristotelian sense, does not signify a possessive relationship between an agent and an entity (like "I have a toaster"); rather, it signifies (as his analogy suggests) the form of an object as it extends from its inherent *telos* (ultimate purpose). For example, the telos (or first actuality) of a wrist-watch is to keep time. It can only do so based on the constituent matter that makes it up—tiny cogs, gears, springs, etc. So, in this sense, the *soul* of the wrist-watch is its capacity to keep time, not some single entity that exists within it.[15]

A relevant point that I wish to stress regarding ancient philosophies of human nature regards the capacities unique to human beings (such as the very act of doing philosophy). It proved difficult to attribute these capacities to matter alone, so philosophers developed theories regarding the addition of an immaterial component that would account for the exercise of reason. In this context, it is easy to see how the soul was a relevant philosophical concern.

Thinkers within the early Church wrestled no less with the issue of human nature. Tertullian (160–220) followed the Stoics in adopting the notion that the human soul was an inextricable part of human corporeal existence and was thus generated with the body.[16] In contrasting fashion, Origen (185–254) held a more Platonic view in teaching that the soul was incorporeal and eternal, thus pre-existing the body. In fact, Origen reasoned that a finite number of souls exist as part of original creation

13. Aristotle, *De Anima*.

14. It is worth noting that that although this concept of the *psuche* can be translated as "soul"; for Aristotle, the concept did not carry with it a religious connotation.

15. This *hylomorphic* conception of reality distinguished Aristotle's use of forms from Plato—it is not a pre-existent entity within the human body, nor is it a substance that survives bodily death. Given these differences it is questionable whether Aristotle's view could be considered dualist at all. As the argument progresses it will become increasingly obvious the importance of this Aristotelian view to my project at large.

16. For a detailed translation of Tertullian's work see Roberts, *Theology of Tertullian*. View this text online at http://www.tertullian.org/articles/roberts_theology/roberts_00_index.htm (accessed 31 May 2006). See especially chapter 8: "The Doctrine of Man and Sin," 149–65. Tertullian's position is often referred to as *traducianism*. This theory states that the soul, along with the body, is derived from one's biological parents.

(although he seems to claim that they were somehow created outside of time). Through a series of events these souls fell from heaven (taking on a fleshly form) with the exception of the "soul of Christ" which remained with God until the appropriate time.[17]

Probably the most influential Christian thinker on this issue was Saint Augustine of Hippo (354–430). Augustine has had substantial influence on both Catholic and Protestant spirituality. Essentially Augustine's concept of human nature is a modified Platonic view—a human being is an immortal soul with the body seen as a mere vehicle for this immaterial entity. Although Augustine's view of the soul was tripartite in nature, it differed from Plato's in that the *will* was viewed as being superior to the intellect.

As mentioned in chapter one, Augustine was successful in combining Neoplatonist ideas with religious concepts thus yielding the development of the notion that salvation was primarily a condition of the soul. Such a move has had vast implications for a Christian understanding of conversion. Following Augustine, it would be through the cultivation of the soul that one would achieve knowledge and relation to God. Such a "cultivation of the soul" was often achieved by the denigration of the body (physical need and desire).

Thomas Aquinas (1225–74) offered a view of human nature in contrast to Augustine's ideas. Aquinas was largely informed by Aristotle's hylomorphic metaphysics—which practically translated into his adoption of Aristotle's thesis that the soul was the form of the body.[18] Aquinas differed from Plato and Aristotle regarding the relationship between soul and body. This is evident in his doctrine of the resurrection. In his commentary on 1 Cor 15, Aquinas writes:

> A man naturally desires his own salvation; but the soul, since it is part of the body of a human being, is not a whole being, and my soul is not I; so even if a soul gains salvation in another life, that is not I or any man.[19]

17. For more on Origen's notion of the pre-existence of human souls see Origen's *On First Principles* (2.6.5), 96.

18. See Aquinas, *Summa Contra Gentiles*, section 65—"That the Soul is Not the Body."

19. Aquinas, "Commentary," 67. Note that with Aquinas, the Christian hope of resurrection is not identical with "immortality of the soul." See also Pegis, "Separated Soul," 131–58.

His elaborate view of human nature was also marked by the development of a hierarchically ordered account of the capacities of the soul. For Aquinas (as with Aristotle), the rational capacities are distinctively human and the intellect is superior to the will (contra Augustine).

The issue of human nature has been widely debated throughout the history of human thought. Some of our most rich resources originate in Greek philosophy—the most notable figures being Plato and Aristotle. The concepts set in motion by these ancient philosophers had a profound affect on early Christian theologians. I have suggested that the most notable of these thinkers is St. Augustine of Hippo. His formulation of Christian spirituality has deeply influenced our modern understanding of what it means to experience conversion.

The epic of understanding human nature continues with the rise of early modern science. The following section will deal with some of the prominent thinkers related to the issue of human nature.

Human Nature and the Rise of Early Modern Science

The transition from medieval to modern science is primarily marked by the Copernican revolution. Inherent in this transition is the philosophical shift from Aristotelian hylomorphism to atomism.[20] Although Galileo Galilei (1564–1642) is widely known for his contributions to astronomy, he played a significant role in the philosophical shift to atomism.[21] Galileo was one of the first modern scientists to reject the Aristotelian notion that all things were composed of both "matter" and "form." Rather, he opted for an atomic or corpuscular theory—he hypothesized (early in his career) that all physical processes could be explained in terms of the properties of atoms (size, shape, and rate of motion).

The work of Isaac Newton (1643–1727) applied the basic philosophical premise of atomism put forth by Galileo. The system of physics developed by Newton depended on taking inertial mass as the essential

---

20. Here "hylomorphism" is meant to refer to Aristotle's basic view of human nature (body and soul) as being an instance of "matter-formism." That is, the soul is the *form* of the body. The essence of atomism is the idea that all matter can be reduced to basic particles whose activity can then be predicted based on the laws of physics. Subsequently, Aristotle's hylomorphic intuition is nested within a teleological (end-oriented) view of human action where an atomic perspective focuses on an individualized mechanical explanation of human action. This aspect of the transition from hylomorphism to atomism is not often emphasized as a significant contributor to the Copernican revolution. This is most likely due to gradual nature of the shift—extending into nineteenth century biology.

21. See Galilei, *Dialogues Concerning Two New Sciences*.

property of atoms. From this basic assumption he explained acceleration as a concept of *force* rather than velocity, further supplanting Aristotle's views.[22]

Atomism found its way to the domain of chemistry through the work of Antoine-Laurent Lavoisier (1743–94) and John Dalton (1766–1844). These two scientists made great headway in demonstrating that chemistry could basically be understood as phenomena characterized by the properties of the elements that made up a particular substance—atoms. The work of Lavoisier and Dalton proved to be not only a triumph for atomic theory, but also led to an interest in reductionism as a scientific strategy, that is, not only analyzing a thing by looking at the parts that make it up, but explaining the behavior of a thing as the sum of the behaviors of its constituent parts.[23] This concept of *reductionism* is an important one to which I will return at length in a subsequent section of this chapter.

I have intentionally left a quite significant figure out of the chronologically ordered discussion above. René Descartes (1596–1650) is considered by many to be the originator of modern philosophy. His work has had far reaching effects in both science and theology. I suggest that not only is Descartes the father of modern philosophy, but the father of modern dualism as well. So important is this point that I will spend the following section laying out how Cartesian philosophy has contributed to our contemporary concept of the inner life—soul or mind.

The Emergence of Cartesian Dualism

René Descartes, closely connected with the atomist revolution in physics, distinguished two basic forms of reality—*res extensa* (extended substance) and *res cogitans* (thinking substance). With Descartes there was a semantic shift from "soul" to "mind"; nevertheless, both concepts are understood as the most basic life principle.

Descartes's work marked a dramatic upheaval in modern European thought. To some degree, his philosophical concepts had much in common with Aristotelian scholasticism, but he demonstrated a radical departure on four primary issues.[24] First, Descartes held that the mind is the *whole*

22. For Newton's clearest exposition of atomism see *Isaac Newton*, Querie 31 of *Opticks*, 127–40.

23. Dalton built on the work of Lavoisier to derive his unique view of chemical atomism. For more see Dalton, *New System of Chemical Philosophy*.

24. I follow Bennett and Hacker in describing these four departures. For a more detailed account see *Philosophical Foundations of Neuroscience*, 25–27.

soul. In contrast to Aristotle, he held the soul not as the principle of *life*, but as the principle of *thought* or *consciousness*.

> The functions of the Aristotelian nutritive soul (nutrition, growth, reproduction) and of the sensitive soul (perception, physiologically conceived, and locomotion) are *not* essential functions of the Cartesian mind, but of the body. All the essential functions of animal life are to be conceived in purely mechanistic terms.[25]

Second, Descartes redefined what was meant by the *mental*. In his view, the human person is essentially a *res cogitans*—a thinking thing. Descartes's concept of a "thinking thing" extended far beyond anything that Aristotle or the scholastics ascribed to the rational soul. Descartes conceived *thought* to include "everything which we are aware of as happening within us, in so far as we have awareness of it. Hence *thinking* is to be identified here not merely with understanding, willing, imagining, but also with sensory awareness."[26]

> *Thought, therefore, was, in a revolutionary step, defined in terms of consciousness*—that is, as that of which we are immediately aware within us. And consciousness was thereby assimilated to self-consciousness inasmuch as it was held to be impossible to think and to have experiences (to feel pain, seem to perceive, feel passions, will, imagine, cogitate) without knowing or being aware that one does.[27]

Third, Descartes held that the union of the body and mind is constituted by *two distinct substances*.

> Contrary to scholastic thought, according to which a human being is a unitary substance (an *ens per se*), Descartes intimated that a human being is *not* an individual substance, but a composite entity. The person (the *ego*), on the other hand, is an individual substance, and is identical with the mind. . . . [T]he mind, *because* it is united with the body, can bring about movements of the body through acts of will.[28]

The fourth and final departure noted by Bennett and Hacker involved the essential property of matter. Just as Descartes considered *thought* to be

---

25. Ibid., 26.
26. Descartes, *Philosophical Writings of Descartes,* 195.
27. Ibid., 26. Emphasis added.
28. Ibid., 26–27.

the essential property of the mind, he claimed that *extension* was to be considered the principal property of physical substance.

These four points which Bennett and Hacker claim mark Descartes's departure from an Aristotelian concept of human nature signify the basis of his thought on the human person. It was from these concepts that Descartes's ideas flowed. Allow me to quote Descartes at length—from *Meditations on First Philosophy*:

> It is indeed possible (or rather, as I shall say later on, it is certain) that I have a body closely bound up with myself; but at the same time I have, on the one hand, a clear and distinct idea of myself taken simply as a conscious, not an extended, being; and, on the other hand, a distinct idea of body, taken simply as an extended, not a conscious, being; so it is certain that I am really distinct from my body, and could exist without it . . . I must begin by observing the great difference between mind and body. Body is of its nature always divisible; mind is wholly indivisible. When I consider the mind—this is, myself, in so far as I am merely a conscious being—I can distinguish no parts within myself; I understand myself to be a single and complete thing. Although the whole mind seems to be united to the whole body, yet when a foot or an arm or any other part of the body is cut off I am not aware that any subtraction has been made from the mind. Nor can the faculties of will, feeling, understanding and so on be called its parts; for it is one and the same mind that wills, feels, and understands. On the other hand, I cannot think of any corporeal or extended object without being readily able to divide it in thought and therefore conceiving of it as divisible. This would be enough to show me the total difference between mind and body, even if I did not sufficiently know this already.[29]

This shift from hylomorphism to atomism (in the context of modern science) and substance dualism (in the case of Cartesian philosophy) led to what is now seen by many to be a philosophical conundrum—the mind-body problem.[30]

The central issue of the mind-body problem is that of mind-body *interaction*. Simply stated, if one holds the immateriality of mind, then

---

29. Descartes, *Descartes*, 111–15.

30. This is essentially a problem of mental causation. Lynne Rudder Baker states that the problem of mental causation is insoluble. He notes that "We simply have no answer to the question 'How can mental events, in virtue of having mental properties, make a difference to behavior?' because the very assumptions that generate the question render it unanswerable." See L. R. Baker, "Metaphysics," 77.

there is no way to account for its causal role in physical behavior. Even if one interprets mental force as a quasi-physical force, the effects of such a process should prove to be both measurable and quantifiable by scientific means—alas, such an option is not available within the realm of current science.[31]

Owen Flanagan emphasizes the nature of this problem by stating:

> If Descartes is right that a mind can cause the body to move, for example, we decide to go to a concert and go, and then physical energy must increase in and around our body, since we get up and go to the concert. In order, however, for physical energy to increase in any system, it has to have been transferred from some other physical system. But the mind, according to Descartes, is not a physical system and therefore it does not have any energy to transfer. The mind cannot account for the fact that our body ends up at the concert. If we accept the principle of the conservation of energy we seem committed either to denying that the mind exists, or to denying that it could cause anything to happen, or to making some very implausible ad hoc adjustments in our physics. For example, we could maintain that the principle of conservation of energy holds, but that every time a mind introduces new energy into the world—thanks to some mysterious capacity it has—an equal amount of energy departs from the physical universe—thanks to some perfectly orchestrated mysterious capacity the universe has.[32]

This problem regarding the law of conservation of matter and energy exemplifies the type of issues that arise in the mind-body problem.[33] As with most scientific and philosophical revolutions, there were a number of

---

31. Descartes considered mental force to be mediated through the pineal gland in the brain, thus presenting itself as quasi-physical in nature.

32. Flanagan, *Science of Mind*, 21.

33. Murphy notes that the triumph of Cartesian dualism over Aristotelian hylomorphism presents other issues as well, not least of which is the epistemological problems that arise. From an Aristotelian perspective, sensory knowledge was understood as the transference of the *form* of a perceived object to the intellect of the person perceiving it. In this view, it was possible to know the essence of a thing based on observation—only perceptual *error* needed explanation. In an atomistic world, sensory perception is dependent on the impinging of atoms on sensory membranes which results in information being transmitted to the brain, then ultimately to the mind (in Descartes's case). In this latter view, concepts in the mind are no longer identical to the forms of particular objects (that which makes them what they are), but *mere representations* produced through complex physical processes (*Whatever Happened to the Soul*, 8). The end of which is the rise of modern scepticism regarding sensory perception. For more see Meyering, *Historical Roots of Cognitive Science*.

thinkers that challenged the Cartesian view of human nature on a number of counts. The culmination of atomist thinking in science and the widespread influence of Cartesian philosophy led to the articulation of what has come to be known as *reductive materialism*. In the following section, I will sketch the evolution of thought leading to this popular philosophical position.

Reductive Materialism

Descartes's contemporary, Thomas Hobbes (1588–1679) offered an alternative to the dualist view of human nature. Hobbes, a materialist, described thinking to be "motions about the head" and emotions to be "motions about the heart."[34] Such theories of human thought and nature represent attempts to deal with the repercussions resulting from a dualist view of human nature. As mentioned above, the basic problem is that of causal interaction between the material (body) and the immaterial (soul or mind).

A number of attempts to explain this problem arose and subsequently yielded an increased rigor in the area of philosophy of mind. One such attempt, *psychophysical parallelism* is the view that "physical events cause physical events, that mental events cause mental events, and that the *appearance* of causal interaction between the mental and the physical is an illusion created by the fact that there is a pre-established harmony between these two independent causal chains."[35] Such a harmony is either established in the beginning by God or is the result of a constant chain of divine interventions.[36]

This view, however, proves to be undesirable due to its lack of ability to deal sufficiently with the complexities of mental causation and free will. Owen Flanagan argues that "to have to introduce God to explain the workings of the mind, however, is to introduce a big Spirit in order

34. According to Hobbes, human beings are purely physical objects—highly complex machines whose function could be described in mechanistic terms. In this sense, thought is understood as an instance of the physical operation of the human body; likewise, sensation involves a series of mechanical processes operating within the human nervous system, by means of which the sensible features of material things produce ideas in the brains of the human beings who perceive them. See Hobbes, *Leviathan*, 85–222.

35. Murphy, "Human Nature," 9.

36. Gottfried Wilhelm Leibniz (1646–1716) was a proponent of such a view. See Leibniz, *Discourse on Metaphysics and the Monadology*. From Leibniz's point of view, no interaction or causation is necessary because, like two clocks that keep the same time, the behavior of the two substances were in complete harmony. The main problem with pre-existent harmony is that of free will.

to get rid of the perplexities of a world of little spirits, and to magnify the complications one presumably set out to reduce."[37]

A further attempt to solve the issue of mental causation is known as *epiphenomenalism*. Here, the central idea is that conscious mental life is the by-product of physical brain processes. Subsequently, these mental by-products lack any form of causal efficacy over the physical realm—behavior. As with the case of pre-existent harmony, epiphenomenalism is problematic on two main counts. First, there are "intuitive objections" claiming that it is simply absurd that one's thoughts, feelings, emotions, etc., have no causal influence over behavior. A second, and perhaps more subtle problem, occurs when one raises the question of physical-to-mental causality. It would seem that the same epiphenomenalist logic that disallows mental-to-physical causality would also by necessity not allow the physical to express causal efficacy over the mental.[38]

The point in discussing these attempts to reconcile the interaction between mind and body is to demonstrate how they naturally move from the dualist view of human nature to a more physicalist or materialist explanation. Such a motion is no less prominent in a contemporary context.

The twentieth century brought a number of research projects aimed at providing a reductive view of human nature. A classic example is found in *logical behaviorism*. The behaviorists held prominence roughly between the 1930s and early 1960s. Logical behaviorism was in opposition to *methodological behaviorism* in that it did not deny the existence of mental states; rather, the logical behaviorists (the most notable being Gilbert Ryle) claimed that the talk of mental phenomena is a misleading way of talking about actual and potential behavior. Despite Ryle's rigorous defence of the position (and notable critique of Cartesian dualism), it has not proved possible to successfully translate mind-language into language about behavior and physical dispositions.[39]

Prior to advances in philosophical analysis, one of the most popular positions in the philosophy of mind was known as the *mind-brain identity thesis*. There are two types of identity theses that have subtle, but important distinctions—*token identity* and *type identity* (referring to the identity of

37. Flanagan, *Science of the Mind*, 64.

38. I acknowledge that there are a number of issues to address in overcoming epiphenomenalism. The epiphenomenalist suggestion that cases of mental causation merely appear to be so is a difficult claim to counter. For a helpful resource see van Gulick, "Three Bad Arguments," 311–32. Jaegwon Kim refers to this issue as the "problem of Causal Exclusion." See Kim, *Mind in a Physical World*.

39. In addition to *Concept of Mind* see Ryle, *Dilemmas*.

events). The token identity thesis holds that every particular mental event or property is identical with *some* physical event.

The second option, type identity, is a strong version of the token identity thesis in that it states that every *type* of mental event is identical to some *type* of physical event. For example, the mental event of experiencing a particular pain is identical to the activation of a particular neuron assembly (or *type* of neuron assembly) corresponding to the physical realization of the pain. Thus, type identity readily leads to the reduction of mental descriptions to physical descriptions. In response to the identity thesis, Flanagan comments:

> [I]f type-type identity theory is true then reduction of psychology to neuroscience will eventually be possible. It is easy to see why reduction requires that all the concepts of the science to be reduced be translatable into the concepts of the reducing science. These translations are called "bridge laws" and once they are in place reduction merely involves replacing, synonym for synonym. Type-type identity statements, of course, are precisely the necessary bridge laws.[40]

The type identity explanation does not raise much objection when dealing with basic physiological processes—pain response, reflexes, etc. However, more serious issues arise when the theory is applied to "higher-order" capacities such as belief. Murphy states that "when conjoined with the thesis that brain events obey causal laws, type identity implies not only that beliefs could be redescribed in purely neurological language, but also that our beliefs are caused by neurophysiological laws."[41]

There are some philosophers who are comfortable with this reductive move and even anticipate that scientific advances will one day replace any attempt to explain human phenomena via "folk psychology."[42] The discussion of "token" and "type" identity theories make it possible to better articulate an important goal of this chapter—clearly laying out the differences between *reductive* and *nonreductive* versions of materialism (or

40. Flanagan, *Science of the Mind*, 218.

41. Murphy, "Human Nature," 10.

42. "Folk psychology" refers to the psychological theory implicit in the "everyday" descriptions of the actions of others. This notion addresses concepts such as belief, desire, pain, pleasure, love, hate, etc. Two of the most well-known philosophers advocating the identity theory in relation to higher order capacities are Paul and Patricia Churchland. For more see P. M. Churchland, "Toward a Cognitive Neurobiology," 83–96; *Engine of Reason*; "Eliminative Materialism," 67–90; and P. S. Churchland, "The Neural Mechanisms of Moral Cognition," 169–94; *Neurophilosophy*; and "A Perspective," 185–207.

physicalism). Thus, the following discussion will present, in an explicit fashion, the nature of *reductive materialism.*

Recall that with the rise of early modern science and the importation of atomist thinking, the uses of "reduction" as a scientific method gained widespread acceptance. In this way, much of modern science can be understood as the development of research programmes that are based on this metaphysical theory. Murphy refers to this as "the era in which Democritus has triumphed over Aristotle."[43]

The reductionist approach has produced a hierarchical model for the relations among the sciences. From about the beginning of the seventeenth-century a distinct hierarchy of complex systems began to form within science.[44] The hierarchy is arranged according to the complexity of the entities being investigated. Physics appears at the base level, because it studies the smallest and most basic constituents of matter. The analysis of molecules or interactions between atomic particles leads to the next level in the hierarchy—chemistry. The next level presents biology as the study of complex molecular formations that result in living organisms.[45]

As we return to the general theme that led to the creation of the reductive thesis, mind-body causation, and consider the problem by applying the hierarchy of complex systems. Here, causation occurs in a *bottom-up* manner—"the parts of an entity are located one rung *downward* in the hierarchy of complexity, and it is the parts that determine the characteristics of the whole, not the other way around. So *ultimate* causal explanations are thought to be based on laws pertaining to the lowest levels of the hierarchy."[46]

So then, what is needed is a framework to consider the ramifications of this reductive notion of causality. I follow Murphy in distinguishing six related elements in the reductionist programme.[47]

---

43. Murphy, "Supervenience," 466. Democritus (460–370 BCE) was a Greek philosopher known most for his primitive atomic theory. Aristotle discussed his ideas at length due to the fact that he rejected Democritus's atomistic concepts.

44. This hierarchy of *complex systems* replaced the ancient "hierarchy of beings" that originated in ancient Greek thought.

45. It is worth noting a point that will become increasingly important throughout this book, namely, the hierarchy of complex systems can be extended beyond biology to even more complex systems—psychology, sociology, and eventually to the realm of ethics and metaphysics.

46. Murphy, "Supervenience," 466.

47. Ibid., 466–67. Also see Ayala, "Introduction," vii–xvi; Barbour, *Religion in an Age of Science,* 165–68; and Peacocke, *God and the New Biology,* especially chapters 1 and 2.

1. Methodological reductionism: a research strategy of analyzing the thing to be studied into its parts.

2. Epistemological reductionism: the view that laws or theories pertaining to the higher levels of the hierarchy of the sciences can (and should) be shown to follow from lower-level laws, and ultimately from the laws of physics.

3. Logical or definitional reductionism: the view that words and sentences referring to one type of entity can be translated without residue into language about another type of entity.[48]

4. Causal reductionism: the view that the behavior of the parts of a system (ultimately, the parts studied by subatomic physics) is determinative of the behavior of all higher-level entities. Thus, this is the thesis that all causation in the hierarchy is "bottom-up."

5. Ontological reductionism: the view that higher-level entities are nothing but the sum of their parts. However, this thesis is ambiguous; we need names here for two distinct positions. One is the view that as one goes up the hierarchy of levels, no new kinds of metaphysical "ingredients" need to be added to produce higher-level entities from lower. No "vital force" or "entelechy" must be added to get living beings from non-living materials; no immaterial mind or soul needed to get consciousness; no *Zeitgeist* to form individuals into a society. Let us reserve the term "ontological reductionism" for this position.

6. Reductive materialism: I shall use this term to distinguish a stronger claim than the previous one, that only the entities at the lowest level are *really* real; higher-level entities—molecules, cells, organisms—are only composite structures made of atoms. It is possible to hold ontological reductionism without subscribing to this thesis. Thus, one might want to say that higher-level entities are real—as real as the entities that compose them—and at the same time reject all sorts of vitalism and dualism.

The very nature of science is characterized by methodological reductionism and thus lends credence to the other types of reductionism listed above. There is a crucial "metaphysical" view that follows from the reductionist position—that all the constituent parts in a given system determine the character and behavior of the whole system. Such a view necessarily

---

48. This type of reductionism is discussed at length by John R. Searle. For more see *Rediscovery of Mind*, 112–14.

disallows for causal efficacy of the whole system on the base constituents. *I claim that one can hold ontological reductionism without prescribing to reductive materialism.*[49] This latter position proves to not only be philosophically faulty, but also theologically undesirable in that it rejects human uniqueness and any type of free will.[50]

Before moving forward, it will be useful to summarize recent scientific discoveries that challenge traditional views of human nature in various ways. There are a number of disciplines that offer data relevant to the present discussion (evolutionary biology, genetics, etc.). After a brief discussion of the pertinent changes in biology, I will focus on the cognitive sciences and neuroscience in particular. My purpose in doing so is to offer practical examples of how advances in science are challenging our understanding of human nature.

Recent Scientific Discovery

Darwin's theory of evolution has had a substantial impact on contemporary culture. This impact can be likened to that which the revolution in physics and astronomy brought to modern science. The primary issue raised in Darwin's theory is that of continuity between humans and animals; thus, there sprung a further reason to question body-soul (mind) dualism.

A consequence of the rejection of Aristotelian hylomorphism and the adoption of modern atomism was the dismissal of the idea that plants and animals possessed any type of "soul"—which was understood as the substantial *form* of their bodies. From Descartes forward, it was common to conceive of plants and animals as purely material entities. In light of this context—Darwinian evolution and Cartesian philosophy—the kinship of humans to the lower animals led many to conclude that humans were likewise purely material in nature.

Theologians were keenly aware of the challenges that Darwin's ideas presented, so many concluded that although the human body was the product of an evolutionary process, God instilled souls within each human person at conception. Such a move was intended to avoid the pitfalls that

---

49. In other words, I believe it possible to posit that higher-level capacities are *real*—in that they have the power of causal efficacy—without adopting any form of vitalism or dualism.

50. It is worth noting that, due to the strains created by a reductive materialist view, there are those who call for a revival of the concept of the soul. These rightfully claim that a reductive-materialistic worldview yields a deterministic concept of the human person that is practically undesirable. For an example see Boyd, "One's Self-concept," 207–27; and *Reclaiming the Soul.*

reductive materialism posed for human uniqueness. There are a number of problems with this view however, not least of which is the challenge of identifying exactly when in the evolutionary process human beings became distinct from their "animal" ancestors—at what point did the species become sufficiently human to be granted a soul?[51] If this is not the question to ask, that is, if the reductive materialist thesis is true and human distinctiveness cannot be attributed to the possession of a soul, what hope have we for the complex relational nature of human beings that we experience? These are pertinent questions that I will address in the following sections.

Probably the most significant advances in the investigation of the human mind have occurred in the realm of the cognitive sciences. In its essence, cognitive science is the science of *thinking*. It informs and involves several disciplines including artificial intelligence (AI), neuroscience, cognitive psychology, cognitive ethology, and philosophy of mind. The cognitive sciences focus on research concerning the study of language, reasoning ability, memory, perception, and the role of emotions in human cognition.

Many scholars with interest in both science and theology consider the cognitive sciences to have great potential for advances in theological thought. Gregory R. Peterson suggests "that all forms of theology stand to be affected by a serious dialogue with the cognitive sciences. Insofar as methodology and content are connected, the content of the cognitive sciences can affect the way we go about *doing* theology."[52]

Of particular interest to the present discussion are the data provided by neuroscience.[53] As a discipline, neuroscience focuses on three major areas of investigation: (1) neuroanatomy (mapping of brain regions), (2) neurophysiology (studying the functions of the various regions), and (3) neuropsychology (investigating how various brain processes influence behavior). The significance of neuroscientific discovery should not be underestimated. One philosopher points out that "neuroscience has in a sense

51. For more on the topic of theological concerns and evolutionary biology see Ayala, "Human Nature," 31–48; and Ayala, "Evolution of Life," 21–58.

52. Peterson, *Minding God*, 12.

53. The prominence of neuroscientific explanations of human nature has led to an increased interest among philosophers. For examples see Bechtel, Mandik, and Mundale, "Philosophy," 5–22; Bechtel and Stufflebeam, "Epistemic Issues" 55–81; Bennett and Hacker, *Philosophical Foundations of Neuroscience*; P. S. Churchland, *Neurophilosophy*; Daugman, "Brain Metaphor," 23–36; and Mundale, "Neuroanatomical Foundations," 37–54.

completed the Darwinian revolution, bringing not only the human body but the human mind as well, into the sphere of scientific investigation."[54]

In short, neuroscientists are, at a rapid rate, presenting data indicating that many of the faculties once attributed to the mind or soul can now be explained as complex functions of the human brain.[55] There are a number of such examples available from within the field of neuroscience. I will briefly discuss two and expound in more detail on a third—(1) religious or spiritual experiences, (2) the experience and expression of love, and (3) moral attitude and behavior.

By "religious experience" (also referred to as "peak spiritual experiences"), I am referring to experiences of religious transcendence. Such experiences are marked by feelings of awe and divine presence. Most persons, religious and non-religious, would identify these religious experiences as manifestations within the soul.

Current neuroscience is redefining how we understand religious experiences of this nature. At present, there is significant literature suggesting that these experiences are correlated to abnormal neural activity (seizure-like activity) in structures of the temporal lobes and limbic system.[56] Michael A. Persinger and colleagues even claim to be able to create "spiritual experiences" among volunteers in the laboratory by inducing electromagnetic stimulation of the temporal lobe.[57]

While there are a number of issues that need to be addressed to deal fully with these neuroscientific claims, the point here is to emphasize how a realm of experience once exclusively dealt with in terms of the soul or mind is now being investigated through brain sciences. The possible implications are this: if religious or spiritual experiences can be shown to

---

54. Murphy, "Human Nature," 1.

55. This point rings clear in the neuroscience literature. Antonio R. Damasio states that "philosophers, neuroscientists and laypeople have long wondered how the conscious mind comes to be. A more complete understanding of the workings of the brain ought to lead to an eventual solution." See Damasio, "How the Brain Creates the Mind," 112–17.

56. This neural activity has been recorded in patients with temporal lobe epilepsy. In some cases, these patients report experiences similar to recorded accounts of religious experiences. For more see Naito and Matsui, "Temporal lobe," 123–24; and Ogata and Miyakawa, "Religious experiences," 321–25.

57. See Persinger, "Neurobehavioral effects," 89–118; "Experimental simulation," 267–84; and Cook and Persinger, "Experimental induction," 683–93. It is worth noting that a heated debated surrounding this research has ensued. Using the experimental setup from Persinger, et. al., Pehr Granqvist has attempted, and failed, to reproduce these religious experiences in the laboratory; thus, the legitimacy of Persinger's claims are in question. For more on this see Granqvist et al., "Sensed presence."

correspond to certain types of brain activity (i.e. "caused" by certain types of brain activity), then what place does this leave for manifestations of an immaterial soul?[58]

The second area of neuroscientific investigation that I want to mention is that of the experience and expression of love. The feeling of love is not only an honored human capacity, but theologically speaking, is a critical responsibility within human communities. Such a capacity has commonly been considered to be an internal working of the soul.

There are documented cases of neurological impairment that results in the inability to experience or express love. Consider the following account of Capgras Syndrome:

> *Capgras Syndrome* is a disorder of the experience of familiarity and regard for close friends and family. In these rare cases, damage to particular brain areas can result in a disorder characterized by the individual's conviction that close and familiar *persons* are not *real*, but are "doubles" and imposters . . . the person with Capgras Syndrome does not experience an accompanying feeling of familiarity and deep personal significance associated with the visual experience.[59]

A critical aspect of our ability to love is based on the experience of familiarity and relatedness produced by our history with the loved one. What patients with Capgras Syndrome have shown is that these feelings can be dissociated from visual recognition, thus lending weight to the notion that the experience of loving someone is a physical process able to be inhibited by neurological disorder.

The final example involves neuroscientific research on moral attitude and behavior. Human moral behavior, that is how we relate in a social context, is a concern to the religious and non-religious alike. At the center of the Christian faith, rests a mandate for proper relation toward God and creation. Such "spiritual" relationships have traditionally been viewed as faculties of the soul. This area of human experience, once left completely to the realm of religious thought (and later included within the scope of psychology proper), has now been taken under investigation by neuroscientists.

58. I place the term "cause" in scare quotes to emphasize the problematic nature of the term. I will deal with this issue in more detail in a following section.

59. W. S. Brown, "Evolution," 506.

Researchers are uncovering intrinsic links between biology and morality.[60] Research from neuroscience has demonstrated that moral reasoning and behavior is dependent upon the proper function of various subsystems within the brain, particularly in the prefrontal cortex.[61] This aspect of human functioning, once inaccessible to science, can now be investigated via various experimental techniques.[62] Some neuroscientists believe that these new technological advances will unlock the deepest secrets of the human species and eventually render the insights gained from religion obsolete.[63]

Such discoveries have broken the barriers between research disciplines and new approaches are being forged. Perhaps the most notable of these is Social Cognitive Neuroscience.[64] Regarding this new approach to understanding the complexities of human behavior, Ralph Adolphs comments:

> We are an intensely social species—it has been argued that our social nature defines what makes us human, what makes us conscious or what gave us our large brains. As a new field, the social brain

60. For a fascinating discussion involving evolutionary biology and the emergence of morality as a distinctly human phenomenon see Goodenough and Deacon, "From Biology," 801–19. Goodenough and Deacon suggest that moral frames of mind emerge from primate prosocial capacities. These "frames of mind" are then transfigured and valenced by the host of symbolic languages, cultures, and religions that are characteristic of the human species. Also see Deacon, *Symbolic Species*.

61. There is a significant amount of data now available supporting this claim. Leslie Brothers is credited for being a catalyst to much of the present work regarding neuroscience and social interaction. See Brothers, "Social Brain," 27–51. For a survey of other well-known publications see Adolphs, "Cognitive Neuroscience," 165–78; Anderson et al., "Impairment," 1032–37; Bechara et al., "Characterization," 2189–2202; Bechara et al., "Different Contributions," 5473–81; Bechara et al., "Insensitivity," 7–15; and Eslinger et al., "Developmental outcomes," 84–103.

62. Neuroscientists use a number of experimental techniques to gather relevant data. The most common, and reliable, techniques involve neuroimaging. The most widely utilized forms of neuro-imaging are Positron Emission Tomography (PET) and Functional Magnetic Resonance Imaging (fMRI). The importance of neuroimaging cannot be overstated. Dima Amso and B. J. Casey state that "understanding the development of pathways underlying cognition and the experiences that alter those pathways is imperative to the study of cognitive development." See Amso and Casey, "Beyond What Develops When," 24.

63. Truett Allison says that "as we learn more about the development and operation of the system for social cognition . . . it is likely, perhaps even desirable, that the domain of understanding provided by neuroscience, evolutionary psychology, and cultural anthropology will expand, while the domain that is properly a function of ethics and religion will shrink." See Allison, "Neuroscience," 360–64.

64. See Liebermann, "Intuition," 109–36; and Ochsner and Lieberman, "Emergence," 717–34.

sciences are probing the neural underpinnings of social behaviour and have produced a banquet of data that are both tantalizing and deeply puzzling. We are finding new links between emotion and reason, between action and perception, and between representations of other people and ourselves. No less important are the links that are also being established across disciplines to understand social behaviour, as neuroscientists, social psychologists, anthropologists, ethologists and philosophers forge new collaborations.[65]

Rather than delve into the depths of the neuroscientific explanation of socio-moral attitude and behavior, I wish to offer a story which is meant to exemplify the intimate connection between neurobiological processes and morality. Perhaps the most famous case study in the research toward understanding the relationship between brain activity and moral behavior is that of Phineas Gage.[66]

The year was 1848. Phineas P. Gage was a twenty-five year old construction foreman in New England. He was employed by Rutland & Burlington Railroad. At that time, his assignment was supervising a group of railroad workers responsible for laying down new tracks for a railroad expansion across Vermont. The task was shaping up to be a difficult one due to the large amount of hard rock formations through which the workers would have to blast to lay the new track. Although a foreman, Gage works closely with the men, able and willing to perform every task as an equal.

His interpersonal charisma was matched only by his athletic ability to work quickly and precisely around the work site. He was labelled by his superiors as "the most efficient and capable man in their employ."[67] Gage had earned this distinction because of his ability to not only work the long difficult hours, but also because of his ability to plan, design and implement the steps necessary to complete the railroad.

The tedious work proceeded on schedule day after day as the men under Gage's supervision mechanically blasted rock and laid track systematically toward their goal. On 13 September 1848, an accidental explosion occurred that blew a tamping iron through Gage's head. The tamping iron

65. Adolphs, "Cognitive Neuroscience," 165. I also want to add here that an increasing number of theologians are considering these data and have equally valuable contributions to the discussion. Such will become obvious throughout this work.

66. For a detailed account of the life of Phineas Gage see Macmillan, *Odd Kind of Fame.*

67. From the journal of John Martyn Harlow (1819–1907). Quoted by Damasio, *Descartes' Error,* 4.

measured over three feet in length, one and a quarter inches in diameter, and weighed over thirteen pounds. Propelled by the explosion, the rod entered Gage's skull point first under his left cheekbone and passed completely through the top of his head, landing about twenty five yards behind him.

Gage was knocked off of his feet, but onlookers claim that he did not loose consciousness despite the fact that he suffered extensive brain trauma. His men gathered him up, sat him in an ox cart and drove him to a nearby hotel where a town physician was immediately called. Gage arose from the cart himself with minimal assistance and walked to the porch where he sat awaiting the doctor. When the physician, Dr. John Harlow, arrived he found Gage sitting on the front porch sipping lemonade delivered to him by the hotel owner. Note the entry in Dr. Harlow's journal concerning the visit:

> I first noticed the wound upon the head before I alighted from my carriage, the pulsations of the brain being very distinct; there was also an appearance which, before I examined the head, I could not account for; the top of the head appeared somewhat like an inverted funnel; this was owing, I discovered, to the bone being fractured about the opening for a distance of about two inches in every direction. I ought to have mentioned above that the opening through the skull and integuments was not far from one and a half inch in diameter; the edges of this opening were everted, and the whole wound appeared as if some wedge-shaped body had passed from below upward. Mr. Gage, during the time I was examining this wound, was relating the manner in which he was injured to the bystanders; he talked so rationally and was so willing to answer questions, that I directed my inquiries to him in preference to the men who were with him at the time of the accident, and who were standing about at this time. Mr. G. then related to me some of the circumstances, as he has since done; and I can safely say that neither at that time nor on any subsequent occasion, save once, did I consider him to be other than perfectly rational.[68]

To be able to survive the sheer magnitude of the injury alone was a medical miracle, but to be able to walk and talk coherently almost immediately following the accident was astounding to the onlookers. Gage's accident made many newspaper headlines and found its way into several medical journals. With only a few minor complications, Dr. Harlow pronounced Gage cured in less than two months.

---

68. John Martyn Harlow, as quoted by Damasio, ibid., 6.

This was such an incredible case that Harlow devoted a great deal of time to studying Gage for the remainder of his life. He noted that Gage had regained his strength and dexterity and his physical recovery was outstanding. With the exception of the loss of vision in his left eye (the tamping iron had severed the optic nerve as it passed through his skull); none of his physical faculties or senses were hampered in any way.

Despite this, Harlow recounts, "the equilibrium or balance, so to speak, between his intellectual faculty and animal propensities had been destroyed."[69] He was now "fitful and irreverent, indulging at times in the grossest profanity which was not previously his custom, manifesting but little deference for his fellows, impatient of restraint or advice when it conflicts with his desires, at times pertinaciously obstinate, yet capricious and vacillating, devising many plans of future operation, which are no sooner arranged than they are abandoned."[70]

Still having the strong stature that he possessed prior to the accident, Gage had taken on an entirely new personality. In fact, he displayed such a different personality that his friends sadly noted that "Gage was no longer Gage."[71] As a result of the accident, Gage's life dramatically changed leaving him unemployed and without a home. He spent a season of time as a circus attraction and as a feature display in Barnum's Museum in New York City. He held various positions of employment but was unable to carry out any meaningful responsibilities. Gage died in San Francisco, California, on May 21, 1861.

How could this be? How could he make an apparent full recovery from such a tragic accident yet somehow experience a negative change in personality? Neuroscientists have claimed "that it was selective damage in the prefrontal cortices of Phineas Gage's brain that compromised his ability to plan for the future, to conduct himself according to the social rules he previously had learned, and to decide on the course of action that ultimately would be most advantageous to his survival."[72] So this once responsible and esteemed individual was reduced to an unreliable and quick-tempered outcast through an alteration of his neurobiological substrate.

69. Ibid., 8.

70. Ibid.

71. Ibid.

72. Damasio, *Descartes' Error*, 33. Also see Barker, "Phineas," 672–82; Cato et al., "Assessing the elusive cognitive deficits," 453–65; Damasio et al., "Return of Phineas Gage," 1102–5; L. F. Haas, "Phineas Gage," 761; Macmillan, "Inhibition," 72–104; and Wagar and Thagard, "Spiking Phineas Gage," 67–79.

The point of Gage's story is to emphasis that although we might consider morality or spirituality an ethereal concept only accessible through religious inquiry, it is becoming increasingly evident that these are emergent human capacities having a physical basis. So, once again, the postulation of a separate entity (the "soul") is deemed unnecessary to explain complex human phenomena.

To summarize, scientific advances have played a significant role in formulating the way one conceives of human nature. From Darwin's theory of evolution to the rise of social cognitive neuroscience, researchers have conducted extensive research into areas that have traditionally been relegated to matters of religion. I have cited three such examples above—peak spiritual experiences, the experience and expression of love, and finally moral attitude and behavior. The latter is of particular concern to the present work.

To be clear, the relevance of this immediate discussion is to emphasize that, within the realm of science, those characteristics once attributed to a "soul" can now be explained in neurobiological terms. This semantic move removes the *necessity* to speak of the soul as the causal agent in human life. As I have discussed in an earlier chapter, this strikes at the heart of many presuppositions about the role of religion in human life.

In light of these data, and the evolving views of human nature among scientists and philosophers, attention turns to theological notions of personhood. I have already mentioned some of the historical theological views regarding human nature; however, there is little doubt that there is a theological conundrum nigh at the door.

Francis Crick has delivered what he refers to as the "astonishing hypothesis." Crick says that

> "You," your joys and your sorrows, your memories and your ambitions, your sense of personal identity and free will, are in fact *no more than the behaviour of a vast assembly of nerve cells and their associated molecules.* As Lewis Carroll's Alice might have phrased: "You're nothing but a pack of neurons." This hypothesis is so alien to the ideas of most people today that it can truly be called astonishing.[73]

In Crick's view, religious life (and Christian spirituality in particular) consists of the cultivation of the inner world of the soul. So, it follows from Crick's hypothesis that if science can show the implausibility of the existence of the soul, then the Christian faith falls in one fell swoop.

73. Crick, *Astonishing Hypothesis*, 3. Emphasis added.

This is obviously an undesirable conclusion for the theologically oriented community. A number of theologians have addressed these concerns in an effort to preserve traditional Christian ideals, not least of which is the integrity of the human person. As these accounts emerge, the issue of the soul—its existence and its function—is a crucial theme. So we see a critical debate exacerbated over the question of the existence of the soul. The following section will include a discussion of some of the theological developments related to this issue.

Theological Developments

The concept of the soul has played an important role in the history of Christian thought, particularly in ethics.[74] It is surprising, however, that the metaphysical makeup of the human person appears to not have been a central topic in ancient Christian thought. Etienne Gilson comments that

> It would probably surprise a good many modern Christians to learn that in certain of the earliest Fathers the belief in the immortality of the soul is vague almost to non-existence. This, nevertheless, is a fact, and a fact to be noted, because it casts so strong a light on the point which Christian anthropology turns and on the course of its historical development. A Christianity without the immortality of the soul is not, in the long run, absolutely inconceivable, and the proof of it is that it has been conceived. What really would be absolutely inconceivable would be a Christianity without the resurrection of the Man.[75]

How is it then that the soul seems to be at the center of so many modern conceptions of Christian life and spirituality? Although the issue of human nature has not been a consistent theme through Christian history, it has been an issue that arises at various transitional points in theological thought.[76] The modern period has brought another such transitional period. The development of biblical criticism and critical church history has once again brought the nature of the human person into consideration.

---

74. For a helpful work on the ethical implications of theological anthropology see Post, "Moral Case," 195–212.

75. Gilson, *Spirit of Medieval Philosophy*, 172.

76. Nancey Murphy identifies two such transitions. The first was the adaptation of Christian teaching to the gentile world. In this case there were assorted Greco-Roman philosophical concepts that were adopted and adapted to Christian practice. The second point was the Aristotelian revival in the Middle Ages. The writings of Thomas Aquinas exemplify this transitional thought.

What I intend to show in the following is that the issue of human nature has been treated in a quite indecisive fashion in modern theology and biblical studies.

How we conceive of the person has been influenced through historical criticism of the Bible. There was a trend among many scholars in the late eighteenth and nineteenth centuries that led to doubt concerning the historical resurrection of Jesus.[77] This scepticism led to a revival of the treatment of the soul as the basis for Christian hope in the afterlife.[78]

One example of the confusion regarding the nature of the soul appears in the work of H. Wheeler Robinson.[79] Robinson questioned the biblical support offered to the notion of body-soul dualism. He concluded that the Bible presented the human person as an animated body rather than an incarnated or immortal soul (contra the Greek metaphysical explanations). Despite this claim, he goes on to posit that one of the most important assertions in the New Testament is the belief that person survives bodily death.[80] Such an argument necessarily reinserted the need for a nonmaterial entity that represents the true or essential "self"—such can only be conceived of as a soul or spirit. So, once again confusion abounded.

Likewise, theological literature in the early twentieth century exemplified the same type of confusion.[81] Following World War I, there was

77. A prominent source of such ideas was David Friedrich Strauss. See Strauss, *Life of Jesus Critically Examined.*

78. There is little doubt that Immanuel Kant's transcendental proof of the immortality of the soul reinforced these convictions. Kant held that we are justified in affirming that we have an "afterlife" in the sense of an unending and enduring existence after death. Such exists outside the framework of spatio-temporal causality and its purpose was to continue the task of seeking moral perfection. See Kant, *Immanuel Kant's Critique of Pure Reason,* especially the section regarding the "Transcendental Dialectic."

79. H. W. Robinson, *Christian Doctrine of Man.*

80. It is important to note that the debate of whether or not the essence (soul) of a person survives bodily death does not encompass the issue of resurrection. I hold that resurrection is a central and critical component of Christian theology and does not necessarily depend on the existence of an ontologically distinct entity such as an immaterial soul. See further below.

81. See Murphy for some interesting examples. See "Human Nature," 20–21. She demonstrates this confusion by pointing to various reference works within theology and biblical studies. For example, C. A. Beckwith claimed that "the human soul is indeed bound to corporeality, yet it survives death because it possesses the Spirit of God as its immanent principle of life ("Biblical Conceptions of Soul and Spirit" in Macauley, 11:12–14). Yet, in a slightly earlier work J. Laidlaw claims that throughout the Bible the term "soul" is intended to designate the embodied life of living creatures ("Soul," in Hastings, *Dictionary of the Bible,* 4:608). In the same publication, E. R. Bernard states that resurrection is to be understood as "the clothing of the soul with a body which has to be reconstituted . . . the

an increase in theological literature that stressed the distinction between Hebraic and Hellenistic concepts. Karl Barth was a significant player in this regard. He stressed the prominence of the resurrection to a proper understanding of Christian theology.[82] Such an emphasis encouraged a more Hebraic interpretation of theological concerns. As a result, theologians began to grasp a more holistic view of the human person. Contributions from Rudolf Bultmann and John A. T. Robinson exemplify these views.[83]

A cursory survey of the literature within theology and biblical studies reveals a trend (throughout the twentieth-century) from dualistic views of human nature to more holistic notions. The issue seems to revolve around concepts of the afterlife, where on one hand there is the immortal soul that lives beyond bodily death, and on the other, the hope of resurrection.[84] Murphy observes that one way of highlighting this shift is to note "that in *The Encyclopedia of Religion and Ethics* (1909–21) there is a lengthy article on 'soul' and no entry for 'resurrection.' In *The Anchor Bible Dictionary* (1992) there is no entry for 'soul' but a very long set of articles on 'resurrection.'"[85]

So, in many ways what holds the issue of human nature in contention is the way one interprets the Christian notion of the after-life, particularly resurrection. This is a vastly unsettled issue within theological circles.[86] Paul Badham has performed a substantial survey of the literature regarding the Christian notion of the afterlife and has found that while most scholars

---

only self which we know is a self constituted of a body as well as a soul" (ibid., 4:236).

82. Barth claims that God is revealed in Jesus only by an event that breaks the bounds of history. Jesus' true identity is revealed in the act of resurrection. See *Church Dogmatics*, volume 4. Also, Colin Gunton states, "Barth is above all a theologian of the resurrection, rather than of the incarnation or cross." See "Salvation," 143–58.

83. Bultmann claims that a correct reading of Paul's use of the term *soma* renders a holistic view of the human person. See Bultmann, *Theology of the New Testament*. Robinson's latter work reflects a similar idea. See J. A. T. Robinson, *Body*.

84. My "cursory" look at this issue tends toward oversimplification. There are a number of complexities that I will not cover in the present work, not least of which is the fact that liberal and conservative (primarily evangelical) traditions have different opinions on these issues. For example Robert Gundry rejects Bultmann's arguments regarding theological anthropology. See Gundry, *Soma in Biblical Theology*. The idea of body-soul dualism is much more prominent in evangelical scholarship.

85. Murphy, "Human Nature," 21.

86. Joel B. Green claims that the Christian notion of resurrection does not require the existence of a ontologically distinct soul. See "Resurrection of the body," in Green, *What about the Soul?*; "What Does It Mean to Be Human?," 179–98; "Restoring the Human Person," 3–22; and "Bodies," 149–73. For a critique of Green's work on this topic see Cooper, *Body, Soul & Life Everlasting*.

share the view that, "I shall be 'I'" at resurrection; such a view requires a type of "re-embodiment" that can only be described in terms of an immaterial essence that extends beyond bodily death, thus, the existence of the soul is a necessary condition.[87]

Although the status of the soul is critical to many contemporary issues within theology and biblical studies, the debate itself has had a speckled past. While the issue of the "intermediate state" has kept the controversy between dualists and physicalists alive in contemporary eschatological debates; the Bible does not explicitly teach either body-soul dualism or a strict physicalism.[88] Despite the contention on the issue, Christian spirituality continues to be marked by an inherent assumption of body-soul dualism (see chapter one).

As previously mentioned, for a number of reasons this dualist view of human nature does not fare well under philosophical or theological scrutiny. In addition, it can be argued that the assumption of an immaterial soul as being the true "self" has led to a host of ethical issues.[89]

The historical sketch that I have provided in this chapter shows that the traditional alternative to dualistic thinking has been some type of materialism or physicalism. There are, however, problems with these positions as well—historically, materialism has commonly led to reductionism. This is true from both a philosophical and scientific perspective.

From a theological perspective reductive materialism is a highly undesirable position. If human beings can be *completely* described in terms of the firing of neurons or the working of biological machinery, then it would seem that the integrity of the human person, which is critical to a Christian worldview, is gravely at risk. Murphy has described the situation as follows:

> It is undeniable that a serious theological problem awaits solution. Philosophers see dualism as no longer tenable; the neurosciences have completed the Darwinian revolution, bringing the entire human being under the purview of the natural sciences. Scientists and philosophers alike associate dualism with Christianity, and the "evangelical atheists" among them (such as Daniel Dennett) use

87. Badham, *Christian Beliefs about Life Death*, 93.

88. Note the previous insights from Dunn's *partative* and *aspective* views of the human person in the biblical text.

89. Stephen G. Post notes that, although one cannot claim that dualism is the "cause" of poor social practices, history does reveal a certain affinity between dualist thought and practices such as patriarchy, slavery, the debasement of sex, the denial of physical pleasure, and callous speciesism. See Post, "Moral Case," 203–10.

these scientific and philosophical developments as potent apologetic tools.[90]

There is, I claim, a third alternative to Platonic or Cartesian forms of dualism and reductive notions of materialism. This "third alternative" is constituted by an interactive holism claiming that consciousness or sense-of-self is an emergent quality of the human person. While there are several forms of "emergent dualism" in the literature, I will argue for a position commonly known as *nonreductive physicalism*.[91] I claim that the nonreductive physicalist view of human nature is able to avoid the problems of dualism while maintaining the integrity of the human person that is threatened by reductionism. The following section is dedicated to providing a cogent description of this view.

A Case for Nonreductive Physicalism

I offer the following argument: human nature should be viewed as intrinsically and inextricably embodied. This is to say that the human person is ultimately a physical being who operates on such a level of complexity as to allow for the emergence of human capacities such as morality and spirituality. Such dimensions of the human experience are capable of emerging without the addition of any immaterial entity such as a soul or spirit.

This view of human nature clearly separates itself from any form of dualism that leads to a body-soul/material-immaterial dichotomy. Such dichotomies move away from a central argument that I wish to put forward—a person should not be characterized *only* by "interior" thoughts or beliefs, but should rather be understood as a holistic being whose values are inseparably bound to his or her embodied life.[92] Here, values are not

90. Murphy, "Human Nature," 24.

91. It is worth noting that there are various types of dualism whose proponents use holistic language to describe their position. For example, John W. Cooper's account of "holistic dualism" (the roots of which he attributes to Thomas Aquinas). See Cooper, *Body, Soul & Life Everlasting*. Also William Hasker has offered an account which he calls *Emergent Dualism*. Hasker's claim is that consciousness (or soul) "emerges" from human biological complexity. Once such an entity exists, it has the capacity to live beyond bodily death. See Hasker, *Emergent Self*. A popular account is provided by Charles Taliaferro. His "integrative dualism" presents the human person as essentially *non-physical* individuals, integrally related to their bodies, but capable of being separated. Taliaferro's approach is primarily from the standpoint of "philosophy of mind" and he seeks to preserve central tenets of orthodox Christianity. For more see Taliaferro, *Consciousness and the Mind of God*.

92. I do not deny the existence of an "interior" life. The point is that this interior life can only be understood as "embodied" within the context of one's entire life narrative (i.e. one's "interior" life cannot be lived apart from the physical body).

only experienced as inner convictions, but expressed in a social context. In this view, the idea of an interior life at battle with material existence dissolves and the challenge then becomes an embodied life lived in such a way that reflects the values and practices inherent to the community which forms his or her identity.

Furthermore, I want to be clear as to the "type" of physically embodied human nature that I espouse. There are a number of scholars who have engaged this issue from both a philosophical and a theological position.[93] In what follows, I will offer support for the *nonreductive physicalist* view of human nature. This position has been argued most notably by Nancey Murphy, Warren Brown, and others.[94] Their extended treatment of the scientific, philosophical, and theological issues surrounding human nature is a worthy account and one that will inform my overall project.

As discussed above, advances in evolutionary biology and the cognitive sciences are continually closing the gap between the material and immaterial nature of humankind. Indeed, nearly all of the human capacities once attributed to the mind or soul are now understood to be complex functions of the brain. But do these claims not represent an essential conflict with a Christian theological perspective? It is my intention to demonstrate that the nonreductive physicalist view of human nature, in fact, does not present such a conflict.

There are two indispensable aspects of the nonreductive physicalist thesis. The first is the claim that human persons are essentially physical creatures—as such we can function in a fully human manner without the addition of a nonmaterial entity such as a soul or spirit. Second, the position is *nonreductive* in that it rejects any scientific or philosophical claim that insists that human beings are "nothing but" bodies. This means that the human person cannot be *fully* described in terms of his or her biology. There are a host of "higher" capacities (e.g. the experience of passion,

93. For a helpful example see Corcoran, *Soul, Body and Survival*. See also Moreland and Rae, *Body & Soul*; and Ward, *Defending the Soul*. These latter two represent an effort to "rescue" the soul from reductive materialism. I include these to show the existence of the argument; however, for reasons already mentioned, I do not deem this argument necessary.

94. For examples of such work see Brown et al., *Whatever Happened to the Soul?*; Brown, "Resonance," 110–20; "Neurobiological Embodiment," 58–76; "Evolution," 502–23; "Nonreductive Physicalism," 1812–21; Green, "What Does it Mean to be Human?," 179–98; Green, *What About the Soul?*; Jeeves, *From Cells to Souls*; Brown et al., "Whatever Happened to the Soul?," 51–64; "Problem of Mental Causation," 143–58; "Physicalism," 551–71; "Supervenience"; *Anglo-American Postmodernity*; Russell et al., *Neuroscience and the Person*.

morality, free will, and the many aspects of relationship) that are essential to the human experience and cannot be adequately accounted for from a reductive materialist perspective.

In essence, the nonreductive physicalism that I defend refers to the following constellation of positions:

> [T]he acceptance of ontological reductionism, but the rejection of causal reductionism and reductive materialism. Applied to the specific area of studies of consciousness, it denies the existence of a nonmaterial entity, the mind (or soul) but does not deny the existence of consciousness (a position in philosophy of mind called eliminative materialism) or the significance of conscious states or other ment*al* (note the adjective form) phenomena. In brief, this is the view that the human nervous system, operating in concert with the rest of the body in its environment, is the seat of consciousness (and also of human spiritual or religious capacities). Consciousness and religious awareness are emergent properties and they have top-down causal influence on the body.[95]

In order to justify these claims, one must address two primary areas of concern. The first area deals with the challenges offered by a dualistic view of human nature. For the present purposes, I will assume that the philosophical and scientific challenges that I have offered above are sufficient to render dualism undesirable.

The second concern is that of reductionism; unfortunately, overcoming this hurdle is a much more complex task. The central question, of course, is how a physicalist account, such as the one that I espouse, can fail to be reductive. If mental events can be reduced to neural activity, it seems that the notion of free will must collapse beneath the "laws" of neurobiology.

Murphy adds, "If free will is an illusion and the highest of human intellectual and cultural achievements can (*per impossible*) be counted as the mere outworking of the laws of physics, this is utterly devastating to our ordinary understanding of ourselves, and of course to theological accounts, as well, which depend not only on a concept of responsibility before God, but also on the justification (not merely the causation) of our theories about God and God's will."[96] Avoiding reductionism will require

---

95. Murphy, "Nonreductive Physicalism," 127–48. Murphy has arguably been the most influential Christian scholar in this particular area of interest. I follow Murphy throughout the process of providing a cogent description of the nonreductive physicalist view. For a critique of Murphy's description of Nonreductive Physicalism see Jeffreys, "Soul," 205–25.

96. Ibid., 131.

the explication of three interrelated concepts—*supervenience, emergence,* and *top-down causation.* In the following sections, I will address each of these concepts.[97]

Supervenience

The concept of supervenience is a relatively new idea in philosophy. It is rather complex in its application, so for the present purposes I will explore supervenience only as it relates to the issues at hand—that is, demonstrating how a physicalist account of mental life can avoid causal reduction.[98]

Recall from the discussion above, the issue concerns the relationship between physical brain states (B) and mental states (M). It can be assumed that every mental event is *related* to *some* brain event. So, considering the causal connections between neurological events yields something like the following: B1 _ B2 _ B3 . . . ; where B1, B2, etc. represent brain states in a causal sequence. Now, given the relation of mental events to brain events, there would be a sequence of mental events: M1 _ M2 _ M3 . . . that corresponds to the physical brain states.

Traditionally, the relation between these two types of events—brain (B) and mental (M)—have been described in terms of either *identity* or *causation.* In the first case, brain state (B1) is *identical* (in type) to mental state (M1), and so on. In the second case, brain state (B1) *causes* mental state (M1), and so on. In both cases, if causal connections are assumed *at the physical level,* causal reductionism is inevitable. Another way of saying

97. I wish to make an important point at the outset—just as with all philosophical claims, no amount of evidence will amount to a *proof* of the nonreductive physicalist position. For example, it is still possible to claim that there is a substantial mind or soul that controls the body through precisely correlated neural events. See Eccles, *How the Self Controls Its Brain.* For this reason, I consider the epistemological status of nonreductive physicalism not as a mere philosophical thesis, but rather as a viable *scientific theory.* Just as with the justification of any scientific theory, data must be collected through an organized research programme. In the present case, I suggest that the "hard core" of such a research programme consist of the metaphysical thesis of nonreductive physicalism. I am, of course, following the method of Imre Lakatos. See Lakatos, *Methodology of Scientific Research Programmes.* Lakatos' views were in reaction to Thomas Kuhn's account of science as a series of "paradigms." See Kuhn, *Structure of Scientific Revolutions.*

98. I will begin this section by noting that there has been a past debate as to the proper way of defining "supervenience." Jaegwon Kim has argued that it is not possible to grant causal efficacy to the supervenience of the mental (*Supervenience and Mind*). The weakness of Kim's argument is that he ignores that a supervenient property can be multi-realizable. Never the less, Kim has won the day and most current literature regarding supervenience will reflect Kim's sentiments. This does not, however, weaken the argument that I offer in this section.

this is that mental events appear as mere *epiphenomena*. The crucial issue here is not the *causal* sequence from M1 to M2, etc., but the *reasoned relation* between the mental events that are realized by neural states. Murphy poses the central question this way: "How does *modus ponens* get its grip on the causal transitions between *brain* states"?[99]

The concept of supervenience was introduced by Richard M. Hare.[100] He used the term to relate ethical judgments to descriptive situations. As an example, Hare states

> First, let us take that characteristic of "good" which has been called its supervenience. Suppose that we say, "St. Francis was a good man." It is logically impossible to say this and to maintain at the same time that there might have been another man placed exactly in the same circumstances as St. Francis, and who behaved in exactly the same way, but who differed from St. Francis in this respect only, that he was not a good man.[101]

So in this example, the ethical judgment of "goodness" *supervenes* on a collection of circumstances that formally instantiates St. Francis" character.

Donald Davidson made a monumental move in using the concept of supervenience to describe the relationship between mental and physical events.

> Mental characteristics are in some sense dependent, or supervenient, on physical characteristics. Such supervenience might be taken to mean that there cannot be two events alike in all physical respects but differing in some mental respect, or that an object cannot alter in some mental respect without altering in some physical respect. Dependence or supervenience of this kind does not entail reducibility through law or definition."[102]

Although there is no formally agreed upon definition of supervenience, Terrence E. Horgan has provided a widely accepted description. He states that:

99. Murphy, "Problem of Mental Causation," 146. This is a rephrasing of Colin McGinn's inquiry into how "*modus ponens* gets its grip on the causal transitions between *mental events.*" See McGinn, "Consciousness" 305.

100. Hare introduced the term "supervenience" in the context of philosophical analysis; however, G. E. Moore also asserted a similar thesis. Although Moore did not use the term "supervene" he did assert that "one of the most important facts about qualitative difference . . . [is that] two things cannot differ in quality without differing in intrinsic nature." See Moore, *Philosophical Studies*, 263.

101. Hare, *Language of Morals*, 145.

102. Davidson, "Mental Events," 79–101.

The concept of supervenience, as a relation between properties, is essentially this: Properties of type A are supervenient on properties of type B if and only if two objects cannot differ with respect to their A-properties without also differing with respect to their B-properties. Properties that allegedly are supervenient on others are often called consequential properties, especially in ethics; the idea is that if something instantiates a moral property, then it does so *in virtue of*, i.e., as a (non-causal) *consequence of*, instantiating some lower-level property on which the moral property supervenes.[103]

Murphy suggests that Horgan's definition is insufficient because it overlooks an important dimension of the supervenience relation—the condition of circumstance. In Hare's example, the qualifier "placed in precisely the same circumstances" is critical. For instance, the judgment of St. Francis being a good man is contingent upon his behavior, namely the giving away of his possessions and living a life of poverty. Now, assume that his *circumstances* had been different and he had children to feed. In this particular set of circumstances, the relinquishing of resources to provide for his family might have very well led to him to be judged as *not a good man*. In other words, it is conceivable that in circumstance (c) St. Francis is a "good man" and in circumstance (c') St. Francis is "not a good man."

So then, Murphy redefines supervenience in the following way:

Property S is supervenient on property B if and only if something's being B constitutes its being S under circumstance c.[104]

The salient feature of Murphy's revised definition is that it allows the supervenience relation to be *multiply realizable*.[105] So, with the possibility of a multiple supervenience, if S supervenes on B (in circumstance c), then something's being B entails its being S, but its being S does not entail its being B. For example, I can say that "St. Francis was a good man" and I could also say that "Abraham Lincoln was a good man." Although both of these supervenient claims may be justified it does not follow that Abraham Lincoln lived as St. Francis or vice versa.

---

103. Horgan, "Supervenience," 778–79.

104. Murphy, "Nonreductive Physicalism," 135. Murphy's intent is to stress the *functional* nature of supervenient properties. Her definition makes it possible to say that "mental properties supervene on brain properties and at the same time to recognize that some mental properties are codetermined by the way the world is." See "Supervenience and the Downward Efficacy of the Mental," (150).

105. For a detailed account of Murphy's notion of supervenience see "Problem of Mental Causation," 143–58; "Physicalism," 551–71; and "Supervenience," 147–64.

The value of this application of supervenience is to show that the identity relationship (complete *causal* reduction) does not hold in all cases. The pertinent issues are as follows:[106]

1. whether there are multiple circumstances such that B constitutes S in circumstance *c* but is not the case that B constitutes S in circumstance *c'*; and if so

2. whether or not *c*, *c'*, etc. are describable at the subvenient level;

3. whether S is multiply realizable; and if so

4. whether there is a finite disjunctive set of realizands.

Murphy's more complex definition of supervenience leads to the conclusion that

> Reduction will only be possible in the limiting case where B constitutes S under all circumstances and S is not multiply realizable. Reduction will not be possible when: (1) there are multiple circumstances that make a difference to the supervenience relation and these circumstances cannot be defined in terms of the subvenient level; or (2) when S is multiply realizable and there is no finite disjunctive set of realizands.[107]

Warren Brown provides a simple example applying the concept of supervenience as presented above. He says

> You might be able to give a complete (reductionist) neuromuscular description of raising your arm, but that description would miss the fact that raising your arm was for the purpose of casting a deciding vote in a meeting. The neuromuscular explanation would systematically miss the cognitive and social facts of the matter. Thus, the explanation of voting (or intention to vote) as a cause of subsequent effects on the ongoing social intercourse of the meeting in question supervenes on the physiological (neuromuscular) causal explanation. Or, to state it more technically, *the supervenient property of voting allowed the lower level neuromuscular events of arm raising to participate in a broader, more complex causal process.*[108]

In the present case, it is important to understand that the use of supervenience is not intended to eliminate the causal efficacy of subvenient properties or to grant causal efficacy to supervenient properties per se;

106. Murphy, "Nonreductive Physicalism," 136.

107. Ibid.

108. Brown, "Nonreductive Physicalism," 1817.

rather, "the best account we can give of the causal efficacy of mental states is to assume that they supervene on physical states, and *it is the physical states that are causally efficacious.* That is, it is because my thought 'I should take an umbrella' is realized neurobiologically that it is capable of initiating the chain of physical events resulting in my picking up the umbrella."[109]

In this sense, it is the *reasoned relation* between mental states that determines a subsequent brain state, not the supervenient mental state itself. In order to clarify this notion, one must first consider two additional concepts central to the nonreductive physicalist thesis—emergence and top-down causation.

Emergence and Top-Down Causation

My challenge in this section will be to apply the notion of supervenience in the context of emergent properties that possess downward causal efficacy. It is my position that such a task can be achieved without compromising the physicalist nature of the person. Just as with the notion of supervenience suggested above, this section will stress the *functional* character of mental states. In order to properly discuss the concepts of emergence and top-down causation, allow me to review a bit of history.

Roy Wood Sellars is noted for his description of a hierarchy of systems that he dubbed "emergent realism." He argued against the notion that complex systems were mere aggregates of the particles that made them up.[110] This idea of a hierarchy of complex systems was not a new one, but gained prominence through Sellar's work. In theological circles, the hierarchy has been used by Arthur Peacocke to demonstrate the nature of what he calls "whole-part causation."[111]

The hierarchy has been further developed by Nancey Murphy and George Ellis. Figure 1 represents the hierarchy as will be discussed in the present work.[112] Murphy and Ellis expanded Peacocke's version of the hierarchy by distinguishing between the natural and applied human sciences. In addition, they added the level of *ethics* that they consider an essential ingredient of any adequate account of reality.

109. Murphy, "Supervenience," 153–54. Emphasis added.

110. Sellars, *Philosophy of Physical Realism*; and *Principles of Emergent Realism*.

111. For more on Peacocke's use of the hierarchy see "God's Interaction with the World," 263–88; and *Theology for a Scientific Age*.

112. Figure 1 is taken from Murphy and Ellis, *On the Moral Nature of the Universe*, 204.

The purpose in introducing the hierarchy of complex systems is to provide a visual schematic for the following discussion of emergence and top-down causation.

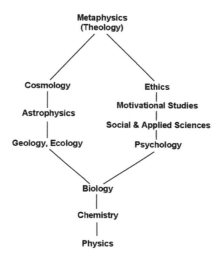

FIGURE I

The term *emergence* refers to the fact that complex entities can exhibit properties that are not present within the constituent elements that make up the complex entity. An *emergent property* is then understood to be a property whose existence is derived from a set of complex interactions. Such "emergent properties" are capable of exhibiting causal efficacy over the base elements from which they emerge. In the case of cognitive properties, emergence allows for the creation of new determinative influences with respect to thought and behavior. Warren Brown states that

> A critical aspect of a truly emergent property is that the configurational regularities of the complex system affect the interactions of the more micro-level elements. So, my conscious thinking, as an emergent function of the configurational regularities of interactions between the micro-level constituents of my nervous system, creates determinative influences on my behavior that cannot be accounted for solely on the basis of the underlying micro-level operations of the brain.[113]

113. Brown, "Nonreductive Physicalism," 1817–18.

Brown offers the following points as critical to the concept of emergence:[114]

1. New functional capacities arise from the *interactions* between the parts of a complex system.

2. Interactions create larger dynamic patterns that bind smaller units into webs of interactive influences.

3. These larger dynamic patterns operate by different rules and causal processes than the parts (i.e., they have emergent properties).

4. What is more, the relational constraints of the larger pattern on the individual parts significantly increase the range of possibilities for the system as a whole.

So, applying this notion of emergence to the hierarchy of complex systems reveals the possibility that entities belonging to higher levels in the hierarchy can have determinative effects on base levels in the hierarchy. The most relevant application of this concept to the present discussion concerns the cognitive processes (deciding, judging, etc.) occurring at the psychological level. So then, the task is to demonstrate how it is that mental events (*reasons*) can have causal influence on physical brain states. This is an extension of the challenge discussed above concerning supervenience. The difference is that we now have the concepts of emergence and top-down causation to apply.

Before proceeding, a brief excursus on the nature of "causation" is in order. Alicia Juarrero has compiled an impressive account of human action by applying the concepts of action theory and complex system dynamics.[115] Juarrero argues that a complete account of downward causation ("self-cause") has not been offered in contemporary theories of action due to a faulty understanding of cause and explanation.

Beginning with Aristotle's claim that an entity cannot act on itself (thus rendering "self-cause" unintelligible), a foundation was laid concerning the nature of "cause" that extended to the realm of Newtonian science.[116] By the end of the seventeenth century the Newtonian world-

---

114. These points are taken from Brown's presentation at the 2005 Fuller Symposium on the Integration of Faith and Psychology (16–18 February 2005, Pasadena, CA), *Science, Faith, and Human Nature: Reconciling Neuropsychology and Christian Theology.* Lectures available online at http://www.fuller.edu/sop/integration/Symposium/Symposium%202005/Symposium2005.html (accessed on 1 June 2006).

115. See Juarrero, *Dynamics in Action.*

116. Aristotle claims that "in so far as [a thing] is a natural unity, nothing is acted upon by itself; because it is one, and not a separate thing." See *Metaphysics,* 1:431.

view had reduced wholes to their component parts with the negative effect of rendering "whole" entities causally impotent by-products.[117] Juarrero comments that

> Newton's physics take place in an absolute, three-dimensional Euclidean space. Inhabiting this universe are material particles: tiny, discrete objects sometimes pictured as minuscule marbles. These atoms constitute the building blocks of all matter and are acted upon according to fixed laws by external forces such as gravity. According to the clockwork mechanism this view describes, things are related to each other only *externally*. One atom activates a second by colliding with it and thereby impressing an external force on the latter. Aristotle's ban on self-cause thus became firmly entrenched after Newton.[118]

Newton's physics left no room for either entities in the external world or particular goal states to serve as the intentional objects of action. The practical result of this form of atomism was the loss of context and environment as constituents of any theory of human action.

Self-"cause" was subsequently reconceptualized as self-"motion." In the context of Descartes's dualism, a nonmaterial entity (soul or mind), distinct from the body became the efficient cause of human action. This immaterial entity did not require anything external to activate it (no goal or end-state intention). However, when combined with the Newtonian understanding of cause (billiard ball, A _ B _ C, etc.), a host of philosophical problems arose—namely the challenge to reconcile how an immaterial mind can insert itself into a causal chain of physical forces.

The alternative, offered by the materialists, placed efficient cause within the physical structure of the brain. In this scenario, a base part of the brain triggers another part, which in turn pushes another, which eventually pushes the skeletomuscular system resulting in an observable action; thus, the goal becomes finding the most basic element in the human brain that initiates action. All the while, "behind these conundrums lurked both the Aristotelian understanding of cause that prohibited self-

---

117. This philosophical move was solidified by the removal of Aristotle's "formal" and "final" cause. As a result, goal-seeking (structuring) causes no longer qualified as "cause." This left the notion of causation open for the insertion of mechanistic concepts of motion typical to Newtonian physics. See Juarrero, *Dynamics in Action*, 15–24 for a detailed account of this transition.

118. Ibid., 21. Emphasis added.

cause, and the modern view of cause as only collision [of individual atomic particles]."[119]

Against the backdrop of this construal of the concept of "cause," Juarrero asserts that the notion of history and context have been eliminated from metaphysics and epistemology. Thus, her project is to rescue action theory from an "inadequate, 350-year-old model of cause and explanation."[120] She does so by claiming that action theory needs an account of how the content of an intention can inform and flow into behavior such that the action actualizes the content of the intention. Juarrero recruits resources from a relatively new branch of thermodynamics referred to as the theory of complex adaptive systems. This theory deals with systems "far from equilibrium" and open to energy exchanges with the environment.[121]

Juarrero insists that "as a result of this reformulation, complex adaptive systems can serve as a 'theory-constitutive metaphor' that allows us to rethink the philosophical concept of cause, particularly as it applies to causal relations between parts and wholes. In turn, this rethinking will radically recast our understanding of intentional causality and human action."[122] Complex adaptive systems are the result of the emergence of relatively autonomous qualities. Within the context of system development, quantitative changes produce qualitative changes in the overall system.[123]

Once a transition point is passed in the development of a complex system, new modes of causal being emerge; thus, "the most essential and characteristic feature of a qualitative transformation is that new kinds of causal factors begin to be significant in a given context, or to 'take control' of a certain domain of phenomena, with the result that there appear new laws and even new kinds of laws, which apply in the domain in question."[124] This aspect of complex systems is an integral part of a theory of top-down causation. An important aspect of Juarrero's argument is that it upholds the notion of self-cause that necessitates the interaction between external

119. Ibid., 23.

120. Ibid., 3.

121. This field was pioneered by Ilya Prigogine. See Prigogine and Stengers, *Order out of Chaos*.

122. Juarrero, *Dynamics in Action*, 119.

123. See Bohm, *Causality and Chance in Modern Physics*.

124. Ibid., 53.

environmental inputs and "intention" on the part of the agent.[125] This is an important point to which we will return in the following chapter.

The notion of top-down causation is not a new concept.[126] A relatively recent and well-known account is Donald Campbell's description of downward causation in the evolutionary process. The purpose of offering such an account is to demonstrate an instance where higher-level systems have a selective effect on lower-level entities *and* their causal effects.

Campbell's account concerns the role of natural selection in the production of jaw structures in worker ants. He points out that the jaws are designed in such a way that conforms to the laws of macromechanics, that is, they are maximally efficient for the work required of the ant. Campbell points out that "we need the laws of levers, *and organism-level selection . . .* to explain the particular distribution of proteins found in the jaw and *hence* the DNA templates guiding their production."[127] This example is intended to illustrate the following four points:

1. All processes at the higher levels are restrained by and act in conformity to the laws of lower levels, including the levels of subatomic physics.

2. The teleonomic achievements at higher levels require for their implementation specific lower-level mechanisms and processes. Explanation is not complete until these micromechanisms have been specified.

3. The emergentist principle: Biological evolution in its meandering exploration of segments of the universe encounters laws, operating as selective systems, which are not described by the laws of physics and inorganic chemistry, and which will not be described by the future substitutes for the present approximations of physics and inorganic chemistry.

---

125. "Complex adaptive systems exhibit true self-cause: parts interact to produce novel, emergent wholes; in turn, these distributed wholes regulate and constrain the parts that make them up" (Juarrero, *Dynamics in Action*, 130).

126. For example Austin Farrer argued that "higher-level patterns of action . . . may do some real work and thus not be reducible to the mass effect of lower-level constituents . . . [I]n cellular organization the molecular constituents are caught up and as it were bewitched by larger patterns of action, and cells in their turn by the animal body." *Freedom of the Will*, 57. Although Farrer was plainly trying to suggest a type of downward causation, language of this sort adds to the confusion over the matter.

127. Campbell, "Downward Causation," 180.

4. Downward causation: Where natural selection operates through life and death at a higher level of organization, the laws of the higher-level selective system determine in part the distribution of lower-level events and substances. Description of an intermediate-level phenomenon is not completed by describing its possibility and implementation in lower-level terms. Its presence, prevalence, or distribution (all needed for a complete explanation of biological phenomena) will often require reference to laws at a higher level of organization as well. Paraphrasing Point 1, all processes at the lower levels of a hierarchy are restrained by an act in conformity to the laws of the higher levels.[128]

Campbell's account can be demonstrated by the schematic below (figure 2):[129]

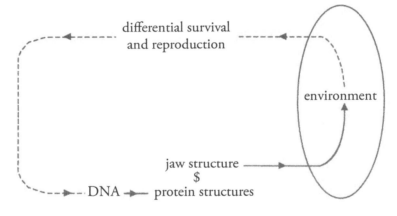

FIGURE 2

The information encoded in the DNA of the worker ant contributes to the production of particular protein structures. The jaw structure of the ant *supervenes* on the protein formation—this is "bottom-up causation." However, downward influences from the environment (represented by the

---

128. Ibid., 180. A similar account of downward causation is offered by philosopher, Robert van Gulick. He adds that "we can say that the causal powers of a composite object or event are determined in part by its higher-order (special science) properties and not solely by the physical properties of its constituents and the laws of physics. . . . Thus the whole is not any simple function of its parts, since the whole at least partially determines what contributions are made by its parts." See van Gulick, "Who's in Charge Here?," 251.

129. Figure 2 is taken from Murphy, "Problem of Mental Causation," 150.

dashed line) play a role in encoding the DNA that lead to the protein structures upon which the jaw structure supervenes, etc. . . . So we have an example of *co-determination*—a process of feed-back loops that involve both "bottom-up" *and* "top-down" causation.

So how does this process relate to mental events? Perhaps it is best to ask the question this way: how does the brain become *structured* in such a way that *causal processes realize rational processes?*[130] Many researchers claim that the structuring of neural systems occurs through a process of random growth of synaptic connections. These connections are then subjected to a subsequent process of strengthening or weakening based on the frequency of their activation—this process can also be called *learning*.[131] Simply stated, useful neural connections that model various relations within the world become strengthened while the unused connections weaken and eventually disappear.

In this sense, the environmental selection of neural connections and the subsequent fine tuning of synaptic weights—top-down causation— provides a plausible account of how the brain becomes structured in such a way to execute rational processes—*the embodied person interacts with his or her environment to select which causal connections will be activated.* As the connections among things in the environment come to be mod- elled by complex neural assemblies, free association becomes "rational" thought.[132]

To claim that the environment conditions human behavior is certain- ly not a new idea (this was central to behaviorism), but the nonreductive physicalist will take this a step further in arguing that neural pathways can be organized via one's *own* mental operations.[133] By this I mean that any of

130. For Murphy, this is the key issue. This notion of "structuring" is based on Fred Dretske's work on "structuring" and "triggering" causes. See Dretske, "Mental Events," 121–36.

131. Some refer to this process as "Neural Darwinism." Gerald Edelman has argued this position in *Bright Air, Brilliant Fire.*

132. Murphy offers an example of how interactions in the social world can structure the brain in ways that eventually lead to rational thought. She considers the social environ- ment of the child's classroom and the teaching of simple arithmetic. The mental condition of (5 X 7) supervenes on a brain state B1 and a brain state B2 represents any number of possibilities for the answer. Feedback from the social environment (i.e. the teacher) strengthens the mental condition that says that 5 X 7 = "35." Subsequently, the mental condition "35" supervenes on a physical brain state B2 that over time becomes *rationally* related to B1. "Problem of Mental Causation," 151–52.

133. This discrepancy with behaviorism can be understood as the difference between *end* states and *goal* states. The idea of "cause" inherent in behaviorist philosophy rightly emphasized environment, but ignored the possibility of an agent being embedded in the

the vast neural assemblies in the brain representing rational norms can exhibit causal efficacy upon the brain itself. Demonstrating this will require moving to the level of information processing. Donald MacKay offers a way of understanding the hierarchical structuring of cognitive processes. Note the feedback system below (*Figure 3*):

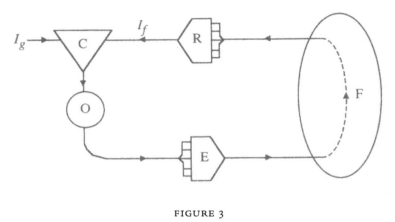

FIGURE 3

> Here the action of the effector system, E, in the field of action, F, is monitored by the receptor system, R, which provides an indication, If, of the state of F. This indication is compared with the goal criterion, Ig, in the comparator, C, which informs the organizing system, O, of any mismatch. O selects from the repertoire of E action calculated to reduce the mismatch.[134]

This schematic can be used to represent simple self-governing systems such as a thermostat. It can also be used to demonstrate how, in a cognitive sense, learning becomes a self-governing process. In the case of learning, *O* can represent a plethora of possible answer selections of which one is selected based on external social forces (as in rote learning), or it can represent an organizing system that involves a skill (learning *how* to perform a particular operation). In the latter case, feedback from the environment not only reinforces "correct" answers, but trains the organising system itself to perform rational operations.

---

environment to the degree that an organism-context system emerges. In essence, behaviorists saw the environment as *only* a triggering mechanism and ignored that environmental influences become part of the external structure of complex human behavioral systems. For more see Juarrero, *Dynamics in Action*, 63–75.

134. MacKay, *Behind the Eye*, 43–44 (including Figure 3).

Once this system has been trained it can take the place of the teacher, selectively reinforcing right answers and thus the neural connections that subserve them. So the brain becomes a self-modifying system, modifying its own neural structure in response to norms incorporated into its operations. The organizing system is trained by the environment and it in turn has downward causal efficacy in governing lower-level cognitive processes and thus the neural structures that subserve them.[135]

MacKay offers a second schematic that involves the internal evaluation of cognitive processes (Figure 4). Here MacKay incorporates a supervisory system (SS). This supervisory system selects from the organizing system (O) parts of the repertoire appropriate to incoming mismatch signals from the comparator (I) and supervises the development, trial, and updating of the repertoire.[136]

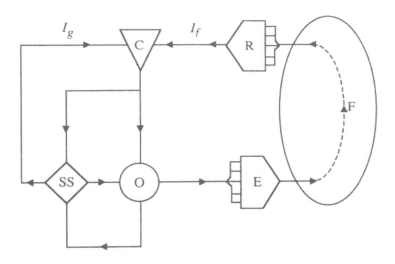

FIGURE 4

This diagram represents the internalization of the cognitive processes required to both evaluate and correct performance. The addition of the supervisory system allows for an additional feedback loop *internal to the*

135. Murphy, "Problem of Mental Causation," 153.
136. *Behind the Eye*, 51.

information-flow system—thus, allowing for a more complex set of top-down causal properties.[137]

MacKay provides yet another more complex schematic (Figure 5) in order to demonstrate the possibility of a system's adoption of "goal-directed" behavior. This aspect of downward causation is important, not only to a nonreductive physicalist view of human nature, but also to the whole of the present work. Here, the supervisory system is replaced by a meta-comparator (MC) and a meta-organizing system (MO). Also, FF represents a "feed-forward" system with feature filters.

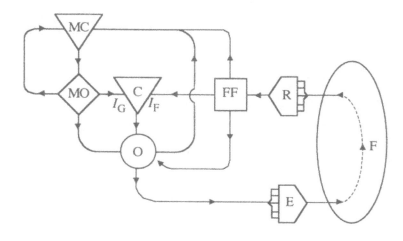

FIGURE 5

In the previous schematic (figure 3), the goal state (I*g*) is set by some criterion *outside the system*, but the addition of a meta-organizer and meta-comparator allows the goal state to be set by higher-level processes within the system itself. MacKay says "we have drawn the meta-organizing system with a meta-evaluative procedure to take stock of how things are going. It adjusts and reselects the current goal in the light of its evaluation of the success of ongoing agency, and it also keeps up-to-date the organizing system to match the state of the world indicated by the feed forward from the receptor system. . . .So there is a meta-organizing system, which organizes

137. It is worth noting here that this notion of top-down causation extends beyond the philosophical framework that I have discussed above. Recent neuroscientific research has demonstrated a "nested hierarchy of control functions within the prefrontal cortex" that bears striking similarity to MacKay's model. See Koechlin et al., "Architecture of Cognitive Control," 1181–85.

the activity of the organizing system in the way that the organizing system organizes the activity in the outside world."[138]

The significance of this more complex schematic is that it allows for the possibility of "moral" reasoning, that is, higher-order *reason*, in the form of goal-directed intention, can play a causal role in behavior—thus arises the option for various sorts of religious and altruistic motivation in behavior. This capacity is a critical component of nonreductive physicalism and is vital to my discussion of religious conversion.

In summary, what I have attempted to show in the previous section is how it is possible that a physicalist account of the person can fail to be reductive. I have done so by showing how the emergence of higher-order capacities supervene on physical brain states. The reasoned relations between supervenient mental states exemplify a sort of top-down causation on base neural constituents. The work of Donald MacKay and Alicia Juarrero has proven to be indispensable in offering a way of understanding downward causation in mental processes, even in the case of moral reasoning.

Many, particularly in theological circles, will take issue with the nonreductive physicalist view of human nature on the grounds that the human uniqueness is lost without the existence of an immaterial self (soul or spirit). The final section of this chapter will be dedicated to showing how one can espouse a thoroughly physicalist view of the human person without compromising theological integrity.

The Human Capacity for Relatedness

Espousing any form of physicalism has its challenges. In addition to the capacities mentioned above, there are a number of dimensions within human experience that have great theological significance. There are properties and attributes of human nature that seem critical in the religious life. These aspects of human nature are thought to be that which makes us unique among creation. Concepts such as sin, redemption, grace, worship, etc. all seem to possess an aspect that extends beyond what can be explained from a physicalist perspective. Another way of posing this question is to ask how a purely *physical* being can be made in the *image of God*.

I claim that nonreductive physicalism does allow for the emergence of human beings as unique among creation. As such, the theological integrity of the human person can be preserved without resorting to claims of an essential self or soul. I follow Warren Brown in submitting that the capaci-

138. McKay, *Behind the Eye*, 141–42.

ties that are considered to be critical to a theological portrait of the human person can be expressed as the capacity for *personal relatedness*.[139] This unique human capability is an emergent property of human cognition.[140]

Recall from chapter two I discussed Wesley's concept of being made in the "image of God." While many would consider this to refer to the "rational" nature of human beings, Wesley suggested that the *imago Dei* refers to our relational nature. It is then through relationship that human identity emerges. This idea resonates with Brown's claim that the "soulish"[141] nature of human beings arise from three dimensions of relatedness:[142]

1. The qualitative and quantitative differences between human and nonhuman *interindividual* relatedness. Differences of depth, scope, complexity, and range in time, space, and topic.

2. The subjective (*intrapersonal*) process of self-relatedness and self-representation.

3. The capacity for, and experiences of, *relatedness to God.*

In this sense, our humanness *emerges* through the expression of relatedness. This emergence is manifest within the boundaries of three critical interpersonal aspects: (1) the complex process of an individual's relatedness to others; (2) the state of *being related to* by a human community; and (3) the act of God's relating to humankind.[143] This last aspect in particular can be understood as the most definitive of human dignity and uniqueness.

Arnold Come supports the notion that human integrity is born from the "God-man" relationship. Come says

> It should be clear by now that in defining the human "soul" we are not seeking some elusive, immaterial substance which is distinct from body even while in a body. Rather, we are trying to isolate the

139. Brown, "Neurobiological Embodiment," 58–76; "Evolution" 502–23; "Nonreductive Physicalism" 1812–21; "Cognitive Contributions," 99–125; and "Conclusion" 213–28.

140. Note that this claim is consistent with the nonreductive physicalist thesis discussed above.

141. Although Brown uses the language of "soul," he is not positing the ontological existence of an immaterial entity. Brown comments, "soul" (or at times "soulful" or "soulish") is used to designate not an essence apart from the physical self, but the net sum of those encounters in which embodied humans relate to and commune with God (who is spirit) or with one another in a manner that reaches deeply into the essence of our creaturely, historical, and communal selves." See "Cognitive Contributions," 101.

142. "Evolution," 507–8.

143. Ibid., 508.

uniqueness of that configuration of life we call "human," which is integrally fleshly or somatic. What are its unique characteristics, powers, capacities, and form which make it a genus of life unlike all others? This uniqueness of life is what a "soul" of man consists of. The Christian understanding of human life . . . derives from that God-man relationship.[144]

From a cognitive perspective there are a number of capacities that must be in order for a proper functioning sense of relatedness. Brown lists the following capacities:[145]

1. *language*: the capacity to communicate a potentially infinite number of propositions; to relate regarding complex, abstract ideas, as well as about the past and the future

2. *a theory of mind*: an ability to consider the most likely thoughts and feelings of another person

3. *episodic memory*: a conscious historical memory of events, persons, times, and places (i.e., more than memory for actions and their consequences)

4. *conscious top-down agency*: conscious mental control of behavior; the ability to modulate ongoing behavior in relationship to the conscious process of decisionmaking

5. *future orientation*: ability to run mental scenarios of the future implications of behaviors and events

6. *emotional modulation* by complex social and contextual cognition that serves to guide ongoing behavior and decisionmaking

These cognitive capacities account for the distinctiveness of the human species. It is the uniquely human capacity for personal relatedness that sets us apart from the rest of creation. This relatedness should be understood as both multi-dimensional *and* multi-directional experiences of relationship both with God and creation.

144. Come, *Human Spirit and Holy Spirit*, 59–60.

145. Brown, "Cognitive Contributions," 103–4. This list is not intended to be exhaustive; rather, it is intended to point out the cognitive capacities to which a good deal of research has been committed. For the purposes of this dissertation, I will simply list these and forgo a lengthy discussion of each.

Process or Event?—A Nonreductive Physicalist Corrective

To reiterate an earlier point, the nonreductive physicalist view of the human person *requires* a process-oriented view of conversion.[146] In the following chapter, I will offer a proper definition of conversion; however, at present, I wish to address the issue of process or event as it relates to the concept of sanctification.

John Wesley's notion of sanctification serves as a critical theological language for my understanding of conversion at large; however, his teachings have been subject to a degree of doctrinal evolution, particularly through the nineteenth-century holiness movement. In this brief section, I will offer a corrective to what I judge as a negative transition from Wesley's view of sanctification as a healing process to a crisis event.

As I mentioned in chapter two, interpretations of Wesley's teaching on "entire sanctification" has remained divided to this day. The concept of being entirely cleansed from the "sinful nature" (entirely sanctified) held a prominent place in the emerging holiness movements in England and America. One of the central questions concerning the phenomenon was how it was to occur—whether by process or crisis event. As the idea of entire sanctification became increasingly nuanced, the tendency arose to resolve the tension between crisis and process by stressing the instantaneous character of a "second blessing" or a "second definite work of grace."

Adam Clarke, an influential biblical commentator from England, claimed that

> In no part of the Scripture are we to seek holiness *gradatim*. We are to come to God as well for an instantaneous and complete purification from all sin, as for an instantaneous pardon. Neither the *seriatim* pardon, nor the *gradatim* purification, exists in the Bible. It is when the soul is purified from all sin that it can properly grow in grace, and in the knowledge of our Lord Jesus Christ.[147]

146. One could claim that a person could attain immediate holiness via God's instantaneous alteration of neurobiological substrates; however, to do so would be to misunderstand both the process of neurobiological transformation as well as the nature of holiness that I am arguing for in the present work. Holiness, in the present context, is not to be equated with an ethereal state of being (condition of the soul, etc.), but with observable socio-moral attitude and behavior, such a transformation is necessarily processive. In addition, as I will argue in the following chapter, God's activity in conversion should be understood as co-operant—that is, God respects the constraints of neurobiological systems.

147. Clarke, *Christian Theology*, 207–8. Also see reference to this discussion in Peters, *Christian Perfection and American Methodism*, 103–7. Clarke's influential commentary on the Bible was published first in America between 1811 and 1825. This set became the exegetical standard for Methodism and the early holiness revivals. See Clarke, *Holy Bible*.

Clarke's commentary seemingly resolved the Wesleyan tendency in favor of crisis event; however, it downplayed the teleological character of Wesley's practical theology by moving "entire" sanctification to an earlier point in the Christian experience—becoming the presupposition for, rather than the goal of, Christian life. The implicit effect of this move was a tendency to stress sanctification in terms of "salvation from sin" rather than "perfection in love."

Another key figure in the evolution of sanctification as a crisis event is the holiness preacher, Phoebe Palmer. Her "altar theology" stressed the immediate availability of the "second blessing" (entire sanctification). Palmer claimed that holiness was a state of grace in which every Christian should live and that all believers could "exercise faith" and claim entire sanctification even without emotional assurance.[148]

Palmer's teachings seemed to dismiss the struggle for Christian growth that characterized eighteenth-century Methodism and encouraged an immediate appropriation of the sanctification experience. This progression seems natural as Palmer asserts that the sanctified life "as it has been purchased for you, it is *already* yours. If you do not now receive it, the delay will not be on the part of God, but wholly with yourself."[149]

The final figure that I will mention is Charles G. Finney, American revival preacher and leader in the Second Great Awakening. Finney is known as the most influential of the Calvinist revivalists of his era. He advocated a "New Measures" style of revivalism. The emergence of this style can be understood as the permeation of primarily Reformed denominations (particularly Presbyterian and Congregational) by Methodist concepts and practices.[150]

Finney's style of evangelism retreated from the traditional Wesleyan understanding of Christian growth and gave increasing support to Palmer and other American revivalists that stressed the crisis nature of sanctification. His sense of immediacy and pragmatism insisted on the availability of salvation "now" and highlighted the place of human agency in the revival phenomenon.

Finney's approach undercut the concern of Jonathan Edwards and his followers to conceive of revival more as a "work of God" and conversion as a "miracle" to be granted in God's own time.[151] William Warren Sweet has

---

148. See Palmer, *Way of Holiness,* 60ff.

149. Palmer, *Faith and Its Effects,* 53.

150. See Carwardine, "The Second Great Awakening," 327–40.

151. For a helpful comparison see McLoughlin, *Modern Revivalism,* 85.

argued that "Finney made salvation the beginning of religious experience in contrast to the older revivalism which made conversion the end."[152] This statement summarizes the difference between Wesley and Clarke/Palmer/Finney and indicates the extent to which the evolution of thought regarding sanctification resulted from the contextualization of Wesleyan thought with American revivalism.

My point in offering this summary of sanctification as a crisis event or "second blessing" is to demonstrate its incommensurability with the model of sanctification that a nonreductive physicalist view of the human person requires. If sanctification is indeed understood as a "cleansing of the sinful nature" or, in Wesley's terms, a "renewal of holy tempers," then such a renewal *must* occur through a complex process of socio-moral transformation—a transformation that is contextual by nature. If one adheres to the belief in an ontologically immaterial soul, then it is possible to conceive of such a radical and instantaneous transition—from unholy to holy, unsanctified to sanctified; however, the argument that I have offered in this chapter makes such a position implausible.

Summary

This chapter has been dedicated to addressing the issue of human nature or theological anthropology. The question "what are human beings?" can be reframed to ask "what are humans made of?" Within the context that I have presented, this question has been met with either dualist or reductive views of human nature. I have proposed that the way one answers this question has a profound impact on his or her view of Christian spirituality.

If the goal of Christianity (even if an implicit goal) is to have a "saved soul" or for our souls to "go to heaven when we die," then the tendency exists to relegate the call to be the visible Kingdom of God in the world (Body of Christ/the Church) to secondary status.[153] To claim, as I have in

152. Sweet, *American Churches*, 126. Here conversion refers to the transformation of the tempers and affections—Wesley's great appeal for the acquisition of "holy tempers" through a therapeutic understanding of salvation. Such an understanding is necessarily process-oriented.

153. There are many examples of this hermeneutic, not least of which is the tendency of some to interpret εντος (*entos*) in Luke 17:21—"The Kingdom of God is *among* you"—to read "The Kingdom of God is *within* you." Although the classical Greek translation literally means "within," the corporate nature of its use should not be ignored. When the interpretation is thought to mean "within" an individual subject, the Kingdom of God can be more easily construed as private and a matter of personal experience. Such a view vindicates itself of the mandate to be a public and political presence in the world—the embodiment of "new creation." For an extended discussion see Fitzmeyer, "Gospel According to Luke,"

this chapter, that humans do not actually possess an ontologically distinct soul—we are not "made" of separable material and immaterial entities—affects the way that Christians conceive of spirituality (a term that often is assumed to imply immateriality), conversion, and essential practices such as discipleship.

I clearly reject any position that would remove the public character of the Christian faith—a spiritualist dichotomy that separates inner from outer to the point of aberration. While I do not deny the existence or value of an "inner life," it would be a serious misunderstanding of the Christian Gospel to ignore the central themes of creation, incarnation, God's action in history, and the resurrection of the body. On this note, William Temple, the distinguished Archbishop of Canterbury, claims that Christianity is

> the most avowedly materialist of all the great religions. . . . Its own most central saying is: "the Word was made flesh," where the last term was, no doubt, chosen because of its specifically materialist associations. By the very nature of its central doctrine Christianity is committed to a belief in the ultimate significance of the historical process, and in the reality of matter and its place in the divine scheme.[154]

My central claim in this chapter is that both dualist and reductive materialist views of human nature are undesirable on philosophical and theological grounds. I offer a third alternative, Nonreductive Physicalism (NrP), as a viable theory of human nature. Such a theory avoids the problems inherent in ontological substance dualism while preserving the causal efficacy of "higher order" capacities necessary for a proper theological anthropology.

The nonreductive physicalist view of human nature that I have argued for in this chapter together with the insights from Wesleyan theology discussed in chapter two, supplies the critical elements necessary to propose a new model of Christian religious conversion. The following chapter will be dedicated to this task.

1160–62. For a profound work on the necessary visibility of the Church see Yoder, *Politics of Jesus*.

154. Temple, *Nature, Man and God*, 478. See also *Christus Veritas* and *Christianity and Social Order*.

CHAPTER 4

Rewired

Re-Imagining Christian Religious Conversion

If perfection can be characterized only by "reference to the wholeness of a human life" then the language of stages is far too abstract. Rather, what is required is the actual depiction of lives through which we can be imaginatively drawn into the journey by being given the means to understand and test our failures and successes. That such is the case, moreover, reflects the kind of journey that Christians are asked to undertake. For the telos of the Christian life is not a goal that is clearly known prior to the undertaking of the journey, but rather we learn better the nature of the end by being slowly transformed by the means necessary to pursue it. Thus, the only means to perceive rightly the end is by attending to the lives of those who have been and are on the way.

—Stanley Hauerwas[1]

THE PURPOSE OF THE present chapter will be to offer a new model of Christian religious conversion based on insights gained from the previous two chapters. In chapter one, we discussed reasons why it is desirable to seek such a nuanced concept of conversion as the one that I propose. I claim that a "correct" (informed as possible) view of conversion and how it occurs is critical to Christian community orthopraxis. The way that Christians understand discipleship or spiritual development is conditioned by a particular view of conversion; that is, what we are as human beings and what we are to "become" through the Christian faith is greatly influenced by one's preconceived notion of how this transformation occurs.

The proposed model of conversion is based on insights gained from Wesleyan theology as well as from a nonreductive physicalist view of human nature. The application of concepts from these two areas will necessarily

---

1. Hauerwas, *Sanctify Them in the Truth*, 128.

involve a multidisciplinary approach; therefore, the following model will be informed by both theological concepts as well as relevant data from various scientific disciplines. As discussed in the opening chapter of this work, I argue that such an approach is not only justified, but arguably necessary to fully understand complex phenomena such as conversion.[2]

In chapter two, I argued that the theology of John Wesley provides a view of creation possessing an inherent "telos." This ultimate end or goal is understood as the redemption of the whole of creation. At the center of this redemption lies Wesley's notion of the "way of salvation." This "way" is informed by Wesley's distinctive *affectional moral psychology*. Here an emphasis is placed on the acquisition of holy tempers; that is, the heart of religion for Wesley is the transformation of those inclinations in human nature that serve as motivators for moral attitude and behavior. Throughout this chapter I will demonstrate how Wesley's notion of the "way of salvation," and his concept of sanctification in particular, provides a necessary language for an approach to the phenomenon of Christian conversion.

I presented three key features of Wesley's theological anthropology: (1) *relational anthropology* where the emphasis is on the relational nature of humankind; (2) *holistic anthropology* where Wesley stresses holistic human nature (i.e., interrelatedness of body and soul); and (3) *affectional moral psychology* which is central to his mature view of salvation.

Wesley presents salvation as constituted by God's *prevenient, justifying,* and *sanctifying* grace. Sanctification is understood as the process whereby the "tempers" are transformed and one's motivations, attitudes, and behaviors are changed to reflect the image of God. Such a change is critical to the creation and cultivation of relationship. My central claim was that Wesley's notion of *sanctification* is equivalent to my concept of religious conversion, and thus provides a theological language for the observed socio-moral change.[3]

---

2. While I do claim that the understanding of any given phenomenon increases as explanations are offered at new levels, my current investigation involves explanations offered by theology and the cognitive sciences (which special emphasis on neuropsychology). I do realize that there are additional levels which offer an explanation of conversion (sociological, anthropological, etc.); however, I will refrain from engaging those resources here.

3. Further support for this notion of conversion can be found in Catholic theology. Jesuit theologian, Donald L. Gelpi, cites the "new" theology of conversion that has developed since Vatican II. This theology of conversion views conversion as ongoing and synonymous with "sanctification." The terminology that Gelpi cites makes it clear that conversion does not happen once and for all, but is rather a lifetime affair. Gelpi states that "one does not understand the meaning of any belief until one has grasped its practi-

In chapter three, I presented a cogent description of the nonreductive physicalist view of human nature. My central argument was that a proper view of human nature is critical to virtually every dimension of religious life. The traditional options fell victim to either dualism or reductionism; thus, I offered a third alternative, nonreductive physicalism, as a means to both avoid the problems of dualism and reductionism as well as preserve the uniqueness of the human species necessary for theological integrity (in terms of personal and communal interrelatedness). In the closing section, I argued for the human capacity for relatedness by demonstrating that the particularly social nature of the human species can be accounted for without requiring a nonmaterial essence such as the soul.

I suggest that the nonreductive physicalist view is crucial to the present work not because it reflects a particular philosophical thesis, but because it represents the "hard core" (in the Lakatosian sense) of a research programme that seeks to explain human nature. As such, various philosophical concepts and scientific data are critiqued and applied respectively.[4] For example, "neuroscience," as a set of data, offers neither support nor refutation for any particular explanation of a phenomenon. It is only through philosophical interpretation that such data become applicable.

So then, the insights from chapters two and three will serve a critical role in my definition and explanation of Christian conversion. This synthesis will appear in the following sections beginning with my proposed definition of Christian conversion.

Defining Christian Religious Conversion

The definition of Christian conversion that I offer is constituted by four salient features:

I claim that (1) *Christian conversion is a process involving normal human biological capacities.* (2) *It is characterized by a change in socio-moral attitude and behavior, and* (3) *is best understood as the acquisition of virtues intrinsic to Christian faith. Such acquisitions are facilitated through social in-*

---

cal, operational consequences. The new theology of conversion insists, therefore, that the experience of *sanctification* defines the very meaning of conversion. See Gelpi, *Conversion Experience*, 102. Similar sentiments have long been a part of Catholic practice. The process oriented nature of conversion is exemplified by the early practice of delaying baptism and first communion until the Easter after the new member had completed catechesis.

4. Nancey Murphy has applied this approach in several instances where there are multidimensional data sets available. Once the "hard-core" is established then a number of "auxiliary hypotheses" are offered to support the central claim. For example, see Murphy and Ellis, *Moral Nature of the Universe*.

teraction and participation in practices inherent to the Christian community. (4) *Furthermore, the conversion process should be viewed as the co-operant result of Divine grace and human participation.*

In the following section, I will offer justification for this definition.

Explaining Christian Religious Conversion

Justification of the proposed definition will involve both theological and scientific data. I will address each of the salient features listed above beginning with the notion that conversion is a process involving normal human biological capacities.

Conversion as a biological process

In chapter three, I made a case for the link between biology and morality. Through the process of evolution, human beings have acquired such a level of complexity as to allow for the emergence of "higher order" capacities such as morality. Ursula Goodenough and Terrence Deacon suggest that moral experience

> entails a coupling of our rich heritage of social orientation with our ability to represent it to ourselves symbolically. During this coupling, the experience of our prosocial capacities, and their role in affecting action, is radically transformed, and what emerges is a major augmentation of our social heritage. We are able to apply these amplified prosocial capacities to experiences, imaginings, and modes of action that are no longer constrained by evolutionary precedents and classes of phylotypic stimuli. Indeed, our capacity for conceptual blending allows us to synthesize moral understandings and emotional experiences that would otherwise be mutually exclusive.[5]

It is then through the evolution of symbolic interaction that our capacity for moral behavior arises.[6] The evolutionary branches of biology and psychology have contributed a great deal of research helping us to understand

---

5. Goodenough and Deacon, "From Biology to Consciousness to Morality," 814. A significant premise follows from this claim—Goodenough and Deacon claim that humans do not acquire morality by means of cultural instruction alone; rather, we "discover" morality or learn to "see" it. This, of course, resonates with virtue theory and the works of Aristotle (*Nicomachean Ethics*). I will return to this notion later in this chapter.

6. This is a complex process that I will not discuss here. For an excellent resource on the issue see Deacon, *Symbolic Species*.

complex human functions.[7] As Deacon makes clear, it is the complex evolution of our brains that leads to capacities particular to human beings. So, we see scientific disciplines emerging which focus on the brain and cognition.

Various disciplines within the cognitive sciences are dedicated to investigating human cognition. At an increasing rate, brain sciences are permeating many scientific disciplines resulting in the emergence of new fields of investigation—such as neuropsychology,[8] social cognitive neuroscience,[9] and even neurotheology.[10] These all point to the significance of the human brain in complex functioning.

Recall that in chapters one and two, I argued for an understanding of conversion that extends beyond "religious experience" per se. Instead, I intend for the term conversion to designate a significant socio-moral transformation.[11] Such a transformation necessarily encompasses all human attitudes *and* behaviors—this is what Wesley meant by "holiness of life." So, properly understood, conversion entails a transformation of the underlying motivations that bring about attitudes and behaviors particular to the Christian faith.

This claim, coupled with my call for a physicalist view of the human person (albeit *non*reductive), leads to the claim that conversion must somehow involve our physical or *embodied* selves—that is, it must in some way be a change recognisable at a biological level of investigation.[12] It follows, then, that we need a way to view conversion as a biological process.

7. For example, research is burgeoning in the area of neuroscience which claims that the human brain has evolved in such a way as to give rise to morality. For example see Moll et al., "Morals and the human brain," 299–305.

8. The aim of neuropsychology is to understand how the structure and function of the brain relates to specific psychological processes. It is a popular field with a rich literary history.

9. See Ochsner and Liebermann, "Emergence of Social Cognitive Neuroscience."

10. The basis of "neurotheology" is the application of brain sciences in order to understand religious phenomena. There are a multitude of publications ranging from an obscure work by Mckinney (*Neurotheology*) to the more scientifically oriented research offered by Newberg and his colleagues See Newbert et al., *Why God Won't Go Away*; Newberg, "Neuropsychology," 251–26; Newberg and D'Aquili, "Creative Brain," 53–68.

11. Recall that I use the term "socio-moral" to designate those behaviors that are necessary for the flourishing of human life, both individual and communal. I will also add, but not argue, that such behaviors are necessary for true happiness. In this vein, Wesley believed that holiness of life was integrally related to happiness; thus he believed that none were truly happy except the "real inward Christian" (Sermon 77: *Spiritual Worship, BE* 3:99).

12. It will be clear at this point that I reject any notion of conversion claiming that

In order to present such a view, I will first offer a way of conceiving of moral sentiment and action in a biological framework. Then, I will demonstrate the way in which a change in these capacities is likely to occur. The purpose for doing this, I argue, is that *given that human persons are biological beings, it follows that any change involving our biological substrate must respect the nature in which such changes occur.*[13] In other words, I am suggesting that conversion be seen as occurring in a "normative" fashion in the sense that biological constraints must be considered.

In order to present conversion as a biological process, I suggest the consideration of three interrelated levels:

1. The *phenomenal level* which, in the present case, is the occurrence of religious conversion.

2. The *cognitive level* which designates the components of a moral cognition. These components are constituent of a sense of moral responsibility; thus, any change in socio-moral attitude and behavior must somehow involve these capacities.

3. The *neural level* which describes the biological correlates of moral cognition.[14]

Here, *moral cognition* generally refers to what researchers in the field of social cognitive neuroscience refer to as *social cognition*. The two are equivalent inasmuch as they both deal with the neural underpinnings of human socio-moral behavior. Ralph Adolphs states that social (moral) cognition refers to "the processes that subserve behavior in response to conspecifics (other individuals of the same species), and, in particular, to those higher cognitive processes subserving the extremely diverse and flexible social behaviors that are seen in primates."[15] There have been two main approaches to the study of the neural systems critical to moral cognition in

---

the change is due to an alteration in "soul" or "spirit"—when these terms are meant to designate an ontologically distinct immaterial entity.

13. I want to stress that this in no way violates my argument for a "top-down" form of causation. At no point do I wish to argue that emergent properties can exert causal efficacy that leads to a violation of the laws existing at the lower levels.

14. While I assume it to be true that *some* relationship exists between various brain areas and moral cognition, I am quick to point out that identifying such neural mechanisms is difficult. I hold that the exercise of moral sentiment and judgment in humans requires multiple cognitive processes and is ultimately an affair of the entire brain and body—in other words, I do not claim that moral cognition is "in the head" or is the result of any particular module within the brain.

15. See Adolphs, "Social cognition," 469–79.

humans. The first involves socio-moral impairments following brain damage to specific parts of the brain (particularly the prefrontal cortices, e.g., Phineas Gage) and the second concerns the social impairments observed in studies of autism. The importance of moral cognition to the present work is to point out the burgeoning evidence showing the biological links to moral behavior.[16]

The top or phenomenal level will represent the occurrence of religious conversion—again, understood as a change in socio-moral attitude and behavior. The cognitive level involves an understanding of the cognitive components that make a change in socio-moral attitude and behavior possible (from a neurobiological point of view). I will assume that the components necessary for such a change to be the same as those constituent of a sense of moral responsibility. I will list these below, but for the purposes of the present work, I will only offer a brief explanation of each.[17]

1. *Self-concept*—Consciousness of one's own identity. Self-concept does not refer to the recognition of an ontological entity within a human person—"There is indeed such a thing as self-consciousness in the philosophical sense of the term, but it is not consciousness of a "self". It is a distinctively human capacity for reflexive thought and knowledge, wholly dependent upon possession of a language."[18] Leslie Brothers has offered research regarding the neurobiological underpinnings of the "person concept." A dimension of this con-

16. For more see Adolphs, "Cognitive Neuroscience," 165–78; Forgas, *Handbook*; and Reis and Collins, "Relationships," 233–37. For a helpful overview of the literature in social cognitive neuroscience specific to moral cognition and the prefrontal cortex see Jacqueline N. Wood, "Social Cognition," 97–114. In addition, William D. Casebeer has offered an insightful investigation into the relationship between moral theory and what science tells us about moral cognition. Casebeer concludes that the moral psychology required by virtue theory is the most neurobiologically plausible. I believe that this conclusion will be valuable to the future of research in moral cognition. For more see Casebeer, "Moral cognition" 841–46; *Natural Ethical Facts*; and Casebeer and Churchland, "The Neural Mechanisms of Moral Cognition," 169–94.

17. These are adapted from a similar list offered by Nancey Murphy. See Murphy and Brown, *Did My Neurons Make Me Do It?*. Also, Francisco J. Ayala claims that human beings exhibit ethical behavior *by nature*. This is due to our biological constitution that involves three necessary and jointly sufficient conditions for moral behavior. These conditions are "a) the ability to anticipate the consequences of one's own actions; b) the ability to make value judgments; and c) the ability to choose between alternative courses of action." See Ayala, "So Human an Animal," 129. Note that some of these components coincide with Brown's suggestions regarding the cognitive components of "soulishness."

18. Bennett and Hacker, *Philosophical Foundations of Neuroscience*, 324.

cept involves the person's ability to locate his or her*self* in a social network with its various interrelational dynamics.[19]

2. *Language*—The capacity to communicate a potentially infinite number of propositions or abstract ideas about the past, present or future.[20]

3. *Episodic memory*—A conscious historical memory of events, persons, times and places—"episodic memory is our recall of the events of our past that are marked in our recollection by specifics of time and place."[21] It is the "cumulated events of one's life, an individual's autobiography."[22] In this sense, episodic memory is critical to our ability to reflect and make future judgments.

4. *Imagination*—The ability to predict outcomes in relation to goals, i.e. imagine the future. Brown refers to this as the capacity to imagine "future orientation." Such is meant to denote "the ability to run a conscious mental simulation or scenario of future possibilities for the actions of oneself and others, and to evaluate these scenarios in such a way as to regulate behavior and make decisions now with regard to desirable future events."[23]

5. *Theory of Mind (ToM)*—The ability to predict the mental states of others. This metacognitive skill has long been researched and found to be a crucial aspect of a properly functional moral cognition. Simply stated, a theory of mind allows an individual to make statements such as "*I* think that *he* thinks."[24]

---

19. It is this dimension of Brother's concept of the person that I wish to relate to "self-concept." See Brothers, *Friday's Footprint*.

20. A seminal work on language and its role in the development of higher order human capacities is offered by Terrence W. Deacon. See Deacon, *Symbolic Species*. In addition Warren S. Brown offers a helpful discussion of language as it concerns the capacity for personal relatedness. See Brown, "Cognitive Contributions," 104–8.

21. Ibid., 113.

22. Squire, *Memory and Brain*, 169. I will challenge Squire on one point—it seems a confusion to speak of memories as *stored in the brain*. Such conjures an image of the human brain as a massive filing cabinet. I follow Bennett and Hacker in understanding the capacity to remember various events as being "*causally dependent* on different brain areas and on synaptic modifications in these areas." See Bennett and Hacker, *The Philosophical Foundations of Neuroscience*, 159.

23. Brown, "Cognitive Contributions," 117.

24. There is a bounty of research on ToM. For some helpful examples see Baron-Cohen et al., *Understanding Other Minds*; Frith and Frith, "Interacting Minds," 1692–95; and Stone et al., "Frontal Lobe," 640–56.

6. *Top-down agency*—The ability of higher-order human capacities to exert causal efficacy over base constituents. Brown asserts that top-down agency designates the ability "to modulate behavior in relationship to conscious thought and intention."[25]

7. *Goal formation*—The ability to form goals in light of abstract concepts including non-embodied ideals such as truth and love. In the case of moral goals, the affective dimension of human cognition plays a critical role.[26]

8. *Action potential*—The physical ability to act on conscious or intuitive judgments.

These cognitive components represent capacities that are necessary for, not only the state of moral responsibility, but they also designate the capacities that must be affected in a change in moral attitude and behavior. To be clear, the components that I have listed are neither exhaustive nor are intended to represent any type of "one-to-one" relationship to the realization of moral action. As stated earlier, moral cognition is a complex state of affairs that can only be understood in terms of whole body relations to dynamic environmental situations. Nevertheless, the list of cognitive components that I have offered allows one to conceive of the type of biological processes that undergird moral inclination and response.

Investigation of the neural correlates of moral cognition strengthens this claim. By "neural correlates" I am referring to a collection of data that point to particular areas within the brain that appear to be "correlated" with various levels of socio-moral attitude and behavior. Jorge Moll and colleagues suggest that the present state of neuroscientific research points to the existence of brain networks specialized for the generation of moral emotions.[27] Such emotions are integral to the formation and implementation of moral action.

To sum up thus far, I began this section by recalling that Wesley's understanding of conversion was characterized by a "holiness of life"—a change in both attitude and behavior. Such a change permeates every aspect of the convert's life. I suggested that such a change can (and should) be considered biological in nature. I then offered as a conceptual framework

25. Brown, "Cognitive Contributions," 117.

26. Perhaps the most notable example can be seen in Antonio Damasio's "Somatic Marker Hypothesis." I will address this hypothesis in detail later in this chapter. For more, see Damasio's *Descartes' Error*.

27. Moll et al., "Neural Correlates," 2730–36. Also see Moll et al., "Functional Networks," 696–703.

the three interrelated levels—*phenomenal* (the occurrence of conversion), *cognitive* (the cognitive capacities underlying moral "selfhood"), and *neural* (the various neural networks correlated with socio-moral function).

At this juncture, I propose that religious conversion, seen as a change in socio-moral attitude and behavior, can be understood (from a neuro-biological point of view) as *learning* a new way of relating. This *process* of change is commensurate with a reorganization of neurobiological substrate and as such can be characterized as neuroplastic in nature.[28] In short, I am suggesting that *religious conversion supervenes on an alteration of neurobiological substrate*. A brief discussion of neural plasticity is in order.

The ability of the brain and/or certain parts of the nervous system to respond and adapt to new conditions is called *neural plasticity*. Specifically, neural plasticity refers to the formation, breakdown, and re-formation of neural synapses, and the subsequent changes in brain function. Synapses are formed or reinforced as an individual experiences or performs particular actions—such actions stimulate simultaneous activity of the presynaptic and postsynaptic neurons. In contrast, synapses dissolve as neural links become less active due to the lack of corresponding experiences or actions. As this process of formation and breakdown occurs, localized subsystems within the brain change and as a result become more or less capable of performing certain tasks.

Research in brain plasticity is well-known in the field of neuroscience. In fact, the nineteenth century scientist, Santiago Ramón y Cajal, described the brain's ability to adapt to environmental change.

> When one reflects on the ability that humans display for modifying and refining mental activity related to a problem under serious examination, it is difficult to avoid concluding that the brain is plastic and goes through a process of anatomical and functional differentiation, adapting itself progressively to the problem. . . . In a certain sense, it would not be paradoxical to say that the person who initiates the solution to a problem is different from the one who solves it.[29]

28. I will use the term *neuroplasticity* or *neural plasticity* in a *descriptive* fashion. By this I mean that I am characterising the change by using this term. I am thereby not implying any causal explanation. In other words, I am not saying that neural plasticity *causes* conversion nor am I saying that neural plasticity *is* conversion in the sense of a type-identity relationship. I am simply saying that a physicalist account of the person requires that a psychological change be commensurate with a change in brain state. I am using the term "neural plasticity" to describe this relationship.

29. Ramon y Cajal, *Advice for a Young Investigator*, 35.

It is obvious that human beings are able to adapt to a multitude of environmental fluctuations. While there has long been research showing neural plasticity and neurogenesis in various areas of the somatosensory and visual cortices, hippocampus, etc.,[30] little research has been done on neural plasticity and changes in personality. Jim Grigsby and David Stevens discuss synaptic (neural) plasticity in such a context. They claim that

> Personality is shaped by the interaction of constitutional processes and the experiences of individuals in unique environments. In other words, we are, at least in part, who we learn to be. As a result of these experiences, learning drives the acquisition and refinement of a wide repertoire of enduring perceptions, attitudes, thoughts, and behaviors. The relative permanence of learning and memory reflects the operation of processes that modify the microscopic structure of the brain, yielding changes in different aspects of functioning over time as a result of the individual's interactions with the world. These experience-dependent changes in brain structure and functioning are known by the general term *synaptic plasticity*.[31]

The challenge then is to understand what type of experiences a person must have for the brain to undergo this process of plastic change. While there are obvious external environmental influences that shape us biologically (through the process of natural selection for instance), there is reason to believe that *self-induced* neuroplastic change can occur.

---

30. An example of plasticity in the somatosensory cortex is noted by V. S. Ramachandran's account of patients experiencing "phantom limb syndrome." See Ramachandran and Blakeslee, *Phantoms in the Brain*. Changes in grey matter related to learning-induced plasticity have been observed by Draganski et al. See "Changes in grey matter," 311–12. Research has shown that neurogenesis (the biological production of neurons) continues throughout the lifespan. These newly generated neurons express unique mechanisms to facilitate neural plasticity, which may be important for the formation of new memories. See Schmidt-Hieber et al., "Enhanced synaptic plasticity," 184–87. Significant research has been offered by Eleanor A. Macquire demonstrating neuroplastic changes in the hippocampus of London taxi drivers. The increased size of the posterior hippocampi in the taxi drivers can be understood as a plastic change resulting from an increased demand for spatial memory and navigation skills. The taxi driver's repetitive stimulation of particular subsystems within the brain has led to the reinforcement of existing structures and the formation of new synapses that aid the drivers in their daily tasks. See Maquire et al., "Navigation-related structural change," 4398–4403. It should be noted here that neural plasticity is not an open door to boundless biological change; the process does have its limits. For an example see Sereno, "Plasticity," 288–89.

31. Grigsby and Stevens, *Neurodynamics of Personality*, 39.

Jeffrey M. Schwartz has more than twenty years of research experience with patients suffering from Obsessive Compulsive Disorder (OCD). He has noted that individuals suffering from OCD show increased metabolic activity in their occipital lobes and caudate nuclei. These brain areas along with the thalamus and cingulated gyrus are involved in a perpetual cycle of error detection that drives the patient to repeat certain actions over and over.

Schwartz has gained significant recognition for his research demonstrating the effectiveness of behavioral therapy in the treatment of OCD.[32] The basic premise of Schwartz's therapy involves the ability of the patient to recognize the obsessive tendency before it is enacted as a compulsive behavior. The individual then intentionally engages in an alternate physical activity while maintaining awareness that the obsessive feeling is "only OCD."

After a period of time, patients notice a reduction in obsessive tendencies commensurate with a reduction in metabolic activity in the brain areas involved in error detection. The "before and after" brain scans of OCD patients participating in Schwartz's behavior therapy are striking. Schwartz attributes the success of the treatment to the individual's ability to exert mental force that alters obsessive/compulsive behavior and ultimately changes the brain.[33]

In addition, Richard J. Davidson has been involved in research designed to examine the biological impact of meditation, particularly as it affects the central circuitry of emotion. Davidson and colleagues assert that the human brain along with various emotional tendencies can be transformed through mental training.[34]

While it is unclear precisely how neuroplastic changes occur in the brain,[35] there is wide agreement that a structural change of some kind

---

32. See Schwartz and Begley, *Mind and the Brain*; Schwartz, "Role for Volition," 115–42; and Schwartz, *Brain Lock*.

33. For an extended discussion see Schwartz et al., "Volitional Influence," 195–238.

34. Urry et al., "Making a Life Worth Living," 367–72. For more regarding plasticity and its implications for transforming emotion and cultivating positive affect and resilience see R. Davidson, "Toward a Biology of Personality," 191–207; "Affective Style," 1196–1214; and Davidson et al., "Emotion," 890–909. It is worth noting that in addition to the "mental training" discussed by Davidson et al., I would add that "physical training" is imperative as well. I will return to this point later in this chapter.

35. One of the most popular notions of how learning (neural plasticity) occurs in the brain was offered a number of years ago by Donald O. Hebb. He suggested that "the persistence or repetition of a reverberatory activity (or 'trace') tends to induce lasting cellular changes that add to its stability. . . . When an axon of cell A is near enough to excite a cell

occurs at the synaptic level in response to experience.[36] The effect of such alters the probability that an action potential from a presynaptic neuron will lead to a discharge in a postsynaptic neuron. Grigsby and Stevens claim that

> On a functional level, the effect of synaptic plasticity is a change in probabilities. Learning induces structural changes that make it either more or less likely that stimulation of a given neuron or (more accurately) a population of neurons will cause the stimulated neurons to fire. . . . The probabilities are determined to a large extent by the overall state of the individual at any given time. Changing one's state can reset the probabilities for almost all kinds of behavioral, perceptual, cognitive, and mnestic activity.[37]

This means that when a person's activity is "effective," it is likely to recur in the future—the

> facilitation of specific behaviors is generally nonconscious and does not necessarily occur because an animal knows that it should behave in a particular manner. Instead, an activity that previously has been adaptive is likely to recur because the brain functions automatically, but probabilistically, to produce that behavior in similar circumstances.[38]

In other words, each repetition of an action realized by a particular brain state has the effect of making the same action more likely to occur in the future.

It should be noted that neuroplastic changes are best understood as a *process* involving complex neural networks situated within one's body and environment at large. Perhaps the best example of neuroplastic change is "learning." Take for example, learning to play the piano or learning to ride a bicycle—both of these *skills* require the process of learning by trial

---

B and repeatedly or persistently takes part in firing it, some growth process or metabolic change takes place in one or both cells such that A's efficiency, as one of the cells firing B, is increased." See Hebb, *Organization of Behavior*, 62. For a critique of "Hebbian Learning," see Cruikshank and Weinberger, "Evidence for the Hebbian hypothesis," 191–228.

36. I recognize that much of the past research on neural plasticity involves infants or early developmental aspects. It is worth noting that there is a surge of recent work emphasising plasticity in the adult primate brain. This punctuates an implicit claim within the present work—learning and transformation (plasticity and neurogenesis) occurs throughout the life-span. For an example see Kozorovitskiy et al., "Experience," 17478–82.

37. *Neurodynamics of Personality*, 53.

38. Ibid., 51. This explanation introduces the potential for "automatic behavior." This is an important concept to which I will return in the following section.

and error. This is usually a slow and tedious task. Such exemplifies the nature of neuroplastic change—it is a gradual process of training resulting in the reorganization of neurobiological substrate on which a particular skill supervenes.

Given the above discussion, I claim that religious conversion can be understood (from a neurobiological point of view) as the *learning* of new skills characterized by a tendency toward a particular moral attitude and behavior. Such learning should be considered a process involving neuroplastic changes in the complex neurobiological substrates necessary for proper socio-moral cognition. In Wesley's terms, such a change requires a transformation of the "tempers" or "affections." In order to more fully understand this claim, I will once again turn to Wesley's affectional moral psychology.

Conversion as a Transformation of the Tempers

A salient feature of the analysis that I offered in chapter two was the emergence of a theological language for religious conversion as a process of the transformation of socio-moral attitude and behavior. For Wesley this language was rooted in his theological anthropology and especially in his affectional moral psychology.

A key aspect of this psychology was the place given to the "will"—here meant to signify the presence and actuation of "affections." For Wesley, these affections were not simply feelings, but "indispensable motivating inclinations behind human action. In their ideal expression they integrate the rational and emotional dimensions of human life into holistic inclinations toward action (like love)."[39]

So then, an *affection* is properly understood as "transitory feeling state"[40]—e.g. *feeling* love for another. Another concept, perhaps more frequently applied by Wesley, was that of the *tempers*. A temper is a "habituated affection, or said differently, an enduring disposition to perceive/feel/think/act in a consistent manner (e.g. to *be* a loving person)."[41]

For Wesley, moral attitude and behavior is *motivated* by the inclinations established by the affections and tempers. Wesley held that holiness of life was possible through the transformation of these dispositions; thus, he identified the goal of Christian practice as the recovery of "holy tempers." True religion—attitude and behavior marked by love—would then

---

39. Maddox, "Reconnecting the Means to the End," 41.

40. Strawn and Brown, "Wesleyan Holiness," 121.

41. Ibid., 121.

flow from a purity of intention. In short, for Wesley, "conversion" was concerned with the transformation of unholy affections and tempers to those characterized by the love of God.

Wesley recognized that such a transformation was unlikely to occur as a crisis event; rather, the renewal of the affections and tempers should be understood as a gradual *process*. Such a claim resonates with the discussion above regarding conversion as a biological "process." This, together with the view of human nature offered by nonreductive physicalism, requires one to seriously consider the embodied nature of the conversion process. I propose, then, that science can once again prove to be helpful in understanding conversion at large.

In the remainder of this section, I will offer scientific insights that help us to better understand what is meant by a transformation of the "tempers." I will follow Brad D. Strawn and Warren S. Brown in offering four concepts from cognitive science that aid in this endeavor: *procedural knowledge, affect memories, somatic markers,* and *automaticity*.

PROCEDURAL KNOWLEDGE

Larry R. Squire and Daniel L. Schacter have identified two "kinds" of memory—*declarative* and *nondeclarative*.[42] Both involve anatomically distinct neural substrates[43] and contribute to different functions within the realm of human cognition. Declarative memory[44] is knowledge of particular facts or events that can be directly recalled. In contrast, nondeclarative memory designates a type of *implicit* knowledge of which is not easily accessible using language. An important type of implicit knowledge is known as *procedural knowledge*.

Procedural knowledge deals with the learning of *processes* as opposed to facts or events. These processes include "motor skills (e.g., gymnastics), perceptual abilities (e.g., visual pattern recognition), cognitive skills (e.g., solving mental arithmetic problems), cognitive-perceptual skills (e.g., reading), and more complex kinds of tasks (e.g., playing music or *learning social and relational processes*)."[45]

---

42. Squire and Schacter, *Neuropsychology of Memory*.

43. Declarative memory is primarily hippocampus-based, while nondeclarative memory has "other neural loci (e.g., amygdala, striatum, or cerebellum)." Rosenblatt, "Insight," 202.

44. Declarative memory is generally further subdivided into *episodic* and *semantic* memory. See Grigsby and Stevens, *Neurodynamics of Personality*, 87–89.

45. Ibid., 91. Emphasis added.

N. J. Cohen describes procedural knowledge as a type of memory system that eludes verbal expression (and thus not constituting "knowledge" in the same sense as declarative knowledge). As one gains procedural knowledge, "experience serves to influence the organization of processes that guide performance without access to the knowledge that underlies the performance."[46] Procedural knowledge is therefore well-learned, complex behaviors that are often elicited outside of an individual's conscious awareness.[47] So, actions elicited by procedural knowledge can be likened to "habits" in that they are formed over a sustained period of time, become "automatic" and are consequently "hard to break."[48]

Procedural knowledge has an intimate connection to the concept of top-down "causation" that I discussed in chapter three. Dianne Berry and Donald Broadbent have provided a helpful experiment demonstrating the relationship between procedural knowledge and behavior.[49]

> Berry and Broadbent . . . asked subjects to try to control the output of a hypothetical sugar factory (which was simulated by a computer program) by manipulating the size of the workforce. Subjects would see the month's output . . . and then choose the next month's workforce. [The rule relating workforce and output was a complex mathematical formula.] . . . Oxford undergraduates were given sixty trials at trying to control the output of the sugar factory. Over the sixty trials, they got quite good at controlling the output of the sugar factory. However, they were unable to state what the rule was and claimed they made their responses on the basis of "some sort of intuition" or because it "felt right." Thus, subjects were able to acquire implicit knowledge of how to operate such a factory without corresponding explicit knowledge.[50]

This experiment demonstrates how system-type feedback loops relate to the embodied nature of mental causation. The interaction between the students and the computer programme represents high-order mental activity despite the fact that they were not able to "name" the complex process that contributed to their ability to reach their goal. The "knowledge" of how

46. Cohen, "Preserved learning," 96.

47. E. J. Langer and L. G. Imber have contributed research demonstrating that with repetition, performance of procedurally learned processes become increasingly automatic. See Langer and Imber, "When practice makes imperfect," 2014–24.

48. M. Mishkin et al. defined procedural knowledge as the retention of "habits." See "Memories and habits."

49. Berry and Broadbent, "On the relationship," 209–31.

50. As cited by J. Anderson, *Cognitive Psychology and Its Implications*, 236–37.

to successfully reach their goal exists only in the *interaction* between the students and the programme—the required knowledge was inaccessible apart from the activation of the relevant action-feedback loop.

This example serves to emphasis the role of "cause" in mental "causation" (as discussed in the previous chapter). Brown notes that "causation" does not refer solely to the triggering of particular actions; rather, "'causes' of behavior are the processes by which a continuously active organism evaluates and modulates its action. The causal role of the mental is evident in evaluative modulations of ongoing behavior, not in the initiation of behavior."[51]

Strawn and Brown note that "we are typically only conscious (usually somewhat after the fact) of the initiation and progression of [a] procedural sequence. Certain domains of our procedural knowledge, particularly those procedures that have to do with interpersonal interactions, go into what we call *character*."[52] I suggest that a transformation of the tempers will involve a reorganization of an individual's procedural knowledge. In short, conversion requires the learning of new "habits."[53] In order for the formation of new habits to occur, new *experiences* must be present that result in the formation of new procedural knowledge.[54]

Affect Memories

Closely related to the concept of procedural knowledge are the formation and recollection of *affect memories*. Strawn and Brown claim that

> Affect memories are based on previous life situations. The affective responses that are triggered in new but similar situations are evaluative in that they code for us whether this situation is likely to be pleasant, threatening, sad, frustrating, etc. Sometimes we are aware of our emotional and evaluative responses, and sometimes we are not. If we become consciously aware of our emotional responses,

51. Brown, "Lecture 3," of *Science, Faith, and Human Nature*, 17.

52. Strawn and Brown, "Wesleyan Holiness," 123.

53. The concept of "habits" has a long history. Aristotle considered the capacity to form habits to be a fundamental aspect of human nature. Likewise, his ethics were largely concerned with the formation of "virtuous habits." See Aristotle, *Nicomachean Ethics*, especially Book II, Chapter 1. Within the area of modern psychology, William James referred to living creatures as "bundles of habits." See James, *Principles of Psychology*, 104. As mentioned in chapter one, the concept of habits is a key feature in virtue theory and one to which I will return to later in this chapter.

54. This concept of new "experiences" is a critical component of my overall argument and will be addressed in more detail later in this chapter.

it is after the fact. The emotion occurred automatically, then we became conscious of its occurrence.[55]

Despite the long history of conflict over the role of emotions in moral judgment,[56] current research in cognitive science shows that it is difficult to separate emotion from behavior.[57] Strawn and Brown comment further that "it is most often the case that our subconscious emotional evaluative responses frame our perception of a situation and govern our actions. Affective responses are among the many factors that influence which procedures are activated in a particular situation."[58]

These conclusions are supported by research indicating that socio-moral decision-making involves more than "reasoning." Jonathan Haidt's "social intuitionist" model of moral judgment represents the philosophical amalgamation of this research.[59] Haidt's model is "social" in that it deemphasizes the private reasoning done by individuals and focuses on the importance of social and cultural influences. It is "intuitive" in that it states that socio-moral judgment is generally the result of quick, automatic evaluations to which "reasoning" is applied to ad hoc.

Collaborative research between Haidt and Joshua D. Greene suggests that moral judgment is less concerned with deliberative reasoning and is more a matter of emotion and affective intuition.[60] While "cognitive"[61] processes do play a role in the outcome of socio-moral behavior, the function of the emotions should not be underestimated.[62]

55. Strawn and Brown, "Wesleyan Holiness," 123.

56. Plato argued for the irrationality of emotions. This idea was extended by Immanuel Kant, who characterized emotions as non-moral influences. See Kant, *Groundwork*.

57. There is extensive literature from multiple disciplines that supports this claim. For a helpful article on the issue see Pizarro, "Nothing More Than Feelings?," 355–75.

58. Strawn and Brown, "Wesleyan Holiness," 123.

59. See especially Haidt, "Emotional Dog," 814–34. Also see Haidt, "Dialogue," 54–56; and Haidt et al., "Affect," 613–28.

60. See Greene and Haidt, "How (and where)," 517–23.

61. While it is uncertain how and where to draw the line between "cognition" and "emotion," I will follow Greene in maintaining some sort of distinction. Greene claims that "one may render the emotion/cognition distinction in terms of a contrast between, on the one hand, representations that have direct motivational force and, on the other hand, representations that have no direct motivational force of their own, but that can be contingently connected to affective/emotional states that do have such force, thus producing behavior that is both flexible and goal directed." In this sense, the distinction between cognition and emotion exists as a matter of degree. See Greene et al., "Neural Bases," 397–98.

62. Greene and colleagues find a distinct correlation between what they call "personal"

Affect memories exist as the product of an intricate weaving together of emotion with past life experiences. As such, they have the ability to influence socio-moral behavior.[63] I suggest, therefore, that a transformation of the tempers will necessarily require a change in an individual's emotional reactions encoded in affective memories.

Somatic Markers

Research regarding "somatic markers" offers further support for the role of emotion in the decision-making process. The *Somatic Marker Hypothesis* has been suggested by Antonio Damasio and colleagues.[64] This hypothesis emerged from the study of individuals displaying various types of behavioral disorders due to frontal lobe dysfunction. Damasio and colleagues find that patients with damage to the prefrontal cortex (particularly the ventromedial sector) demonstrate a profound disruption in social behavior.

Like the account of Phineas Gage (offered in the previous chapter), many of these patients show no decrease in intellectual ability; however, they demonstrate a marked reduction in their ability to process emotion and feeling in relation to complex situations or events. It is from this conundrum that the somatic marker hypothesis was born.

Antoine Bechara and colleagues summarize the hypothesis as follows:

> The somatic marker hypothesis proposes that a defect in emotion and feeling plays an important role in impaired decision making. The hypothesis also specifies a number of structures and operations required for the normal operation of decision making. Because emotion is most importantly expressed through changes in the representation of body state, though not solely, and because the results of emotion are primarily represented in the brain in the form of transient changes in the activity pattern of Somatosensory structures, the emotional changes are designated under the umbrella term "somatic state." The term "somatic" thus refers to in-

---

moral judgments and areas of the brain associated with emotion and moral cognition. See Greene, "From Neural 'is'," 847–50; and "fMRI Investigation," 2105–10. For examples of additional supporting research see Bjorklund, "Intuition," 1–15; and Heekeren et al., "fMRI study," 1215–19.

63. For a helpful discussion of emotion and its role in social action see Forgas, "Affective Influences," 596–618.

64. The hypothesis became popular with the publication of Damasio's book *Descartes' Error*.

ternal milieu, visceral and musculoskeletal, of the soma rather than just to the musculoskeletal aspects. It should also be noted that although somatic signals are based on structures which represent the body and its states, from the brainstem and hypothalamus to the cerebral cortex, the "somatic" signals do not need to originate in the body in every instance and can be generated intracerebrally.[65]

To test the hypothesis, Damasio's team devised the now well-known "Iowa Gambling Task." In the basic version of the task, subjects are given four decks of cards and a loan of two thousand dollars (play money). The goal of the game is to maximize profit before the researcher ends the task. The subjects are then allowed to draw from the decks at random. With each card selection, subjects either receive additional money and/or are asked to pay a penalty.

Unknown to the test subjects, the task is rigged so that two of the decks yield greater monetary rewards, yet require higher and more frequent penalties. So, the most beneficial strategy is to draw consistently from the deck yielding the lower immediate monetary reward, but ending in the higher net-gain. Whereas the control group quickly learn this strategy and apply it, subjects with prefrontal brain damage are unable to successfully learn the "moral" of the task.

The researchers have used this task to demonstrate the link between emotion and behavior by recording the Skin Conductance Responses (SCRs) of the test subjects during the process of executing the Gambling Task. The SCRs show that individuals in the control group develop a negative anticipatory response (or negative emotion) to the action of reaching for the "bad decks." These anticipatory responses quickly manifest in the control subjects as an unwillingness to draw from these decks.

An interesting fact is that, in the control group, the occurrence of the negative anticipatory response and the subsequent avoidance of the "bad decks" developed prior to the conscious awareness of the game's contingencies. Strawn and Brown note that these anticipatory SCRs "were being triggered in early stages of learning by mental calculations that were not yet available to conscious awareness. What is more, these preconscious negative emotional responses were modulating and controlling successful card choosing."[66]

---

65. Bechara et al., "Emotion," 295. There are a number of background assumptions concerning the hypothesis; however, for the purposes of the present work I will forgo a detailed discussion and simply refer to the work cited above.

66. Strawn and Brown, "Wesleyan Holiness," 124.

In contrast, subjects with frontal lobe damage did not show anticipatory autonomic responses—negative emotional reactions—and thus failed to maximize profit by continually drawing from the "bad decks." Researchers use these data to suggest that the capricious behavior of patients with frontal lobe dysfunction is attributed to their lack of ability to experience emotional prompts.[67]

This discussion is relevant to the present work because it supports the notion that life experiences cause individuals to develop "anticipatory evaluative autonomic responses" (somatic markers) that are bound to knowledge of the world. As with procedural knowledge and affect memories the actuation of somatic markers is largely a non-conscious event that "feels" like what one might refer to as "intuition" or "gut-feelings."

I suggest that a transformation of the tempers will involve a change of "intuition" as described by the Somatic Marker Hypothesis.

Automaticity

The process of *automaticity* applies the previously discussed concepts of procedural knowledge, affect memories, and somatic markers. The basic premise of automaticity is that a great deal of human behavior occurs "automatically" outside of conscious control (or at least conscious activation). In short, automaticity is understood as the *process* by which particular cognitive *content*, constituted by procedural knowledge, affective memories, and somatic markers, sets in motion certain *goal-directed* behavioral sequences.[68] While this idea is certainly not a novel one,[69] research has

67. See Bechara, "Role of emotion," 30–40; Bechara et al., "Deciding," 1293–95; Bechara et al., "Failure," 215–25; and Bechara et al., "Insensitivity," 7–15. See also Carter and Pasqualini, "Stronger," 901–11; and Tranel, "Emotion," 338–53.

68. Note that "goal-directed" does not imply a *conscious* goal. Francisco Ayala has cited three categories within the realm of biological phenomena where teleological explanations are pertinent. These are: (1) when the purpose or goal is consciously anticipated by the agent, (2) in self-regulating systems, and (3) when structures are anatomically and physiologically constituted to perform a certain function. Ayala asserts that the concept of "goal," together with a correlative concept of function, become essential for understanding causal processes. See Ayala, "Teleological Explanations," 46.

69. The Behaviorists claimed that free will is a mere delusion. Instead, our behavior is under the strict control of our particular environments and individual historical contexts. For a prominent work in this vein see Skinner, *Beyond Freedom and Dignity*. The account of automaticity that I am arguing for is understood as distinct from classical behaviorism in that it does allow for a mental life with determinative potential. This is exemplified by the *goal-directed* nature of automatic processes. That is, the environment is merely activating goals; the source of the *desire* for the goal remains internal—thus, we are not purely controlled by the environment.

continued in the cognitive sciences shedding light on the extent to which this premise is true.

Such research has shown that there are few phenomena that do not occur at least in part automatically. John A. Bargh and colleagues claim that "a person's affective reactions to another individual are often immediate and uncontrolled: attitudes toward social and non-social objects alike become active without conscious reflection or purpose within a quarter of a second after encountering the object. And the emotional content of facial expressions is picked up outside conscious awareness and intent to influence perceptions of the target individual."[70]

There is burgeoning evidence pointing to the fact that social behavior, in general, is based on automatically activated behavioral sequences.[71] While this research has not ruled out the involvement of conscious processes in behavior,[72] it continues to point to new ways which we can understand human *motivation*.

Bargh points out that an automatic process will involve some degree of the following four qualities: *intentionality, controllability, lack of awareness,* and *efficiency*.[73] Accordingly, an "automatic" process will be "*autonomous,* capable of operating by itself without any need for conscious guidance, *once put into motion*."[74] An important question then concerns what it is that puts an automatic process into motion. To address this inquiry, Bargh

70. Bargh, "Automaticity in Social Psychology," 169. Bargh continues that activities such as social stereotyping also become "automatic" responses initiated by the perception of particular features inherent to the target group (169–70).

71. For supporting research see Ferguson and Bargh, "How Social Perception," 33–39; Bargh et al., "Automated Will," 1014–27; Bargh and Ferguson, "Beyond Behaviorism," 925–45; Bargh and Chartrand, "Unbearable Automaticity of Being," 462–79; Bargh, "Automaticity of Everyday Life," 1–62; Bargh and Barndollar, "Automaticity in Action," 457–81; and Bargh, "Goal ≠ Intent," 248–51. For supporting data from Social Cognitive Neuroscience regarding the role of "implicit learning" in attitude change see Lieberman et al., "Do Amnesics," 135–40; and Lieberman, "Intuition," 109–36.

72. Augusto Blasi offers an interesting critique of automaticity and emotions in moral motivation. See Blasi, "Emotions," 1–19. In addition, Josh D. Greene and colleagues have classified moral decisions as involving the competing systems of "social-emotional" and "cognitive" ("cognitive" as defined above). Brain imaging and response times reveal the activation of different neurobiological systems depending on whether a moral judgment is "personal" or "impersonal." See Greene at al., "Neural Bases."

73. Bargh, "Automaticity in Social Psychology," 171–73. It was once believed that for a process to be considered "automatic" that it must be *unintentional, outside of awareness, uncontrollable,* and *efficient* (operates with a minimal level of cognitive attention or focus required). These qualities are now viewed as occurring along a continuum in any given cognitive process. In other words, it is not an all-or-nothing affair.

74. Ibid., 173.

emphasizes the *goal-dependent* nature of automaticity—that is, the *intention* that a process occur must be present, but once the process is set into motion it requires no conscious guidance.

It is important to understand that it is the *goal* in this case that is intentional not necessarily the initiation of the goal-directed process itself—Bargh contends that environmental perception can initiate goal-directed behavior unconsciously.

> [The] goal or intention itself—[the] complex strategy of interacting with the world—can be activated by or triggered by environmental stimuli. In other words, the environment can directly activate a goal, and this goal can then become operative and guide cognitive and behavioral processes within that environment, all without any need or role for conscious decision-making. Because there is no involvement of conscious processing at any point in the chain from the triggering environmental information to the enactment of goal-directed action, such a phenomenon can accurately be described as "unconsciously motivated" behavior. [75]

This could likely explain the intentional "feeling" of our personal behavior. That is, we presume that the majority of our behavior is intentional because our automatic procedures are, in large part, what we would have done had we performed the action as the result of "conscious" reflection.

The concept of automaticity, as the process of the initiation of goal-directed behavior, is critical to the current work. [76] If it is the case that most behavior occurs as the result of automaticity [77] and that the behavior itself is largely determined by previous learning (procedural knowledge, affective memories, somatic markers, etc.), then one's "goals" are critical to desired behavior.

To be clear, I am not suggesting that an individual cannot exert conscious control over his or her moral behavior. Such a "top-down" decision

75. Bargh, "Automaticity in Action," 462. See also "How Social perception can automatically influence behavior." It is important to note that my use of the term "goal" extends beyond basic physiological goals common to living organisms in general (nourishment, reproduction, etc.) to a concept of goal formation that is unique to human beings. These types of goals are established by MacKay's "meta-supervisory systems"—such as moral or ethical goals—in *Behind the Eye.*

76. For more on goal-directed behavior see Aarts and Dijksterhuis, "Habits," 53–63; Dweck, "Implicit Theories," 69–90; Klinger, "Emotional Influences," 168–89; and Ryan et al., "All Goals," 7–26.

77. Strawn and Brown suggest that five percent (or less) of our moment-to-moment behavior is consciously determined or regulated. See Strawn and Brown, "Wesleyan Holiness," 125.

is indeed possible and is no doubt an occurrence that most people would be familiar with; however, *the salient point here is that the type of "conversion" that I am addressing in this book involves a change of those cognitive states that predispose one to a particular socio-moral response.* This is in contrast to a rational deliberative process leading to an alternate course of action different from one's initial unconscious inclination.

Such a change in motivating structures requires the transformation of the *content* of automatic cognitive processes. This transformation occurs through the establishment of goals conforming to "desired behavior."[78] In short, I am suggesting that goals, in this sense, constitute *character.* Grigsby and Stevens comment that character

> consists of habits, to a large extent procedurally learned, in which people engage constantly, repeatedly, automatically, and nonconsciously. Character consists of those habitual behaviors that give people their own distinctive styles of being in the world. The foundations of character are acquired early in life but undergo change over time in association with experience and neurocognitive development. . . . Character, like psychological processes, is an emergent property of the brain's self-organizing activity. As such, expressions of character are actually the behavioral manifestations of the activation of neural networks with a high probability of activation. Thus, no matter how predictable a person's behavior, character is not a *thing*, but rather a set of processes that show variability in the probability of their expression from moment to moment.[79]

So then, to a great degree, automatic cognitive processes are constitutive of our character. Given this understanding, how then does a change in the *content* of automatic processes occur? I suggest that such a change occurs through *"goal-directed" practice*—that is, *not through cognitive understanding alone*. Practice involves purposeful repetition commensurate with the reorganization of frontal lobe systems active in planning, motor command and execution.[80]

---

78. I place "desired behavior" in scare quotes because I am not convinced that it is the individual's "desired behavior" *alone* that serves as the basis for a goal. For example, the "desired behavior" of the religious community is extended to the individual participant (via social interaction), and as such can be seen as a form of *control* or *desired causation*.

79. Grigsby and Stevens, *Neurodynamics of Personality*, 310–11. Recall that I have claimed that "habits" are (at least) constituted by procedural knowledge, affect memories, and somatic markers.

80. Rosenblatt speculates that practice "shifts declarative knowledge and memory to procedural. With many repetitions, the synaptic weightings of a neural net become more differentiated, since extraneous activities are not repeated as often as essential ones. Thus a

In an analysis of moral training, John Bickle concludes that

> Ethical training in a behavioral vacuum (other than speech pro-
> duction and comprehension) is likely not to have much effect on
> people's behavior. . . . Better to get people to *practice* planning
> and executing the specific motor sequences desired, rather than
> training them to construct more sophisticated moral narratives . . .
> One must perform the appropriate actions repeatedly to acquire
> the moral virtues. Theory and argument—narratives, both internal
> and verbally expressed—won't suffice. Our increased knowledge
> of the diverse neural mechanisms that underlie speech produc-
> tion and comprehension on one hand and planning and motor
> execution on the other puts us a step ahead of Aristotle[81] toward
> understanding why theory and arguments (narratives) are less ef-
> ficient for inculcating virtue than is practice (actually performing
> the planning and acting).[82]

Changes in synaptic communication between neurons play a key role in
learning and memory. The way that humans learn and retain knowledge
and experience is critical to moral formation and transformation. In
an analysis of the contributions of neuroscience to theories of learning,
Wickliffe C. Abraham notes that "the fact that both memory and synaptic plasticity remain changeable, even once apparently consolidated, casts
serious doubt on the idea that memory retention requires preservation of
a specific set of synaptic connection strengths. Instead, *continued bouts of
neural activity and synaptic plasticity long after learning may be necessary
to maintain information in dynamic networks.*"[83] This assessment supports
the notion that a life lived in accordance with a particular moral tradition
requires more than "beliefs" per se—continual acting upon these beliefs or
values is required.

In sum, I am suggesting that the philosophical views and empirical evidence that I have presented above is resonant with the notion of
religious conversion that I have proposed. That is, conversion (understood

---

synaptic 'groove' is worn in the net." Rosenblatt, "Insight," 203.

81. Aristotle claimed that humans could acquire virtue by doing just acts. See *Nicomachean Ethics*.

82. Bickle, "Empirical Evidence," 206 (emphasis added). Likewise, Herbert C. Kelman
suggests that significant attitude change always occurs in the context of action. See Kelman, "Role of Action," 117–94.

83. Abraham, "Memory Maintenance," 7. I recognize that the application of neuroscience to theories of learning is a relatively new endeavor which must be approached with
caution. For an account of some "neuromyths" regarding neuroscience and learning theory
see Hall, "Neuroscience and Education," 27–29.

as moral transformation) is a process involving normal human biological capacities and is characterized by a change in socio-moral attitude and behavior. Character, or the disposition to act in certain ways, is constituted (at least) by procedural knowledge, affect memories, and somatic markers. These cognitive features are constitutive of goals enacted through the unconscious process of automaticity.

To be clear, I am not ignorant of the discussion regarding the "eventedness" of conversion. I have simply chosen to focus on the process aspect of the phenomenon. There are works that focus on moral transformation as a crisis event.[84] In regards to this body of literature, I take issue with the idea of "quantum change" in that it generally ignores the tension between expectation and experience—that is to say that beneath one's testimony of crisis or instantaneous change there is a "narrative" involving various social networks that gave him or her the *language* to articulate the change.[85]

This point is also supported by Juarrero's description of system dynamics. A complex system *can* undergo an abrupt reorganization; however, the salient point is that it is a sudden reorganization of the *earlier state space*. That is, the reorganization can be understood as a synthesis of prior historical experiences and intentional states. Thus Juarrero states that these transformations are explainable only with a "retrospective narrative."[86]

Conceived in this way, "conversion" can be equated with Wesley's concept of "sanctification" and thus understood to require a transformation in the content of these automatic processes—such a transformation will manifest itself as a change in the underlying motivation for particular socio-moral attitudes and behavior. In essence, this is what Wesley would have meant by a "renewal of the tempers." What is needed now is a *particularly Christian* account of this change.

Conversion as Acquisition of Virtues

In this section, I will discuss the particularly Christian dimension of religious conversion. I will be describing how conversion can be understood as the transformation of the motivating concepts (tempers) that underlie socio-moral attitude and behavior. This transformation is characterized by the acquisition of virtues intrinsic to the Christian faith and facilitated

---

84. For an example see Miller and C'de Baca, *Quantum Change*.

85. For a helpful resource see Gallagher, *Expectation and Experience*. See also Stromberg, *Language and Self-Transformation*.

86. See Juarrero, *Dynamics in Action*, 9, 179–81.

through social interaction and participation in practices inherent to the Christian community.

In order to proceed, I must return to a concept discussed earlier in this chapter. I suggested that one of the cognitive components of moral cognition is a language-dependent *self-concept*. Here, I will further describe this notion of the "self" as being rooted in narratives. In this sense, I will speak of a *narrative self*.[87]

The basic premise underlying the concept of the "narrative self" is the conviction that narratives or stories are a necessary component to understand the self, social groups, and their histories. It follows that our sense of morality or *character* consists less of rules or principles and more as "collections of stories about human possibilities and paradigms for action."[88] These stories allow us to orient ourselves in the world by disclosing who we are, where we have been, and where we are going.[89]

Despite the "liberal" tendency to regard the self as being detached from societies and personal history,[90] I claim that a more adequate conception of the self "resides in the unity of a narrative which links birth to life to death as narrative beginning to middle to end."[91] In this sense, human

87. The concept of "narrative" is a principle component of a variety of academic inquiries. While each of these levels of investigation offers insight to the concept of a "narrative self," for the purposes of the present work, I have chosen to focus on a limited number of resources from virtue theory. Helpful examples from other areas include (from Narrative Psychology) Crossley, "Formulating Narrative Psychology," 287–300; "Narrative Psychology," 527–46; McAdams, "Psychology of Life Stories," 100–22; Vollmer, "Narrative Self," 189–205.

88. Nelson, *Narrative and Morality*, 9.

89. For an excellent account of how narrative (particularly religious narrative) forms the self see Hauerwas, *Peaceable Kingdom*. Hauerwas claims that all reason and religion is based on particular truth claims which are embodied in the narratives that shape various communities or traditions. In this sense, the Christian narrative must be embodied in the Church, if any one is ever to see that it is true. Thus, on an individual basis, becoming a Christian is in essence making the stories of Israel, Jesus and the Church our own. To do so is to make sense of our past, present and future.

90. I follow Hauerwas' objection on this issue. Hauerwas says that "one of the oddities of the contemporary situation is that what it means to be a person, to be free and/or autonomous, is to be capable of creating or 'choosing' our 'identity'. Thus, we do not think of ourselves as inheriting a family tradition or a group identity with which we must learn to live. Rather, our particular story is that we have no history and thus we can pick and choose among the many options offered by our culture." See Hauerwas, *Christian Existence Today*, 27. Hauerwas vehemently rejects this claim and asserts that humans are more fundamentally formed by stories that we did not create than those we have chosen.

91. MacIntyre, *After Virtue*, 205. I contend that MacIntyre offers the best account of the "narrative self" and his or her status as a moral agent; thus, I will return to frequently

actions are not isolated events independent of a person's intentions, beliefs, and historical context; rather, action flows from a position within particular narratives. The idea that particular actions derive their character from larger wholes is a necessary concept if we are to consider how life may be more than simply a sequence of individual actions. Alasdair MacIntyre claims that a "*narrative history* of a certain kind turns out to be the basic and essential genre for the characterization of human actions."[92]

A key concept of an individual's "narrative history" is his or her ability to be at least a "co-author" of their own narratives. MacIntyre comments that this history can be understood as an

> enacted dramatic narrative in which the characters are also the authors. The characters of course never start literally *ab initio*; they plunge *in medias res*, the beginnings of their story already made for them by what and who has gone before . . . The difference between imaginary characters and real ones is not in the narrative form of what they do; it is in the degree of their authorship of that form and of their own deeds. Of course just as they do not begin where they please, they cannot go on exactly as they please either; each character is constrained by the actions of others and by the social settings presupposed in his and their actions.[93]

Subsequently, the moral legitimacy of individual narrative authorship can only be evaluated in the context of a larger historical narrative. MacIntyre continues:

> Man is in his actions and practice, as well as in his fictions, essentially a story-telling animal. He is not essentially, but becomes through his history, a teller of stories that aspire to truth. But the key question for men is not about their own authorship; I can only answer the question, "What am I to do?" if I can answer the prior question, "Of what story or stories do I find myself a part?"[94]

This sentiment is echoed by cognitive psychologist John A. Teske. Teske speaks of the "social construction of the human spirit" as a way to talk about

---

return to his work.

92. Ibid., 208. Emphasis added.

93. Ibid., 215.

94. Ibid., 216. This claim reflects MacIntyre's central argument that the "Enlightenment project" of grounding morality within the individual limits of reason alone as failed miserably. He contends that the way out of this predicament is to return to the Aristotelian ethic of virtue with its particular teleological character. A key aspect of this renewal is found in MacIntyre's treatment of narrative (although the concept of narrative is not explicit in Aristotle's work).

the interdependent emergence of individual minds. He claims that "any integrity that we have as spiritual beings is likely also to be an achievement contingent upon the character of our relationships with other persons, and our memberships in larger communities."[95] In this sense, if human lives are historically developed constructions, it is possible to realize the transformation of these lives in various ways by recognizing relevant social interdependencies as a key source of human behavior.

Building on John Searle's "constitutive rules," Teske suggests a mode of social construction based on events viewed by psychologists to be intrinsic or "natural" properties of individuals.[96] These events include characteristics of the human mental life which may be locatable as much in structure and operation as in content. This means that they can only exist socially—*between* persons rather than *inside* persons.

The salient point here is that I reject any notion of the human person that takes the "self" to be an isolated moral automaton. The concept of the "narrative self" suggested by MacIntyre and Teske does justice to the embodied view of human nature that I have espoused throughout this work. We are persons only in so far as we exist as narrative selves in complex social networks with other persons (as narrative selves). Likewise, our *character* is formed (*or transformed*) through shared narratives set within a historical framework.[97]

Additional support for intimate connectedness between character, narrative and learning can be found in the field of philosophy of education. Peter Kemp claims that "the process of formation and education, the object of philosophy of education, is in an of itself an art. . . . This art requires a talent that comes out in praxis and which is learned in praxis, as it is modelled in Plato's Socrates and Aristotle's 'wise man'."[98] Kemp uses

95. Teske, "Social Construction," 189. By "human spirit" Teske is referring to "that aspect of human mental life by which we can apprehend meanings and purposes extending beyond our individual lives." See 190.

96. Searle's "constitutive rules" create new forms of behavior or "institutional facts" which would not exist without the rules (e.g. mating would exist based solely on biological drive, but marriage would not exist without relevant constitutive rules). These "institutional facts" cannot be defined in terms of any particular physio-chemical description; however, they are ontologically subjective in that they are (language dependent) facts only relative to the intentionality of agents. See Searle, *Construction of Social Reality*.

97. The relevance of this dimension—character formation or "transformation"—to the present work cannot be over emphasized.

98. Kemp, "Mimesis," 171.

the concept of philosophical hermeneutics to help illuminate the place of *mimesis* (creative imitation) in education.[99]

The concept of mimesis plays an important role in various strands of pedagogical theory, particularly as it relates to the teacher-student relationship. From this context, Paul Ricoeur's theories of storytelling and narrative language have crucial significance. The key point of his work in this area is that through the process of narrative[100] humans mimetically appropriate educational content, thus shedding light on one's life story and his or her place within a larger narrative.[101] Ricoeur describes the relation between the following three moments of an individual's formation:

1. We are already formed—there is a *pre-figuration* of action and consciousness.

2. We form narratives (plots and stories) and theories—a *con-figuration* of the language and discourse.

3. We form and teach ourselves the moment we appropriate stories and ideas—which is a *re-figuration*. This is the actual *mimesis*, the creative representation (the putting forth) of a "hermeneutic identity."[102]

The *pre-figuration* stage refers to the pre-understanding of life in its practical aspects. Humans are predisposed to certain linguistic capabilities that allow them to interpret various occurrences in life including abstract notions such as meaning and values. Such an ability renders one able to construe time in general—that is, the relation of past, present and future.

The *con-figuration* aspect of narrative expresses the reason or theme of a story as one has followed the entire plot, recalled and retold the story.

99. The idea of "mimesis" formally originates with Aristotle. He defines art (*epos*) as mimesis (creative imitation) and tragedy as that particular mimesis that cultivates personal fear and compassion for others. Aristotle develops this idea in his *Poetics*, see especially Halliwell, *Aristotle's Poetics*, 109–37. The concept of "mimesis" has a great degree of resonance with the scientific study of imitation. While I will not explore this area of research in the present work, it should be noted that a wide array of evidence spanning the disciplines of developmental psychology and cognitive neuroscience show that imitation based on mirrored neural activity ("mirror neurons") and reciprocal interpersonal behavior act to scaffold human development throughout the lifespan. For a helpful resource see Hurley and Chater, *Perspectives on Imitation*.

100. For Ricoeur, narrative refers to a linguistic course of events from beginning to end.

101. See Ricoeur, *Time and Narrative*.

102. These points are derived from Ricoeur's *Time and Narrative* and summarized by Kemp. See "Mimesis," 175.

This stage involves extracting a coherent course of events out of a multitude of occurrences and then combining these into a single coherent plot (the *telos* of the narrative).

The final or *re-figuration* stage completes the mimetic process by asserting that educational content (a text, etc.) is not learned until it is experienced as narrative by appropriating the story in one's own context. Kemp asserts that "something happens to us as we follow the story line. We become 'new persons.' This is the *re-figuration* of our lives."[103] In this sense, narratives reconstruct the world of personal and corporate action. Kemp comments further that "there is no individual formation without a tradition of ideas that the individual inherits, and that there is no individual formation without a cultural community wherein the individual resides."[104]

Using Ricoeur's language, learning is the process of character formation through the concept of narrative. Such a concept of learning and narrative is helpful to the development of ideas central to the present work and our discussion of conversion and virtues. If, as I have suggested, Christian conversion is best understood as the acquisition of *virtues* intrinsic to the Christian faith, then I must articulate what is meant by "virtues" and their connection to a "narrative self." MacIntyre's argument in *After Virtue* settles on the notion that a return to an Aristotelian ethic of virtue requires the concept of a "narrative self."

MacIntyre observes that in ancient cultures the primary means of moral education was through the telling of stories—morality was not something distinct from social structures. Those in ancient cultures recognized that "human life has a determinative form, the form of a certain kind of story. It is not just that poems and sagas narrate what happens to men and women, but that in their narrative form poems and sagas capture a form that was already present in the lives which they relate."[105] In this sense, *narratives and human character are constitutive of one another.*

MacIntyre asserts that virtues are understood only within the context of particular narratives[106] and types of *practices*. He defines a practice as

> any coherent and complex form of socially established cooperative
> human activity through which goods internal to that form of ac-

103. Ibid., 176.

104. Ibid., 176–77.

105. MacIntyre, *After Virtue*, 124.

106. "Every particular view of the virtues is linked to some particular notion of the narrative structure or structures of human life." Ibid., 174.

tivity are realised in the course of trying to achieve those standards of excellence which are appropriate to, and practically definitive of, that form of activity, with the result that human powers to achieve excellence, and human conceptions of the ends and goods involved, are systematically extended.[107]

Practices provide the context in which virtues can be understood. MacIntyre proposes that a *virtue* be defined as "an acquired human quality the possession and exercise of which tends to enable us to achieve those goods which are internal to practices and the lack of which effectively prevents us from achieving any such goods."[108]

Here, virtues serve as the *intentional* content of practices which in turn constitute cooperative forms of human inter-relational activity. In other words, virtues can be seen as the *motivational* force (or skill) behind practices particular to a given *tradition*. The concept of tradition is also critical to MacIntyre's account of a social being (or moral agent). The story of one's life (self-identity) is inextricably embedded in a community of collective stories held together by a common understanding—or narrative tradition. MacIntyre claims that

> A living tradition is then an historically extended, socially embodied argument, and an argument precisely in part about the goods which constitute that tradition. . . . Hence the individual's search for his or her good is generally and characteristically conducted within a context defined by those traditions of which the individual's life is a part, and this is true both of those goods which are internal to practices and the goods of a single life. . . . The narrative phenomenon of embedding is crucial. . . . The history of each of our lives is generally and characteristically embedded in and made intelligible in terms of the larger and longer histories of a number of traditions.[109]

107. Ibid., 187. It is important to note that practices themselves require moral evaluation based on their contribution to the *telos* of human existence. That is, in terms of a moral theory, any practical "ought" is to be evaluated in light of the ultimate end to which all virtuous action is to achieve. Murphy says that "the original form of an ethical claim (implicitly, at least) is, 'if you are to achieve your *telos*, then you ought to do (or be) *x*.' This sort of ethical claim can be straightforwardly true or false; the 'ought' is no more mysterious than the 'ought' in 'a watch ought to keep good time.' Furthermore, it can and in fact *must* be derived from certain sorts of 'is' statements: about the nature of ultimate reality, about regularities in human life regarding the achievement of ends as a result of adopting certain means. . . . " See Murphy, "Supervenience," 485.

108. MacIntyre, *After Virtue*, 191.

109. Ibid., 222. MacIntyre further describes a tradition as "an argument extended through time in which certain fundamental agreements are defined and redefined in terms

Only when we know the narrative traditions of which we are part can we know what we are to do. Morality "embodies practices, and practices require virtues and intentions—in brief, the development of human character—that can only appear in lives displaying a narrative coherence."[110]

I suggest that the Christian community embodies a "narrative tradition" in so far as it satisfies the description offered above by MacIntyre. That is, Christianity is a "historically extended, socially embodied argument" whose existence implies that a distinction cannot be made between communal beliefs and practices.[111] These practices require virtues intrinsic to the Christian faith—that is, they require that an individual be a particular "kind of person" characterized by these virtues that are subsequently enacted within the context of a particularly Christian way of relating.

So then, in order to justify my claim that conversion is best understood as the acquisition of virtues intrinsic to the Christian faith, I will attempt to place the concept of virtues within the larger discussion of this chapter. I do so by clarifying the nature of virtues themselves.

I have shown that much of socio-moral attitude and behavior can be considered intuitive and occurring automatically, particularly in regards to underlying motivations and inclinations (tempers). The entire realm of socio-moral functioning is dependent upon (constrained by) our biology. In this sense, the formation or transformation of socio-moral attitude and behavior should be seen as a process likened to learning or skill acquisition. In their commentary on *Intuitive Ethics*, Jonathan Haidt and Craig Joseph state that

> Virtues are social skills. To possess a virtue is to have disciplined one's faculties so they are fully and properly responsive to one's local sociomoral context. To be kind, for example, is to have a perceptual sensitivity to certain features of situations, including those having to do with the well-being of others, and to be sensitive such that those features have an appropriate impact on one's motivations and other responses. . . . Virtues, on this understanding, are

---

of two kinds of conflict: those with critics and enemies external to the tradition . . . and those internal, interpretive debates through which the meaning and rationale of the fundamental agreements come to be expressed and by whose progress a tradition is constituted." See MacIntyre, *Whose Justice?*, 12. In Christianity, scripture represents the communally recognized set of "fundamental agreements."

110. McClendon, *Ethics*, 171.

111. L. Gregory Jones' analysis of moral judgment resonates with this claim. He states that moral judgment "is an activity through which people give form not only to actions but also to themselves. It is when human life is construed narratively that the inextricable interrelation between acts and agency becomes clear." See Jones, *Transformed Judgment*, 21.

closely connected to the intuitive system. A virtuous person is one who has the proper *automatic* reactions to ethically relevant events and states of affairs.[112]

So then, it can be said that a virtue (or virtuous behavior) supervenes on a particular human biological or psychological (depending on the level of analysis) characteristic (or event). Recall that MacIntyre defines a virtue as an *acquired* human quality, thus it follows that virtues are not genetically determined traits; rather, they should be seen as habitually cultivated behavioral states based on genetically produced biological propensities.

In this case, *acquiring* a virtue refers to a complex process involving the re-interpretation of particular biological propensities in relation to a specific *tradition-dependent* purpose or *telos*. In order to clarify this claim, I will offer a practical example involving the experience of empathy or compassion.

Before proceeding to this example, I pause for a brief summary. I am suggesting that one's narrative self is formed by the stories of which he or she is a part, and likewise, *transformed* through acquisition of virtues intrinsic to a particular tradition, in the present case, the Christian tradition. This transformation occurs through social interaction and participation in *practices* inherent to the Christian community. Practices are therefore crucial for the activity of moral judgment and action. MacIntyre states it this way:

> The general form of the thesis which I have defended is that genuinely human consciousness is such that our abilities to reflect upon and thus to be knowledgably conscious of our inner lives—insofar as those inner lives are a matter of intending, doing, having reasons for action and believing—depends upon our abilities to interact socially with others within practices and to understand what they impute to us. We learn to recognize what is true about ourselves in this area and we learn to describe ourselves only as others recognize and describe us and we learn to recognize and describe those others precisely as beings capable of recognizing and describing us in the way that they do.[113]

In this vein, Stanley Hauerwas speaks of conversion itself as the acquisition of practices. He likens the process of Christian discipleship to

112. Haidt, "Intuitive Ethics," 61 (emphasis added). Likewise, Jones argues that people "*learn* to acquire and exercise the virtues ingredient in making wise decisions. Such learning occurs in and through social contexts of particular linguistic communities." See Jones, *Transformed Judgment*, 2.

113. MacIntyre, "Intelligibility of Action," 77–78.

the learning of a craft where "Christian education is not what happens in Sunday school. Rather, what is crucial for Christian formation is to have people engaged in activities through which they learn habits that shape them *before they can name what the shaping is about.*"[114]

Just as in MacIntyre's account, Hauerwas affirms the critical role that narrative plays in the formation of self-identity. He states that "A narrative must not only provide an intelligible pattern that links the contingent events of our lives; it must also provide us a way to go. A story of who we are must give us the power to make our actions consistent with our identity—it must, so to speak, shape the world."[115]

Simply stated, *becoming* a Christian is the process of "naturalization" into a narrative tradition which has been (and is being) shaped by the story of Jesus.[116] This "becoming" constitutes the process of Christian religious conversion. The transformation requires an acquisition of *Christian* virtues which necessarily involve the *learning* of skills and language particular to the Christian narrative tradition.[117] The importance of the relationship between conversion and language acquisition cannot be overstated. To fully

114. Hauerwas and Willimon, *Where Resident Aliens Live*, 82 (emphasis added). Hauerwas claims that, "The Enlightenment tried to show that the mind was immediately appropriate to a factual world without training. In contrast, our minds are adequate to that which we come to know only by being formed by the skills and practices of a tradition. Such training, or course, not only transforms us but transforms what it is that we think we need to know." See also Hauerwas, *After Christendom*, 105. It is worth noting here the resonance between Hauerwas' account of conversion and the research that I have discussed from cognitive science. The establishment of cognitive features (procedural knowledge, affect memories, and somatic markers) that are expressed unconsciously through the process of automaticity supports the notion of habits that shape us "before we can name what the shaping is about."

115. Hauerwas, *Christian Existence Today*, 31. This idea of self-identity being shaped by narrative or goal structures is discussed, from a psychological point of view, at length by Robert A. Emmons. See Emmons, *Psychology of Ultimate Concerns*. Emmon's work is based on the concept of "ultimate concern" offered by twentieth-century theologian Paul Tillich. Tillich claimed that religion itself "is the state of being grasped by an ultimate concern, a concern which qualifies all other concerns as preliminary and which itself contains the answer to the question of the meaning of our life." See Tillich, *Christianity and the Encounter of World Religions*, 4.

116. I borrow the "naturalization" metaphor from Brad J. Kallenberg. See Kallenberg, "Conversion Converted," 335–64. See also Kallenberg, *Live to Tell*, 38–42.

117 Alasdair MacIntyre claims that any attempt to enter a narrative tradition other than ones own requires the acquisition of a "second first language." See MacIntyre, *Whose Justice?*, 374–88. Such a consideration of language also requires insights offered by Ludwig Wittgenstein. For an analysis of Wittgenstein's work relevant to the current topic see Kallenberg, *Ethics as Grammar*, and Kerr, *Theology After Wittgenstein*.

explicate this issue would require a volume within itself; however, at this juncture, it is appropriate to point out some points relative to the present discussion.

George A. Lindbeck has delivered a seminal work regarding language and religious experience.[118] Lindbeck stresses the importance of cultural-linguistic forms in the shaping of human experience. In this paradigm, religion is not simply an array of beliefs or symbols that express inner attitudes or sentiments. Rather religion is a cultural-linguistic system that makes possible the descriptions of realities—including the formulation of beliefs and the ability to experience attitudes and feelings characteristic of the religious tradition. Lindbeck claims that just as a language is cor-related with a particular form of life (having both cognitive and behavioral dimensions), so it is also in the case of a religious tradition—"Its doctrines, cosmic stories or myths, and ethical directives are integrally related to the rituals it practices, the sentiments or experiences it evokes, the actions it recommends, and the institutional form it develops."[119]

The key feature of Lindbeck's proposal is that the inner-outer distinc-tion of religious experience is switched from the traditional understanding (as supposed in an experiential-expressive model of religious experience).[120] In his case, inner religious experiences are derived from external features embodied within a particular religious tradition rather than vice versa. If this is the case, "there are numberless thoughts we cannot think, senti-ments we cannot have, and realities we cannot perceive unless we learn to use the appropriate symbol systems."[121]

118. Lindbeck defines religions as "comprehensive interpretive schemes, usually em-bodied in myths or narratives and heavily ritualized, which structure human experience and understanding of self and world. . . . A religion can be viewed as a kind of cultural and/or linguistic framework or medium that shapes the entirety of life and thought." See Lindbeck, *Nature of Doctrine*, 32–33.

119. Ibid., 33.

120. Lindbeck is critical of the philosophical tradition stemming from Schleiermacher (ibid., 20–21). He offers Bernard Lonergan as the token representative of the experien-tial-expressive model. Lonergan summarizes his theory of religion through theses that are characteristic of experiential-expressivism in general. These are 1) Different religions are diverse expressions or objectifications of a common core experience. It is this experience which identifies them as religions; 2) The experience, while conscious, may be unknown on the level of self-conscious reflection; 3) It is present in all human beings; and 4) In most religions, the experience is the source and norm of objectifications: it is by reference to the experience that their adequacy or lack of adequacy is to be judged. See Lonergan, *Method in Theology*, 101–24.

121. Lindbeck, *Nature of Doctrine*, 34. This claim is based on Ludwig Wittgenstein's contention that private languages are logically impossible. For a helpful summary see

Thus, a religion is above all an *external* reality that shapes one's identity rather than an expression of the pre-existing self or one's pre-conceptual experiences. So then, Lindbeck asserts that

> To become religious involves becoming skilled in the language, the symbol system of a given religion. To become Christian involves learning the story of Israel and Jesus well enough to interpret and experience oneself and one's world in its terms. . . . To become religious—no less than to become culturally or linguistically competent—is to interiorize a set of skills by practice and training. One learns how to feel, act, and think in conformity with a religious tradition that is, in its inner structure, far richer and more subtle than can be explicitly articulated. The primary knowledge is not *about* the religion, nor *that* the religion teaches such and such, but rather *how* to be religious in such and such ways. . . . In short, it is necessary to have the means for expressing an experience in order to have it, and the richer our expressive or linguistic system, the more subtle, varied, and differentiated can be our experience.[122]

This point is echoed in Murphy's exposition on soul and body and its effect on how we perceive spirituality. Murphy states that

> The traditional notion of spirituality has assumed that the inner encounter with God is the *source* of the external forms of religious observance. . . . Instead we need to recognize the ways in which language (which is necessarily public) and other social practices provide the individual with the resources for private, inner experience. . . . To put it quite simply, the lone individual might indeed have an experience of God, but without any theological language would have no way of *knowing* what the experience was. The more linguistic resources and expectations provided by one's tradition the more nuanced one's experiences will be.[123]

The role of social context and language acquisition in the transformation process cannot be overstated. *All of this amounts to a transformation of character that supervenes on a complex series of biological changes.*[124]

Fogelin, *Wittgenstein*, 153–71.

122. Ibid., 34–37. It should be obvious that this view stands in direct contrast with the evangelical conversion methods cited it chapter one. In that case, one *becomes* Christian solely by intellectual assent—by *believing* this or that—not by being transformed within the context of a particularly Christian cultural-linguistic community.

123. Murphy, *Bodies and Souls*, 33.

124. For an interesting discussion of the relation between character formation and biological change see Harak, *Virtuous Passions*. Harak proposes that the practice of virtu-

Recall that a key feature of Wesley's theological anthropology was his assertion that human identity is ineluctably nested in a network of social relationships. As such, a change in socio-moral attitude and behavior—a transformation of self-identity or character—must occur within a social context.[125]

It is clear from Wesley's writing that he affirmed both the transcendent and immanent *means* through which God's grace interacted with creation. That is, while he typically equated the work of God with the movement of the Holy Spirit, he firmly believed that grace was relationally mediated.[126] Maddox emphasizes the ways in which Wesley's holistic anthropology informed his advice to the Methodists. He states that

> [Wesley's] recommendations to his followers interwove both means that present rational enlightenment or challenge and means designed to nurture our affective openness and responsiveness to God's loving Presence. Reflecting his appreciation for the variety of ways in which God's love is mediated, including particularly its mediation through other persons, *Wesley made communal means*

---

ous behavior actually alters biological systems making the recurrence of the same behavior more susceptible to automaticity. He asserts that after prolonged interpersonal interaction "we become physically disposed toward continuance of that interaction, because that interaction has, for better or for worse, reconfigured our bodies. . . . Prolonged interaction with a specific other gives a kind of integrating order to the self" (17).

125. This accusation has earned multidisciplinary support. For instance, from the area of educational psychology, Ronald Lee Zigler has offered an interesting account of "moral impulses." He concludes that one's social environment plays a crucial role in the development of morality in that these experiences "shape the brain's emotional dispositions *from which future actions will stem*." See Zigler, "Formation," 456 (emphasis added). In addition, development psychologists have long had interest in the development and cultivation of moral behavior. The work of William Damon is of particular interest to the present discussion. He describes a change in socio-moral attitude and behavior as "goal transformation through social influence." These are the type of goals that are established within the context of a particular "narrative tradition" and can change throughout the lifespan. Damon asserts that "This process—*the transformation of goals through social influence*—is the foundation of moral development throughout the lifespan. This process results in a building of commitments toward justice, caring, truthfulness, and other concerns of rights, responsibility, and benevolence." See Damon, "Lifelong Transformation," 202. See also Damon and Colby, "Social Influence," 3–19.

126. This is particularly evident in his *mature* view of the "way salvation." For a helpful discussion of this issue see Leffel, "Prevenient Grace," 130–39. Also see Strawn and Leffel, "John Wesley's orthokardia," 351–59. Strawn and Leffel state that "Wesley held that contrary dispositions of the heart might be transformed and a loving *temper* of heart might be developed in an interactive human community of character formation" (354).

of grace central to his movement, rejecting the solitary search for holiness.[127]

So this concept of the *means of grace* was critical to Wesley's view of Christian development. In addition to the Eucharist, prayer, corporate worship, etc. Wesley stressed the importance of interrelational discipleship. As the result of Wesley's conviction that genuine Christian faith could only be developed and sustained in a communal context, he established an organizational structure to provide such nurture—these were known as societies, classes, and bands.[128]

The salient point is that there are a bounty of resources from both theology and scientific disciplines supporting the claim that significant socio-moral transformation (conversion in my terms) occurs within the context of social interaction.[129] A particularly Christian conversion occurs within the specific context of the Christian tradition. This claim strikes at the heart of the claim that one can "become Christian" in isolation or in any single moment of time. Instead, what is required in order to become Christian is a process of holistic change that affects those aspects of an individual's life that constitutes his or her *character*.

As I have claimed, and will expound upon further in a subsequent section, this process occurs as the result of cooperation between divine grace and human participation. So, having claimed that conversion is best understood as a socially mediated process of virtue acquisition, I will now turn to the task of offering a practical example of what it means to "acquire a virtue."

Conversion and Empathetic Response

I have proposed that the acquisition of a virtue refers to a complex process involving the re-interpretation of particular biological propensities in relation to a specific *tradition-dependent* purpose or *telos*. The basic presupposition behind this statement is that virtues *supervene* on psychological

127. Maddox, "Reconnecting the Means to the End," 41. Emphasis added.

128. There is an abundance of literature regarding Wesley's "small groups." For a few helpful examples see Henderson, *John Wesley's Class Meeting*; Runyon, *New Creation*, 114–28; and Watson, *Early Methodist Class Meeting*.

129. Further support for this claim can be seen in Bargh's work on automaticity. Bargh and Williams note that "close relationships" play a key role in automatic behavior. This is due to the context in which goals are pursued and the high frequency of interaction that one has with environmental forces that act as triggers for goal directed behavior. Thus, "significant others in one's life are likely to become external triggers of nonconscious goal pursuits." See Bargh and Williams, "Automaticity of Social Life," 2.

traits which are constituted by genetically produced capacities. While the process of conversion involves a multitude of biological and psychological changes, I will offer a single example in order to clarify my position.

Not only is empathy[130] the most studied of the moral emotions, but some consider it the foundation of morality itself.[131] I claim that the cultivation of empathetic response is a key feature of socio-moral transformation, here referred to as "conversion." In what follows, I intend to show how the Christian community, understood as a narrative tradition, acts to "re-interpret" empathetic reactions as "feelings" of *compassion*—a Christian virtue.[132]

It is important to stress that I am not claming that empathy, in and of itself, is a virtue; rather, I submit that empathy be considered as a genetically produced *capacity*. There is multidisciplinary evidence to support this claim. For instance, there is extensive research showing that children develop emotional reactions to the suffering of others very early in life.[133] In addition, evolutionary biologists have shown empathetic behavior to exist in non-human primates as well.[134] These findings suggest that empathy is a *biologically innate* capacity.[135]

From the area of developmental psychology, Martin L. Hoffman asserts that

> The brain structures required for affective involvement with objects
> in the external world, including people, were apparently present

130. Defining "empathy" is indeed an ongoing struggle. The term *einfühlung* (perhaps best understood as "sympathy") was translated as "empathy" by American psychologist Edward Titchener. For more see Gustav, "Theodor Lipps," 151–63; and Wispé, "History," 17–37. Following Nancy Eisenberg et al., I will assume empathy to be "an emotional response that stems from another's emotional state or condition and is congruent with the other's emotional state or condition." See Eisenberg et al., "Empathy-related responding and cognition," 65.

131. Writers such as Adam Smith, David Hume, and Jean Piaget have identified empathy (or "sympathy" as they used the term) as the root of morality. For a helpful discussion see Haidt, "Moral Emotions," 852–70. Haidt defines a "moral emotion" as "those emotions that are linked to the interests or welfare either of society as a whole or at least of persons other than the judge or agent" (854).

132. Of course, I am not claiming that compassion is an exclusively "Christian" virtue, only that it is central to the Christian way of relating.

133. For an example of such research see Harris, *Children and Emotion*.

134. See de Waal, *Good Natured*.

135. Goodenough and Deacon have suggested that empathy is an "inherited pro-social capacity." See Goodenough and Deacon, "From Biology to Consciousness to Morality." See also Goodenough, "Religious Naturalism," 101–9; and Goodenough and Woodruff, "Mindful Virtue," 585–95.

early in man's evolution. The more recent addition of newer brain structures along with the acquisition of connective neural circuits have made it possible for such affect to be experienced in conjunction with a cognitive, increasingly sophisticated social awareness or insight into others—and all of this appears to be independent of the neural base for egoistic, self-preserving behavior. In brief, the neural basis for a primitive empathy was apparently present in early man's evolution.[136]

This claim is further strengthened by research offered from the neurosciences. In *A Biological Perspective on Empathy*, Leslie Brothers states that

> Evidence from comparative primatological studies suggests that sophisticated social communication is a hallmark of primate evolution. When taken to subsume somatic—including neural—events, empathetic processes are found to be analyzable in terms of brain activity. . . . In the absence of organic disease or social deprivation, primitive response systems become elaborated into mature social communication, by processes as yet incompletely understood.[137]

All of this points to the fact that, barring neurological disorder, empathic experience is indeed a biologically innate capacity. In this sense, empathy should be understood as an *emotion*, that is, it is an *unlearned*[138] response to particular objects or events external or internal to the one perceiving the stimuli. In order to proceed, I will offer a formal definition of an "emotion." I do so because I claim that there is a relevant distinction between an emotion—as an unlearned biological reaction—and the *felt* experience of an emotion and the role this *feeling* plays in subsequent moral behavior.[139]

136. Hoffman, "Developmental Synthesis," 610. See also Hoffman, "Empathy," 275–301.

137. Brothers, "Biological Perspective," 17. In relation to Brother's work on empathy, Vittorio Gallese has offered a helpful discussion of *mirror neurons* and their role in empathy. See Gallese, "'Shared Manifold' Hypothesis," 33–50. The role of "mirror neurons" in moral development is a burgeoning area of research. See Dobbs, "Revealing Reflection," 22–27. There are also numerous works that demonstrate the neural correlates of empathetic experience. For helpful examples see Decety, and Chaminade, "Neural Correlates," 127–38; Eslinger, "Neurological," 193–99; Jackson et al., "How do we perceive," 771–79; Shamay-Tsoory et al., "Characterization of Empathy Deficits," 324–37; and T. Singer et al., "Empathy," 1157–62.

138. By "unlearned," I am implying that emotions are the product of an evolutionary process and are thus genetically inherited capacities.

139. Research indicates that empathetic reactions contribute to "prosocial behavior."

I am aware that defining an "emotion" is one of the most perilous tasks in psychological science.[140] Going forward, I will adopt the description of emotion offered by Antonio Damasio. He offers the following five point definition of emotion:[141]

1. An emotion-proper, such as happiness, sadness, embarrassment, or sympathy, is a complex collection of chemical and neural responses forming a distinctive pattern.

2. The responses are produced by the normal brain when it detects an emotionally competent stimulus (an ECS), the object or event whose presence, actual or in mental recall, triggers the emotion. The responses are automatic.

3. The brain is prepared by evolution to respond to certain ECSs with specific repertoires of action. However, the list of ECSs is not confined to those prescribed by evolution. *It includes many others learned in a lifetime of experience.*[142]

4. The immediate result of these responses is a temporary change in the state of the body proper, and in the state of the brain structures that map the body and support thinking.

5. The ultimate result of the responses, directly or indirectly, is the placement of the organism in circumstances conducive to survival and well-being.[143]

In contrast to this understanding of emotions, Damasio defines a *feeling* as "the perception of a certain state of the body along with the perception of a certain mode of thinking and of thoughts with certain themes."[144] That is, a "feeling" is a mental representation of an "emotion." This "mental representation" is constituted by myriad neural states which

---

For examples of such research see Batson et al., "Adults' Emotional Reactions," 163–84; N. Eisenberg et al., "Affect and Prosocial Responding," 787–803; Hoffman, "Contribution of Empathy," 647–80; "Empathy," 65–85; and "Interaction," 103–31.

140. Keith Oatley and Jennifer M. Jenkins comment that the heterogeneous nature of the literature on emotions makes it difficult to make sense of the data let alone establish a universal definition. See Oatley and Jenkins, *Understanding Emotions*, 33.

141. Damasio, *Looking for Spinoza*, 53.

142. Emphasis added. This last point resonates with the research that I have presented involving procedural knowledge, somatic markers, etc.

143. I would extend this last point to include the placement of the organism in circumstances that predispose it (him or her) to a particular socio-moral action.

144. Damasio, *Looking for Spinoza*, 86.

not only include various chemical and musculoskeletal reactions, but by the *content* of automatic cognitive processes.

I submit that a feeling includes a particular attitudinal and behavioral predisposition. In the case of empathy, an individual experiencing an empathic reaction to certain stimuli will interpret the reaction (in a largely nonconscious fashion) in a particular way thus leading to a specific behavioral response. *Note, at this juncture, that an empathic reaction is not a candidate for a virtue; however, an acquired predisposition to act in a certain way based on empathetic arousal can be considered a virtue.* I suggest that this acquired predisposition, or virtue, is best understood as *compassion.* In short, compassion can be said to supervene on the biological state of affairs referred to as an empathetic emotional reaction.

With this understanding, I offer the following claim: The Christian community acts as the social context for the acquisition of the virtue of compassion by re-interpreting empathetic responses in such a way that these experiences are felt as compassion and likewise manifested as moral action. The "practice" of such moral behavior reinforces the content of our automatic cognitive processes, thus yielding a transformation of character—"conversion."

If one interprets automatic emotional responses in a particular way, thus leading to a specific action (say an action characterized by compassion), and this process is repeated then one becomes the "type of person" that is characterized by those actions—this is true because the actions become more automatic as new procedural knowledge is established and reinforced by continued social interaction and physical repetition. The view of human nature that I have espoused throughout this book makes it highly unlikely that such changes could occur apart from one's naturalization into a narrative tradition characterized by practices that reinforce such behavior.

In his analysis of the Christian moral life, Charles M. Shelton recognizes a similar need for the transformation of empathetic experience. He states that "It is this transformation of our empathetic development that molds and shapes a response to the call of Jesus to 'come and follow me' (Mark 10:21)."[145] Shelton continues by offering the following definition of a particularly *Christian* empathy:

> Christian empathy is defined as the human capacity, transformed by grace, that leads to experiencing to some degree on an affective level another's situation; meaning is given to this experiencing

145. Shelton, *Morality of the Heart*, 102.

through a personal relationship with Jesus Christ, thus motivating one to offer willingly his or her gifts, nurtured in a believing community of faith, for the building of God's Reign.[146]

This particularly Christian experience then leads to the formation of "social compassion." Shelton continues:

> It is this empathic arousal, nurtured by modelling and supportive community environments that articulate valued stances, that offers the optimum strategy for fostering social compassion. Moreover, it is precisely this empathic component of a social compassion orientation that enables one to respond to the question, "Lord when did we see you hungry and feed you or see you thirsty and give you drink?" (Matthew 25:37). It is an empathic response, nurtured in a relationship with Jesus and one's Christian community, that provides the capacity to respond to the very hunger and thirst so necessary for building God's Reign here and now.[147]

This development and cultivation of social compassion is precisely the type of transformation of socio-moral attitude and behavior that characterizes the process of religious conversion.

In summary, I have suggested that all "normal functioning" human beings possess an innate capacity for the emotional response we label "empathy." I have proposed that compassion supervenes on empathetic responses and as such can be considered a virtue. The *acquisition* of the virtue of compassion necessarily occurs within the context of a narrative tradition (Christianity in the present case) whose very existence is marked by practices that embody the telos of the tradition.

No doubt, some may argue that this description of conversion is completely sociological in nature and lacks the need for any metaphysical or religious explanation. While I do concede that the sociological dimension of conversion is a necessary consideration, I nevertheless claim that the conversion process should be viewed as the co-operant result of divine grace and human participation.

Conversion as Co-operant Grace

United Methodists understand prevenient grace to be "the divine love that surrounds all humanity and precedes any and all of our conscious impulses. This grace prompts our first wish to please God, our first glim-

---

146. Ibid., 107.
147. Ibid., 115.

mer of understanding concerning God's will, and our 'first slight transient conviction' of having sinned against God. God's grace also awakens in us an earnest longing for deliverance from sin and death and moves us toward repentance and faith."[148]

This image of God's *action* in the world is a critical component of Christian theology. In this section, I will address the following question: While fully acknowledging the presence of God's grace (as defined above) in human affairs, how can this divine presence be understood to *act*—have determinative effects—in the world, and more specifically in the process of religious conversion? Although it is unlikely that human scholarship will ever be able to describe in detail what Austin Farrer calls the "causal joint" between God and matter, we are bound to accept that God does indeed act in the physical world.[149] In particular, this section will deal with the crude issue of how God changes people—how does God bring about conversion?

Theologians have long claimed that the concept of *divine action* is central in the biblical texts. Such a claim necessarily raises questions as to how exactly this action occurs. Nicholas Saunders offers a helpful taxonomy of the different types of questions one should consider when conceiving of God's "action" in the world. These are:

1. By what means does divine action occur? (E.g. quantum manipulation or overruling the laws of nature).

2. What is the relationship between divine and finite causation? (E.g. complementary or mutually exclusive).

3. How often does SDA [Special Divine Action] occur? (E.g. continuous, only fitful or not at all).

4. What is the effect that SDA achieves? (E.g. to heal diseases or inspire an individual).

5. What is the purpose of the action having taken place? (E.g. promotion of divine justice or peace).[150]

In recent years, there has been a revival of interest in understanding the particulars of divine action. Such interests have taken the form

---

148. *Book of Discipline of the United Methodist Church*, Section 1: Our Doctrinal Heritage: Distinctive Wesleyan Emphases.

149. See Farrer, *Faith and Speculation*, 66. See also Hebblethwate and Henderson, *Divine Action*.

150. Saunders, *Divine Action and Modern Science*, 17. This list is a modified version of one presented by Owen C. Thomas. See Thomas, *God's Activity in the World*, 234–35.

of both theological *and* scientific investigations.[151] David Wilkinson has offered a helpful summary concerning contemporary models of divine action.[152] He suggests the following seven models as the most prominent considerations:

1. *The "working in the mind" God.* This position, perhaps best represented in the work of Rudolf Bultmann,[153] creates a strict dichotomy between the worlds of science and religion. The former is of an "external" nature where data can be observed through physical observation. Religion, in contrast, can only be understood through "interior" experience—"God does not act in the physical world in any particular physical way, but achieves his purposes by "acting" in the person of faith as he or she encounters God's Word."[154] This view has experienced a good deal of opposition on several points, not least of which is its failure to explain how God could interact in this "interior" manner without engaging humanity in their embodied physical natures.

2. *The "sit back and watch" God.* Maurice Wiles argues that God's action is limited to the initial act of creating the universe and establishing the "laws" which sustain its existence.[155] Likewise, this view allows "radical freedom to human creatures and indeed radical self-limitation on God's part."[156] This view receives the same criticism as classical deism in that it fails to give an adequate account of incarnation and resurrection—vital aspects of Christian faith.

3. *A "persuasive" God.* This position is identified with process theologians such as Ian G. Barbour.[157] Process theology "uses an analogy between God's action and our experience as agents, and attempts to proceed by assimilating the nature of the universe to our nature. Each event in the universe has a psychic pole and a material pole, and God works as an agent at the subjective level, exercising power

---

151. Perhaps the best example of this multi-disciplinary investigation is the Divine Action Project (DAP) co-sponsored by the Vatican Observatory and the Center for Theology and the Natural Sciences in Berkeley, CA. For a helpful discussion of the DAP and its results see Wildman, "Divine Action Project," 32–75.

152. Wilkinson, "Activity of God," 143–47.

153. See Bultmann, "Meaning," 61–76.

154. Wilkinson, "Activity of God," 143.

155. Wiles, *God's Action in the World.*

156. Wilkinson, "Activity of God," 144.

157. Barbour, *When Science Meets Religion.*

by persuasion or lure rather than coercion."[158] Despite the strength of process theology's ability to offer an explanation for the problem of evil, it experiences a number of other theological difficulties including the seemingly passive concept of God that it portrays.

4. *An "open" God.* This view is similar to process theology in that it considers the world to be created by God yet with a future not completely settled—human action is critical in the future state of the world. Clark Pinnock has been a major proponent of this view.[159] Pinnock argues that the traditional view of God's sovereignty is profoundly unbiblical. He proposes a much more cooperative notion of God, thus granting human action a more determinative role. This view has the theological advantage of being more "scripturally based" than process theology, which is typically philosophically motivated; yet, it does face many of the same objections as process theology.

5. *A "bodily" God.* This view appears in two forms. The first is represented in the work of Grace Jantzen.[160] In this view, the world is seen as God's body where divine action can be construed in the same manner as the soul working in the human body. The second, more popular, option appears in the work of Arthur Peacocke.[161] Peacocke uses the term "panentheism" to denote the type of relationship that God has with the world. He views the world as a foetus in the "womb" of God; thus, "God can act on any part of the world in a way similar to our action on our bodies, but God is also greater than the world."[162] This view offers a number of advantages, particularly in its ability to hold together immanence and transcendence; however, it does face its share of difficulty. Wilkinson suggests that panentheism can be seen to "threaten God's otherness and freedom while also compromising the world's freedom to be itself."[163]

6. *A "chaotic" God.* This view's greatest proponent is John Polkinghorne.[164] Polkinghorne argues that chaotic systems allow the "room" for God to work in the world. Similar to the previ-

158. Wilkinson, "Activity of God," 144.
159. See Pinnock, *Most Moved Mover*. See also Pinnock et al., *Openness of God*.
160. Jantzen, *God's World, God's Body*.
161. For a recent example see Peacocke, *Paths From Science Towards God*.
162. Wilkinson, "Activity of God," 146.
163. Ibid., 146.
164. See for example Polkinghorne, "Metaphysics of Divine Action," 147–56.

ous models, the "chaos" view presents the universe as inherently open to the future. Polkinghorne suggests that God works through the flexibility of these open systems. Here "providence becomes a subtle interaction between our freedom, the freedom inherent in the physical nature of the universe and God's freedom."[165] This view possesses many strengths. The objections usually relate to questions of necessity, that is, if God where to act in more bottom-up manner, would this seemingly "God of the gaps" approach be necessary?

7. *A "double agency" God.* In opposition to scientific attempts to describe divine action, Austin Farrer argued that the "causal joint" between divine and human action will always be hidden. In his understanding, every event has a double description, that is an event can be spoken of in terms of God's action while at the same time having a "full natural description in the laws of nature or the action of human agents."[166] The major objection to this view is that it is seen as a retreat into mystery when faced with theologically problematic ideas.

In addition to these models of providence presented by Wilkinson, there is another area that merits our attention—the relationship between divine action and quantum mechanics. Robert John Russell is a major proponent for understanding divine action at the quantum level. Russell asserts that

> If quantum mechanics is interpreted philosophically in terms of ontological indeterminism (as found in one form of the Copenhagen interpretation), one can construct a bottom-up, non-interventionist, objective approach to mediated direct divine action in which God's indirect acts of general and special providence at the macroscopic level arise in part, at least, from God's objective direct action at the quantum level both in sustaining the time-development of elementary processes as governed by the Schrödinger equation and in acting with nature to bring about irreversible interactions referred to as "quantum events."[167]

In this sense, God's action at the quantum level can be seen as bringing about both the general law-like character of the universe as well as specific events in the world. We can describe these as *general* and *special*

165. Wilkinson, "Activity of God," 147.
166. Ibid., 147.
167. Russell, "Divine Action," 293–328.

divine action respectively. The idea of God working at the quantum level is not a new idea. Sir Edmund Whittaker argued for the importance of quantum indeterminacy in a theory of agency and divine action. Whittaker observed that there was a tendency in "Newtonian circles" to conceive of the relationship of God to creation as being unnecessary and detached.[168] Relying on quantum theory, Whittaker argued for the plurality of causes for a single given effect. He claims:

> Thus it does not warrant the view, so common among the deistic Newtonians of the eighteenth century, that the system of the world is absolutely closed and has developed according to purely mechanical laws. . . . On the contrary, the recent trend of physical thought (as will be evident from what has been said about the principle of causality) is in favour of the view that in the physical domain there is a continual succession of the intrusions or new creations. The universe is very far from being a mere mathematical consequence of the disposition of the particles at the Creation, and is a much more interesting and eventful place than any determinist imagines.[169]

There are both theological and scientific weaknesses with this view. As with many "non-process" related views of divine action, there are issues of theodicy to sort out—if a "good" God acts in *every* event at the quantum level, why is there evil in the world? This challenge does not necessarily need to be viewed as a defect in the theory of divine action at the quantum level. Based on the view of "causation" discussed in the previous chapter, together with the notion of "structural constraints" through which God can act, it can be seen as an asset because it helps to explain why a benevolent God does not act more frequently and dramatically in the face of human and animal suffering.

The primary scientific challenge to a theory of quantum divine action is bound up with the science itself. Uncertainties at the quantum level tend to cancel each other out when a very large number of such events are combined to describe the behavior at the macroscopic level sufficient to be relevant to what is occurring at the level of human perceptibility. Likewise, if microscopic quantum events are to have macroscopic consequences, such can occur only through an enhancement of their effect due to their being part of a much larger system which is extremely sensitive to the fine details of its circumstance.

168. Whittaker, *Space and Spirit*, 95–96.
169. Ibid., 126–27.

This criticism proves to not be as strong as it may first appear. For instance many critics of quantum divine action assume that a particular macro-level effect would have to be the result of God's determining the outcome of a single quantum event. If God's action is located at the quantum level, then the scope of God's control would indeed be limited. It is impossible to determine the extent of this limitation without a better understanding of the relation between quantum physics and the rest of science—the limitation itself would be inherent to the nature of the processes.

The accusation that micro-level events do not give rise to macro-level phenomena is a disputed idea. Phillip Clayton argues that "given the billions and billions of such minute [quantum] interventions—the potential number would be limited neither by science nor by inability on the part of God—God might be able to effect significant changes on the macroscopic level."[170] Clayton also asserts that divine interventions at the quantum level can be further amplified by "chaotic" dependencies to achieve macroscopic aims.

I propose that, to date, Nancey Murphy has provided the most theologically coherent account of divine action at the quantum level.[171] Murphy's account is critical to my present purpose; thus, I will turn to a brief summary of her view.

Murphy's account of divine action demonstrates a high degree of resonance between both theological considerations and consistency with the findings of contemporary science.[172] Murphy asserts that "the problem of divine action is, at base, a metaphysical problem—one that cannot be solved by anything less radical than a revision of our understanding of natural causation."[173] Murphy's most basic assumption is that divine action necessarily includes a "bottom-up" approach, that is, if it is assumed

170. Clayton, *God and Contemporary Science*, 194.

171. See primarily Murphy, "Divine Action," 325–58. A basis to Murphy's theory can be found in the work of William Pollard. See Pollard, *Chance and Providence*. There are a number of problems with Pollard's view of divine action at the quantum level; however, Murphy has addressed these issues and offers a more nuanced and theologically desirable theory.

172. This account is based on the type of multi-level explanatory account discussed in chapter one.

173. Murphy, "Divine Action," 326. By "metaphysical," Murphy is referring to metascientific *and* metatheological accounts. She asserts that such accounts are capable of solving problems at the interface of science and theology, thus advancing the credibility of the claim (in the Lakatosian sense).

that God is active in *all* events, then consideration must be given to divine action at the most basic level—quantum phenomena.[174]

Theological requirements for such theory of divine action should be consistent with a number of general—widely accepted—tenets of the Christian faith.[175] Murphy suggests that the two main theological requirements for a theory of divine action include—(1) a way to distinguish between divine and natural (or human) events;[176] and (2) an account of extraordinary acts of God (miracles).[177] In short, this means that an adequate account of divine action must avoid opposite poles of deism[178] and occasionalism.[179] A theologically adequate view of divine action will provide a "picture of the relation of God's action to the world of natural causes that allows us to represent God's sustenance, governance, and cooperation in such a way that we can make sense of revelation, petitionary prayer, human responsibility, and of extraordinary acts such as the resurrection, without at the same time blowing the problem of evil up to unmanageable proportions."[180]

A theory of divine action must also be consistent with scientific investigation. Murphy suggests two salient aspects of science that must be

174. It is worth noting that there is some debate as to what constitutes an "event" in quantum theory. Saunders argues that "no quantum 'events' take place until the point of measurement" (*Divine Action and Modern Science*, 139); thus, God must act interventionistically in the form of measurement in order to "cause" a particular quantum state to be realized. The result is that non-interventionist incompatabilist quantum divine action is impossible because approaches to measurement turn out to be deterministic (ibid., 144). It seems, however, that Saunders objection is answered by John von Neumann (more on this below).

175. For Murphy, the most basic of such tenets is the consistency of God's action that is manifest in the story of Jesus; thus, she claims that "the relevant feature of God's action in Christ, displayed analogously throughout the whole, is its non-coercive character." See "Divine Action," 330.

176. Murphy asserts that "since our knowledge of a person comes primarily from the person's actions, including speech acts. Knowledge of God, therefore, must come primarily from seeing what God has done." Furthermore, to assume that God is entirely responsible for every act in human history exacerbates the problem of evil, so there is a distinct need for discrepancy. Ibid., 331.

177. Murphy prefers not to use the term *miracle* because it is often associated with the violation of the laws of nature. She sees no reason why divine action must occur in such a fashion.

178. As discussed above—the "sit back and watch" God.

179. Occasionalism denies the causal interaction of created things, thus providing only an "occasion" for divine action. In short, God is the *sole cause* of all events.

180. Murphy, "Divine Action," 333.

preserved—(1) the *law-like*[181] behavior of macroscopic objects and events (notwithstanding indeterminacy at the quantum level); and (2) the organization of the world into a hierarchy consisting of levels of complexity. Furthermore, Murphy suggests that an account of divine action must give attention to three different "regimes" within the hierarchy—the quantum level, the realm of human freedom, and an intermediate regime wherein the behavior of entities is describable by means of deterministic laws.[182]

Murphy submits that since the demise of the Newtonian worldview,[183] philosophical accounts of causation have not kept pace with science—"If scientists after Newton are willing to do without Newton's version of Prime Mover, they must be assuming, *contra* Descartes and Newton, that matter is inherently active."[184] So a number of questions arise regarding the ultimate source of the world's processes, not least of which regards the question of what "causes cause."[185] This situation only enhances Murphy's claim that what is needed is a "radical revision of our understanding of natural causation."

A cogent account of divine action must make sense of God's sustaining and cooperative role in the universe—that is, God must somehow be involved in all events, but respect the law-like character of the world. In addition, a metaphysical account of causation that takes divine action seriously must consider the non-reducible hierarchy of complexity which offers two starting points for causation based on either a top-down or bottom-up view.

A top-down view of causation is essential because it describes how free human agency is possible in a deterministic universe. While the top-down concept is crucial to any view of divine action, I propose that it alone does not provide a sufficient account of God's activity in the world.

---

181. Murphy stresses the "law-like character" of the natural world rather than the existence of "natural laws." She states that while many scientists presupposed the existence of such laws, "[she does] not believe such a view is either a necessary prerequisite for doing science or necessarily supported by the findings of science." Rather, she argues that the "de-ontologizing" of the "laws of nature" is helpful in understanding divine agency. Ibid., 334.

182. Ibid., 333.

183. The "Newtonian worldview" to which she refers concerns the change from an Aristotelian view of causation rooted in *primary substances* to the modern view of causal analysis seen as *changes* in the motion of inert material objects.

184. Murphy, "Divine Action," 336.

185. Murphy offers the following example (ibid., 336). Suppose we describe an event as a change from one state of affairs S1 to another S2. Then, is it S2 or the change from S1 to S2 that requires causal explanation? And is S1 the cause, or merely a necessary condition?

The problem occurs at the *causal joint*—that is, an explanation is needed as to how an assumed disembodied God exerts causal efficacy over the natural world.[186] Although Murphy acknowledges the value of a top-down approach to divine action,[187] she considers a bottom-up method to be necessary. She states her position as follows:

> In addition to creation and sustenance, God has two modes of action within the created order: one at the quantum level (or whatever turns out to be the most basic level of reality) and the other through human intelligence and action. The apparently random events at the quantum level *all* involve (but are not exhausted by) specific, intentional acts of God. God's action is at this level limited by two factors. First, God respects the integrity of the entities with which he cooperates—there are some things that God can do with an electron, for instance, and many other things that he *cannot* (e.g., make it have the rest-mass of a proton, or a positive charge). Second, within the wider range of effects allowed by God's action in and through sub-atomic entities, God restricts his action in order to produce a world that *for all we can tell* is orderly and law-like in its operation.[188]

Having ruled out the option of God being the *sole* cause of action at the quantum level—as this is an instance of occasionalism—it is necessary to grant that every created entity has some measure of existence independent of God.[189] Despite this independent potential for particles to act at

186. Most accounts of top-down divine action are presented as an analogy of human (top-down) agency in the inanimate world. This analogy is itself unclear because human agency is brought about by bodily action (physical force, conservation of energy, etc.).

187. Arthur Peacocke has offered the most helpful account to divine action through top-down processes. See *Theology for a Scientific Age*. Murphy contends that Peacocke's top-down approach requires the supplement of a viable bottom-up account of divine causation.

188. Murphy, "Divine Action," 339–40. Murphy contends that by taking quantum events as the primary locus for divine action it will be possible to adequately address theological requirements without running into insuperable theological or scientific objections. It is worth noting (as in an earlier instance) that there is some debate as to how exactly quantum events influence action at the macroscopic level. It seems that quantum uncertainties only relate to those particular kinds of events that we call measurements. Since measurements only occur intermittently, agency exercised in this way would have a problematically sporadic character.

189. Murphy argues that although God keeps all things in existence, created entities have a measure of independence from God. That is "if God were completely in control of each event, there would be no-*thing* for God to keep in existence. To create something, even so lowly a thing as an electron, is to grant it some measure of independence and a nature of its own, including inherent powers to do some things rather than others. . . . To

the quantum level, it is not possible to predict exactly *when* they act—is the "when" completely random or determined by God?[190]

Murphy claims that the better option is divine determination—"God's governance at the quantum level consists in activating or actualizing one or another of the quantum entity's innate powers at particular instants, and that these events are not possible without God's action."[191] Furthermore, divine action at the macro-level (the level of everyday human experience) is realized through God's interaction with *all* quantum events via bottom-up causation. Murphy states that

> God is not one possible cause among the variety of natural causes; God's action is a necessary but not sufficient condition for every (post-creation) event. In addition, I claim that God's participation in each event is *by means of* his governance of the quantum events that *constitute* each macro-level event. There is no competition between God and natural determinants because, *ex hypothesi*, the efficient natural causes at this level are insufficient to determine all outcomes. . . . Notice that this is a radical revision of the meaning of "cause" as it is used in science and everyday life, since on the view presented here no set of natural events or states of affairs is ever a sufficient condition for an event. One necessary condition will always be an element of divine direction; nothing ever happens without God's direct participation.[192]

Murphy uses the analogy given by the medieval philosopher John Buridan (~1300–61) to make her point. Buridan supposed that if a starving donkey were placed midway between two equal piles of hay it would starve to death for want of sufficient reason to choose one pile rather than the other. Murphy claims that entities at the quantum level are "miniature Buridian asses"—the asses have the "power" to do one thing rather than

---

be is to be determinate, and to be determinate is to have certain innate properties, including actual or potential behaviors." Ibid., 341.

190. This is true by process of elimination. Theoretically speaking it could be possible for the "when" to be internally determined by the entity itself or externally determined by environmental forces outside of the entity; however, "insofar as epistemological interpretations of quantum theory and the quest for hidden variables are rejected, we are left with the conclusion that there is no 'sufficient reason' either *internal* or *external* to the entities *at this level* to determine behavior" (ibid., 341, emphasis added). The central question is what causes an entity to take a particular course of action at a particular time.

191. Ibid., 342.

192. Ibid., 343–44.

the other, but the pertinent question is what induces them to take a particular action at a particular time.[193]

This idea resonates with John von Neumann's work regarding quantum measurement. The notion of wavefunction collapse was first formulated by von Neumann as a deduction from experiments involving the scattering of light by electrons.[194] Von Neumann's complex postulate has important implications for the relationship between quantum theory and divine action of the type that Murphy suggests.

In fact, "von Neumann's . . . wavefunction collapse as it is known, is the only place in the "orthodox" theory of quantum mechanics in which true ontological indeterminism might be accommodated."[195] This is true because the indeterminism of the quantum state arises from the fact that upon the collapse of the wavefunction (measurement) there is no determination of *which* of the various states of the superposition will be realized. Therefore, it is conceivable that God acts within this level of quantum indeterminacy in precisely the way that Murphy suggests.

Murphy's account is consistent with a long theological history claiming that God acts in all things at all times rather than on rare occasions. In his sermon, *On the Omnipresence of God*, Wesley wrote

> God acts everywhere, and, therefore, is everywhere; for it is an utter impossibility that any being, created or uncreated, should work where it is not. God acts in heaven, in earth, and under the earth, throughout the whole compass of his creation; by sustaining all things, without which everything would in an instant sink into its primitive nothing; by governing all, every moment superintending everything that he has made; strongly and sweetly influencing all, and yet without destroying the liberty of his rational creatures.[196]

Wesley was adamant that there cannot be any place within creation that God is not fully and actively present. Wesleyan theologian, Michael E. Lodahl, echoes this sentiment. Lodahl comments that "If God truly *knows all things* in the Hebraic participatory sense of the word-concept 'to know,' then God's knowing will indeed include a sharing in every creature's experience—including, again, the strange and mysterious world of sub-atomic processes—'from the inside.' The universe of events, things, and relationships can occur nowhere but *in God*, and thus God's knowing

193. Ibid., 342.
194. See von Neumann, "Measurement"; and "Measuring Process," 549–647.
195. Saunders, *Divine Action*, 147–48.
196. Sermon 111, *On the Omnipresence of God, BE* (4:42).

must be intimate, experiential, utterly thorough and, in some analogical sense, *bodily*."[197]

Furthermore, German theologian, Karl Heim, asserts quantum theory allows us to understand how God can indeed be active in *all* aspects of creation. Heim argued that fundamental assumptions in quantum theory demolished the absolute concept of causal necessity and provided a way of understanding causal laws as no longer exact, but containing "gaps" associated with bulk statistical predictions. Therefore when Heim speaks about God being active in the "fall of every sparrow" (Matt 10:29), he asserts

> No quantum transition occurs without your Father in Heaven. . . .
> The great faith . . . which alone is able to give us peace and freedom from anxiety in the midst of storm-ridden world processes, is the belief that precisely in these smallest areas it is not an impersonal causal mechanism which rules, but a personal will which steers every elementary particle, without which no sparrow falls to the ground and no hair can fall from our heads. None of these smallest events, says Jesus, of whose interaction the world is constituted, occurs "Without the Father."[198]

This is a clear assertion that God is active in determining *every* quantum event. This claim supports Murphy's argument that God is active in all of creation from the bottom up.

Having adopted Murphy's understanding of divine action and observed its resonance with both Wesley's notion of the providence of God in all of creation together with Heim's observations that God works in every quantum event, I make the following claim: The conversion process should be viewed as *caused* by God insofar as *general* divine action is understood as prevenient grace acting at the quantum level. In this case, I am equating "general divine action" with a universal morality understood as innate in the created order (like mathematics).[199] Not only is God present in every

197. Lodahl, "Cosmological Basis," 25.

198. Heim, *Wandlung*, 155–57. Translated by Saunders, *Divine Action*, 102–3.

199. For a helpful discussion of the concept of universal morality see Murphy and Ellis, *Moral Nature of the Universe*. Murphy and Ellis designate this morality as a *kenotic ethic*. Therefore, "self-renunciation for the sake of the other is humankind's highest good" (118). Likewise, John Hick states that "The function of religion in each case is to provide contexts for salvation/liberation, which consists in various forms of transformation of human existence from self-centeredness to Reality-centeredness . . . and the salvific transformation is most readily observed by its moral fruits, which can be identified by means of the ethical ideal, common to all the great traditions, of *agape/karuna* (love/compassion)." See Hick, *Interpretation of Religion*, 14. Wesley was keen to point out that the way to holiness was to be found in the transformative power of God's love. This love is not only the agent of

quantum event, but God acts through the course of individual and collective history to move creation to a particular expression of relationship.[200]

To be clear, I am not claiming that God acts *only* at the quantum level. Divine action via top-down causation (Peacocke) and chaotic systems (Polkinghorne) provide important ways of understanding how God may act through human mental processes[201] and in response to petitionary prayer. The great value of my claim is that, in a necessary supplementary role, it provides a way to understand God as active in *all* macroscopic events via God's action at the quantum level.

My description of religious conversion is not complete apart from the role that human beings play in the process. Not only are persons the *object* of conversion but in an important sense, they are the *cause*—more appropriately the *co-operant cause*. What I am suggesting is consistent with Maddox's notion of *responsible grace*. In theological terms Maddox asserts that "without God's grace, we *cannot* be saved; while without our (grace-empowered, but uncoerced) participation, God's grace *will not* save."[202] How can our "participation" be considered a "cause" in the conversion process? We will now turn to this important question.

COMMUNITY AS "CAUSE"

So far, I have argued that conversion is a complex biological process that occurs by way of divine grace. To put it flatly, I claim that God "causes" individual religious conversion to occur. The most viable way of conceiving of God's interaction with creation necessarily includes a bottom-up account of divine action—at the quantum level. The basic way of conceiving this is to suppose that God acts at the quantum level in order to bring about a particular quantum event among a superposition of possible states. God's action at an infinite number of quantum levels results in the

---

moral change, but the defining characteristic of human life in communion with God. For example see *A Plain Account of Christian Perfection, BE* (11:366–446). For more on the universal experience of prevenient grace see Leffel, "Prevenient Grace."

200. Note the resonance between this statement and Wesley's notion of *new creation*—both occur as gradual process and possess and inherent "telos."

201. God acting on the human nervous system in a "bottom-up" manner could stimulate particular thoughts, memories, concepts, etc. The mental representations or goal scenarios that arise from such action can then become part of a metasupervisory action loop that is realized in a "top-down" manner. Such a process could explain the religious experience of "revelation."

202. Maddox, *Responsible Grace*, 19.

realization of particular macro-level phenomena (human level).[203] We can refer to this as the *triggering cause* of conversion.

It is critical to note that due to the model of divine action proposed here, God's action is constrained by the structures through which God can operate. In the case of conversion (psychological phenomena), God can only bring about certain mental states (beliefs, actions, etc.) if the appropriate neurobiological cell assemblies are present. In other words, what is needed is a *structuring cause* for conversion to occur.

This notion is consistent with Murphy's claim that God does not fundamentally alter the nature of quantum entities, but merely triggers quantum events that underlie various aspects of behavioral potential that already exist within the entity's neurobiological repertoire.[204] She states that "God's governance at the quantum level consists in activating or actualizing one or another of the quantum entity's innate powers at particular instants, and that these events are not possible without God's action."[205] God is constrained by the characteristic limitations inherent to the entities through which God acts.

So, what is needed is a way to conceive of *structuring causes* of conversion. It will be obvious from my description of conversion above that the Christian community is a *vital* ingredient in the conversion process. In fact, I claim it is necessary for an individual to be within the context of the community to undergo the process of religious conversion. It is through the practices of the community that cognitive structures (neurobiological assemblies) are formed and sustained. This can be understood as neuro-plastic changes in areas of the brain (and body) contributing to the formation of procedural knowledge and affect memories. This includes the formation of somatic markers and the activation of various automatic, goal-directed repertoires. Particularly Christian virtues then supervene on these various neurobiological states of affairs in order to bring about the character that we call "Christian."

Understood in this way, the religious community is the "structuring cause" of conversion—the community, through its respective cultural-

203. Without properly qualifying this note, I will add that it seems reasonable to assume that quantum level events could also bring about macro-level change via the amplification of "chaotic" processes.

204. This is why Murphy can claim that humans limit the action of God to a significant degree. She says that "God is working at all times in all things to bring about the good, but the extent to which God can realize those good plans is, by divine decree, dependent upon the cooperation of all-to-often-recalcitrant creatures, both human and non-human." See Murphy, "God's Nonviolent Direct Action," 42.

205. Murphy, "Divine Action," 343.

linguistic context, makes possible the particular kind of agent through which God can act. It is an important theological truth that this community is a holy community that God brought into existence through the incarnation. Christians do not submit to just any community, but the community that God initiated through Jesus—a community embodying the dynamic reign of God in the world (Kingdom of God). The primacy of the ecclesial community should be obvious in the concept of divine action that I have presented in this section.

In order to explore this notion to a greater depth, we will return to Juarrero's account of human action as an adaptive complex system. The aim here is to conceive of a way that the community can have causal influence on individual behavior. We can represent this challenge by asking how, at the neurobiological level, the religious community can participate in the formation or transformation of the character of an individual such that his or her behavior will reflect the virtues of the religious tradition.

In Juarrero's model, the human brain can be considered a complex dynamic system. She equates this with an "autopoietic" system as understood to be "a distinguishable complex of component-producing processes and their resulting components, bounded as an autonomous unity within its environment, and characterized by a particular kind of relations among its components and component-producing processes: the components, through their interaction, recursively generate, maintain and recover the same complex of processes [the organization] which produced them."[206]

Juarrero conceptualizes the distributed control of complex autopoietic systems as the operations of *constraints*. Essentially, the environment in which a system is unified and embedded constrains the system. These constraints are properly understood as relational properties that parts of the system acquire in virtue of being unified into a systematic whole.[207] Juarrero holds that "By correlating and coordinating previously aggregated parts into a more complex, differentiated, systematic whole, contextual constraints enlarge the variety of states the system as a whole can access."[208]

When this range of accessibility includes the agent's historical context, an entire realm of possibility emerges. In Juarrero's model, a historical event not only serves as a trigger for a particular action (in Newtonian "bump-and-run" fashion), but the historical event becomes integrated into

---

206. Zeleny, *Autopoiesis*, 5.

207. Juarrero, *Dynamics in Action*, 132–33.

208. Ibid., 138.

the dynamic structure of the system. This point requires quoting Juarrero at length:

> Once the probability that something will happen depends on and is altered by the presence of something else, the two have become systematically and therefore internally related. As a result of the operations of context-sensitive constraints and the conditional probabilities they impose, A is now part of B's external structure. Because A is no longer "out there" independent of B, to which it is only externally related, the interdependence has created a larger whole, the AB system. Insofar as it is part of B's new context or external structure, A has been imported into B.
>
> By making a system's current states and behavior systematically dependent on its history, the feedback loops of autocatalysis also incorporate the effects of time into those very states and behavior patterns. Indeed, precisely what makes these complex systems dynamical is that a current state is in part dependent on a prior one. Feedback, that is, incorporates the past into the system's present "external" structure. Feedback thus threads a system through both time and space, thereby allowing part of the system's external structure to run through its history.[209]

The result is that by embodying these context-sensitive constraints, a system is constrained by its own past experiences—they "carry their history on their backs."[210] The resulting system—a product of both internal and external interactions—appears as a "structured structuring structure" in which the components parts of the system are situated in such a way as to render a whole that changes the prior probability of distribution of various behavioral options.[211]

Juarrero then develops the notion of *phase space* which represents a system's potential behavior over a given time lapse. *Attractors* can be understood as trajectories that converge on typical patterns with a system's phase space—they are "representations of natural precursors of final cause."[212] Within any give phase space, points located within a *basin* of attraction represent states with a greater than average probability of being realized

209. Ibid., 139.

210. Ibid., 140. Juarrero offers the example of a snowflake the very structure of which embodies the conditions under which it was created.

211. Antonio Damasio has shown that various levels of neural architecture function as a "structured structuring structure." See Damasio, "Time-locked Multiregional Retroactivation," 25–62.

212. Juarrero, *Dynamics in Action*, 152.

by the system—*a system's behavior converges on its attractor.*[213] Given this understanding of attractors, Juarrero surmises that in the brain

> coherent wave patterns embodying the emergent properties of consciousness and meaning emerge as neurons entrain and self-organize. These higher levels of organization impose second-order, context sensitive constraints on their components by carving out strange attractors that reset the natural, intrinsic firing frequency of the individual neurons, including those controlling motor processes, and in so doing entrain and constrain these to the attractor's dynamics.[214]

So, allow us to return to my example of a neurobiological predisposition toward empathetic response being transformed to the Christian virtue of compassion. In the language of system dynamics, one may say that the particular (multi-realizable) neural representation for the experience of compassion toward another exists as an attractor state for a particular complex system. The goal of transformation in this example is to "carve out" this particular attractor state to such a degree that one's prior intention for sympathetic response remains the most probable selection down-stream—the probability of "helping" increases while the probability of "walking away" decreases.

> The construction of an attractor, once again, results from interactions between the system's current dynamics and its structured environment, whether physical or social. In the case of proximate intentions, the dynamics involved are the meaningfully self-organized regions of the prior intention's belief, desire, and so forth, together with their logic (their dynamical pathways). These dynamics affected by top-down contextual constraints entering from the environment, and by entraining motor control, explicitly formulating a proximate intention restructures the agent's dynamics even further. . . . By further differentiating a cognitive state space, proximate intentions impose additional context-dependent constraints on that semantic and motor space; they thereby stack the odds that a certain behavior will be performed.[215]

This process described by Juarrero has a great degree of resonance with the "goal-directed" automaticity discussed earlier in this chapter. In

213. Attractors that describe complex patterns of behavior are called *strange attractors*. These often characterize complex dynamic systems. See ibid., 154–55.

214. Ibid., 162.

215. Ibid., 187.

Juarrero's language, the inculcation of habits or skills (virtues) constitutes *automated attractors* that function as a series of initial conditions within an object's relevant phase space.[216] This constitutes one's intent or "inclination" to act in a particular way.

In the context of religious conversion, the goal is to establish a robust system that yields the greatest probability for behaviors characteristic of the religious community. Depending on the prior stability of the system such transformations require varying degrees of restructuring of the physical and social environment in which a person is situated. This environment constitutes the structuring cause of religious conversion referred to above.

This discussion of system dynamics has direct relevance to the field of psychology. Esther Thelen and Linda B. Smith have written a volume regarding the relationship between nonlinear system dynamics and developmental psychology. In it they propose "a radical departure from current cognitive theory."[217] Their central argument is that although behavior and development appear structured and rule-driven, there is in fact no such "rules," rather there is a complex and continuously dynamic interplay of perception and action.

A system, by its thermodynamic nature, seeks certain stable solutions that emerge from *relations*, not from design. They assert that "When the elements of such complex systems cooperate, they give rise to behavior with a unitary character, and thus to the illusion of structure. But the order is always executory, rather than rule-driven, allowing for the enormous sensitivity and flexibility of behavior to organize and regroup around task and context."[218]

This notion is further applied in the field of attachment theory. Using resources from neuroscience and developmental psychology, Daniel J. Siegel has argued for a way of conceiving how experience shapes the human mind.[219] He asserts that "Experiences can shape not only what information enters the mind, but the way in which the mind develops the

---

216. Ibid., 199–200.

217. Thelen and Smith, *Dynamic Systems Approach*, xix. See also Thelen, "Self-organization," 77–117.

218. Thelen and Smith, *Dynamic Systems Approach*, xix.

219. Specific resources from neuroscience regarding the impact of experience on mental processes include Milner et al., "Cognitive Neuroscience," 445–68; Eisenberg, "Social Construction of the Human Brain," 1563–75; and Kandel and Schwartz, *Principles of Neural Science*.

ability to process that information."[220] Siegel has constructed a "neurobiology of interpersonal experience." The three principles are as follows:

1. The human mind emerges from patterns in the flow of energy and information within the brain and between brains.

2. The mind is created within the interaction of internal neurophysiological processes and interpersonal experiences.

3. The structure and function of the developing brain are determined by how experiences, especially within interpersonal relationships, shape the genetically programmed maturation of the nervous system.[221]

In this sense, human connections actually shape the neural connections from which the mind emerges. This point has interesting ramifications for how we think about what it means for one to "change one's mind." In so far as we can conceive of this possibility (and my argument for top-down causation certainly makes this option plausible), such a change of mental state and behavior will necessarily be the result of relational emergence. On this note, Siegel continues:

> Relationship experiences have a dominant influence on the brain because the circuits responsible for social perception are the same as or tightly linked to those that integrate the important functions controlling the creation of meaning, the regulation of bodily states, the modulation of emotion, the organization of memory, and the capacity for interpersonal communication. Interpersonal experience thus plays a special organizing role in determining the development of brain structure early in life and the ongoing emergence of brain function *throughout the lifespan.*[222]

As we have learned from dynamic system theory, the more stable (robust) that a particular system becomes, the more abrupt social interrelationships must be in order to affect a change in behavior. In dynamic systems language, the attractor states have been "carved out" to such a degree that the prior intentional states of an agent have become largely "automatic." In order to change behavior, new environmental conditions must be introduced in order to increase the probability that a new course of action will be chosen. In the context of religious conversion, depending on the initial robustness of the system, socio-moral transformation will

220. Siegel, *Developing Mind*, 16.
221. Ibid., 2.
222. Ibid., 21. Emphasis added.

not only involve experiences resulting in cognitive dissonance, but will require coordinated (repetitive) intentional behavior (over time) in order to "carve out" new attractor sets corresponding to the new behavior.

I claim that this transformation can only occur through one's participation in the religious narrative community. This participation literally (physically) changes an individual in the ways discussed above. Character transformation occurs in this context because, whether explicitly or implicitly, the religious community opens itself to God's grace—*love* characterized by its specific teleological nature.

Summary

The purpose of this chapter was to present a new model of religious conversion. As I suggested in chapter one, the current state of affairs calls for such a re-examination and the present proposal is a synthesis based on Wesleyan theology and a nonreductive physicalist view of human nature.

I have defined Christian religious conversion as a process involving normal human biological capacities. It is characterized by a change in socio-moral attitude and behavior and is best understood as the acquisition of virtues intrinsic to Christian faith. Such acquisitions are facilitated through social interaction and participation in practices inherent to the Christian community. Furthermore, the conversion process should be viewed as the co-operant result of divine grace and human participation.

In the concluding chapter, I will offer some reflections and implications by focusing on the community of the Church as a *sanctifying community*. Drawing from arguments presented above, I make the strong claim that individual religious conversion (sanctification) cannot occur apart from a sanctifying community. Rather than concluding this book with a systematic method for facilitating conversion, I will offer an example of a community in which conversion occurred in dynamic and interesting ways. Communities of this nature constitute a critical "space" for conversion to occur. I refer to this "space" as a "conversion community."

CHAPTER 5

A Sanctifying Community
Reflections and Implications

Questions of the truth or falsity of Christian convictions cannot even be addressed until Christians recover the church as a political community necessary for salvation. What Christians believe about the universe, the nature of human existence, or even God does not, cannot, and should not save. Our beliefs, or better our convictions, only make sense as they are embodied in a political community we call church. . . . For Christians, without the church there is no possibility of salvation and even less of morality and politics.

—Stanley Hauerwas[1]

T HE PRIMARY GOAL OF the present work has been to offer a new model of religious conversion. I have argued that this new model can be viewed as a competing theory (doctrine) of conversion, or in Lakatos's terminology, a competing "research programme." MacIntyre has contributed to this methodological approach by providing the basic framework in which to assess the theory, or perhaps more appropriately, *doctrine* of conversion that we find prominent in many American evangelical churches.

A doctrine of religious conversion should not be understood as a mere collection of propositions reflecting the beliefs of a particular group; rather, such a doctrine should allow members of a particular tradition to understand the narrative sequence in which they live and *form* them in such a way that they know how to move within their respective cultural-linguistic systems, and in the case of Christianity, know how to relate to those outside of their tradition.

Understood in this way, a theory (doctrine) of religious conversion is *formative* (or *transformative* as the case may be) and not simply a statement of "belief." The theory of conversion that a particular tradition holds will shape the way that members of that tradition develop in relation to their

---

1. Hauerwas, *After Christendom*, 26.

stated *telos*. As stated in the previous chapter, Christian religious conversion is properly understood as the co-operant result of divine grace and human participation. I indicated that in terms of divine action, there must be both a "triggering" and "structuring" cause of conversion. I then suggested that the Christian community can be understood as this structuring cause.

This final chapter will be dedicated to providing examples of how the community can be understood as the structuring cause of the conversion process. In order to do this, it will be necessary to engage in a further analysis of the American evangelical model of religious conversion that I criticize throughout this work. The focus of this criticism is not so much of the model itself, but of the community (church) that has inculcated it. Thus, a theology of corporate conversion is required.

A Theology of Corporate Conversion

Before delving into the discussion, allow me to clarify some terminological issues that will extend throughout this chapter. It will be obvious at this point that, in the present work, the phrase "religious conversion" is not meant to designate a particular religious experience, a moment in time, or a substitutionary term for justification. Rather religious conversion should be seen as a process equivalent to Wesley's notion of sanctification. As such, throughout this chapter the terms conversion, discipleship, and spiritual or faith development can be understood as synonymous.

I will begin this section with a quote intended to set the context for the discussion. During an inaugural address at Fuller Theological Seminary, Dallas Willard commented:

> We have counted on preaching and teaching to form faith in the hearer, and on faith to form the inner life and ordered behavior of the Christian. But for whatever reason, this strategy has not turned out well. The result is that we have multitudes of professing Christians that well may be ready to die, but obviously are not ready to live, and can hardly get along with themselves, much less others.[2]

Willard's proclamation not only captures the sad state of affairs in many American churches, it alludes to the difficulty one has in forming a theology of corporate conversion. The challenge extends from the issues discussed in chapter one regarding the highly individualized and interiorized notion of Christian spirituality that we observe in many evangelical

2. Willard, "Spiritual Formation in Christ," cited in Bolsinger, *It Takes a Church*, 31.

churches. This culminates in what Rodney Clapp calls the worship of a "god of Gnostic consumerism."[3]

Clapp observes that church members routinely depart from worship services with the general complaint that their "needs weren't being met" or they "weren't being fed." Such sentiments lead to a God known only in terms of products—a God known only in terms of the desires God satisfies. This highly individualized view leads to a destructive understanding of God and world for "without politics—with a God who wrestles with a people in time and space—God and individual dissolve into one another."[4]

Likewise, Darrel L. Guder laments the reduction of the Gospel to a mere offering of individual salvation. Guder asserts that

> As the gospel proclaimed by the church has been reduced to individual salvation, that salvation has itself become the purpose and program of the church. When the church went through the paradigm shift from its initial shape as a movement to its continuing shape as an institution, its focus was more and more upon the administration of salvation. Its worship centered on the message of individual salvation; its sacraments established and regulated the status of salvation; its doctrines sought to define and delimit salvation.[5]

Questions thus arise concerning the acquisition and assurance of salvation (as if it were an object and not a way of life) and the subsequent administration of salvation by the church. The continued individualization and privatization of faith equated the gospel with the "pursuit of happiness." Thus, in many cases, both worship and preaching are designed to meet the individual need for the assurance of salvation.[6]

What is needed, in the face of these challenges, is a proper theology of corporate conversion. Such a theology views the community as a *necessary* part of the conversion process. In this sense, the community develops, or is converted, together. At the heart of this theology is the understanding that the character of the church is *not* determined by the sum of its individual members; in contrast, the community determines the

---

3. Clapp, *Peculiar People*, 40–42.

4. Ibid., 42.

5. Guder, *Continuing Conversion of the Church*, 133. This "paradigm shift" to which Guder refers can no doubt be described as the "Constantinian shift" which moved Christianity from an obscure sect to a national religion.

6. Ibid., 135.

character of its individual members. Such an approach requires an active and developing community.

In order to offer such a theology, it is necessary to establish a view of the Church that is not shaped by the individualism that I criticize. As Christians live "between the times," the Church is understood to be the visible Kingdom of God in the world.[7] The Church embodies the ministry and resurrection of Jesus. Bishop N. T. Wright states that

> All that we are and do as Christians is based upon the one-off unique achievement of Jesus. It is because he inaugurated the kingdom that we can live the kingdom. It is because he brought the story of God and Israel, and hence of God and the cosmos, to its designed climax that we can now implement that work today. . . . *What Jesus was to Israel, the church must now be for the world.*[8]

This claim should strike Christians as a challenge indeed. However, we should not read this as a challenge for individual Christians to achieve. The whole point of the Church is that it is precisely *not* a collection of individuals, but a community which embodies Jesus' kingdom of God ministry.[9] Individual Christians are subsequently formed by this community. This is in opposition to the view that the character of the church is established by the collective personalities of its individual members.

It is obvious from this claim that the ability of persons to become Christian depends on the character shaping potential of the Christian community. Edward Farley notes that historically, the way the pastor encouraged spiritual maturity in believers was not to focus on their individual needs, but to form and nurture a distinctly Christian community.[10] In this way, religious conversion is rightly understood to be a natural result of a maturing Christian community.

Likewise, the early church understood and taught that to be baptized into the Christian faith was synonymous with undergoing an "extraordinary thoroughgoing resocialization" so that the Christian community

---

7. The phrase "between the times" is meant to designate the period between the resurrection of Jesus and the General Resurrection. See Green, *Beginning with Jesus*, 152–55.

8. Wright, *The Challenge of Jesus*, 53. Emphasis added.

9. Here, Paul's language of the "body of Christ" is quiet interesting. Dale B. Martin has produced an interesting work in this regard. Central to Martin's argument is the Corinthian misunderstanding of resurrection. The Apostle argues that for the Corinthians "to deny the resurrection of their bodies is to deny the resurrection of Christ; [and] to deny the resurrection of Christ is to render any future hope void. The Christian body has no meaning apart from it participation in the body of Christ." See Martin, *Corinthian Body*, 131.

10. See Farley, *Theologia*.

would become "the primary group for its members supplanting all other loyalties."[11] This corporate attitude in the early church was inextricably connected to what it meant to call oneself a Christian or a person of "the Way" (Acts 9:2; 24:14, 22).

This corporate nature of the community of God is so prominent in early Christian theology that Miroslav Volf claims that "Christ's presence is promised not to the believing individual directly, but rather to the entire congregation, and only through the latter to the individual. This is why no one can come to faith alone and live in faith alone."[12] Likewise, New Testament scholar, Richard B. Hays asserts that

> *The church is a countercultural community of discipleship, and this community is the primary addressee of God's imperatives.* The biblical story focuses on God's design for forming a covenant *people.* Thus, the primary sphere of moral concern is not the character of the individual but the corporate obedience of the church. . . . The community, in its corporate life, is called to embody an alternative order that stands as a sign of God's redemptive purposes in the world. Thus, "community" is not merely a concept; as the term is used here, it points to the concrete social manifestation of the people of God.[13]

Given the view of the Christian community presented above, it becomes imperative to conceive of God's action in the conversion process as not an individual and isolated act, but a transformative process that takes place in the context of the community. To overstate the point, religious conversion is not an achievement of individual belief or intellectual assent; rather, it is properly understood as a process that requires intimate interaction with the Christian community.[14] Such a declaration highlights

---

11. Meeks, *First Urban Christians*, 78.

12. Volf, *After Our Likeness*, 162.

13. Hays, *Moral Vision*, 196.

14. This claim is standard doctrine in the Catholic Church. The Catechism of the Catholic Church states that *"extra ecclesiam nulla salus"* (outside the Church there is no salvation). See *Catechism of the Catholic Church* 224. I deny the subsequent claim that it is "absolutely necessary for the salvation of every human creature to be subject to the Roman Pontiff" (Pope Boniface VIII, the Bull Unam Sanctam, 1302). The salient point for the present work is that without the Church salvation (conversion) simply makes no sense. Volf continues, "it is soteriologically and ecclesiologically inappropriate to understand the church as an external aid to salvation. The church is not a mere training subject or training ground for the edification of pious individuals. . . . Salvation and the church cannot be separated." See Volf, *After Our Likeness*, 174.

MacIntyre's claim that "I am never able to seek for the good or exercise the virtues only *qua* individual."[15]

When Friedrich Schleiermacher wrestled with how diverse individuality and social and cultural forms interact, it is interesting that he did not think in the typically modern direction from the individual to the environment, but from the environment to the individual.[16] In regards to moral action, Schleiermacher has little confidence that individual effort might develop the "sentiment" necessary to act in a benevolent matter. However, when others engage in the benevolent activity the sentiment is strengthened.[17] In an analysis of Schleiermacher's commentary, Michael Welker comments that

> Individual benevolent actions normally do little to help disadvantaged human beings. By contrast, a multiplicity of actions, both of one's own and of others, in favour of those who are weaker not only helps them more, but also strengthens the intensity of the sentiments of those performing the benevolent actions. . . . Complex and strengthening sentiments arise in me when my action is embedded in an interconnection with the action of other human beings, strengthening this interconnection and being strengthened by it.[18]

Schleiermacher's notion of helping others in need is directly tied to the promoting God's glorification.[19] This concept of service to those in need is not only at the heart of Jesus' ministry (*For even the Son of Man did not come to be served, but to serve, and to give his life as a ransom for many*—Mark 10:45 (NIV)), but I claim that it is critical to the process of religious conversion. In the following section, I will argue that in essence the church constitutes a social order which inherently stands in opposition to the world. This opposition is not in any way militant or violent. On the contrary, the church should be marked by a kenotic ethic and concerned with justice and care for those in need. It is within this context that the

15. MacIntyre, "Virtues," 105. Stanley Hauerwas makes a similar claim in an extended essay entitled "Sanctified Body," 19–38.

16. See Schleiermacher, "Notes on Aristotle," 164–68.

17. Ibid., 165–66.

18. Welker, "We Live Deeper," 173.

19. Schleiermacher, "Notes on Aristotle," 166. He says that in order to promote God's glorification, "I must structure my free actions, including their impact on others, in such a way that the perfection in the individual parts of the world as a whole becomes increasingly clear both to me and to others, and the apparent imperfections and disharmonies disappear" (166).

nature of God is most tangible and that conversion can fully grasp its *telos*. I will refer to this relational "space" where the people of God are transformed as "conversion communities."

"Conversion Communities"

In order to develop this notion of conversion communities, I must further reflect on the nature of the church. In particular, I will focus on the relationship between atonement and the character of the Church. On the surface this may seem like an odd association, after all, is not atonement an issue of individual interest? Does not the atonement deal with Jesus' substitution for individual sin? In what follows, I will argue to the contrary. Not only does the idea of atonement primarily refer to a social reality, it also carries with it serious ramifications for how we understand a community where people are transformed.

For the purposes of this section, I will not engage in a comprehensive analysis of atonement theories, rather I will focus on one central proposal—the atonement theory dubbed *Christus Victor*. This theory, popularized by Gustav Aulén, is a reiteration of the classic view of atonement which described Christ's work as victory over Satan and thus brought liberation to humankind.[20] Specifically, Jesus was understood to be a ransom paid to Satan for the souls of humanity. This of course turned out to be a clever trick because, unknown to Satan, Jesus was in fact God incarnate. With the resurrection, Jesus was restored and Satan was forever defeated.

J. Denny Weaver presents a "demythologized" version of Christus Victor that is relevant to the present discussion. Weaver states that "Christus Victor is more than a statement about overcoming the devil. Rather, it is—at least can be interpreted as—a statement of the work of Christ which addresses the church in its minority, pre-Constantinian social context, and that it fell out of favor in the aftermath of the Constantinian synthesis."[21] Such a claim necessitates a view of God as acting in history since the notion describes the reality of a non-Constantinian, minority ecclesiology.

Weaver's concept of "demythologizing" Christus Victor resonates with Walter Wink's description of "powers and principalities" in the biblical narratives. According to Wink, these principalities, powers, demons, etc. are not personal beings with a physical location; rather, they reflect the "spiritual" dimension of material structures. All powers in the world, including state, corporate, and economic structures, have spiritual and

---

20. See Aulén, *Christus Victor*.

21. Weaver, "Atonement," 307–8.

material dimensions. The spiritual dimension constitutes the collective cultural ethos of a material structure. Thus, powers and principalities are "real" in the sense that they are embodied by political structures and can be assessed according to their relationship to the Kingdom of God.[22]

Given this view of principalities and powers, the great cosmic battle between the forces of God and Satan found in the classic theory of atonement can be understood as the confrontation that occurs between forces in the material world. This conflict is obvious between Jesus and the ruling powers and institutions of the Roman and Jewish world. Jesus' struggle with the temporal powers of his day culminated in his death and resurrection. The Kingdom of God, which he initiated, is subsequently embodied in those that follow Jesus throughout history. The salient point, as Weaver notes, is that "the work of Christ—atonement—as described in this historical version of Christus Victor establishes a new social order which stands over against—in confrontation with—the structures of this world."[23]

This notion of the church as a "new social order" fell into disarray with the "Constantinian shift"—Christianity moved from an illegal and persecuted minority to the established religion of the empire.[24] Weaver notes that prior to Constantine, it was the community of the church that made God's work visible to the world. It was also clear that the church existed in a state of non-violent confrontation with the world. Once Christianity became the official religion of Rome, the life of the church became identified with the success of empire. The church could now sit comfortably within the social structure of Rome.[25]

It is worth noting that Christus Victor is an approach to atonement that depends on an imagery of confrontation. Weaver claims that "Christus victor fell out of the theological matrix with the Constantinian shift, not so much because of its imagery of demons or objections to tricking the devil but because the church had lost its sense of confrontation with the world."[26] The church's gradual shift in social context thus altered its eccle-

22. See Wink, *Naming the Powers.*

23. Weaver, "Atonement," 309.

24. This move was in reality a gradual transition. The term "Constantinian shift" is used in recognition of Constantine who formally legalized Christianity. For an excellent resource see Yoder, *Priestly Kingdom,* especially chapter 7: "The Constantinian Sources of Western Social Ethics," 135–50. Yoder cites two main dimensions of the shift—(1) the shift from church to civil government, and (2) the transition to empire as God's agent (138).

25. Weaver, "Atonement," 310.

26. Ibid., 311.

siology to the point that discussing atonement in terms of confrontation no longer made sense.

With lessening emphasis on social context in a theory of atonement, other views arose. According to Weaver, the most notable of these "theories" are offered by Anselm (substitution) and Abelard (Exemplary).[27] This difference primarily concerns the subject of the atoning act. Weaver emphasizes this difference in the following:

> Salvation as understood by the Anselm-Abelard axis has an inherently individual component, whichever side of their argument one wants to pursue. The satisfaction or substitutionary theory of Anselm defines the problem of the sinner in inherently individual terms. The sinner owes a debt and that debt in personal. When it is paid, the sinner is saved. Abelard's moral influence theory is equally individualistic. Upon perceiving the loving death of Christ, the rebellious sinner perceives his or her own alienation and rebellion and turns to God. In each case, the answer to sin envisions the status of the individual and God, and is complete at that level. One can, of course, go on to discuss how that saved individual may or can or should engage in community and be socially responsible and establish relationships with other saved individuals. That social component, however, is logically an afterthought, something to consider *after* one has dealt with the prior, fundamental and individualistic problem of personal guilt and penalty.[28]

This emphasis on the social component of salvation is critical to the present discussion regarding conversion. If, as I have argued, the community of the church shapes and gives expression to individual religious conversion, then becoming Christian means being part of a community that has a clear presence in the world as the agent of God's will for creation. To be clear, the critical aspect of the community in the conversion process is not being a part of just any community, but being a part of a community that embodies the Kingdom of God. I am claiming that the *character* of the pre-Constantinian church constitutes the transformative nature of the Christian community. This nature is marked by social engagement for the sake of love and justice.

This is the difference between "communities of togetherness" and "conversion communities." While communities of togetherness share af-

27. It is worth noting that neither Anselm nor Abelard would have sought to offer a "theory" of atonement per se. Focus on atonement "theories" is common in evangelical theology; however, to do justice to the work of Anselm and Abelard would require a much more substantial engagement than that offered by Weaver.

28. Weaver, "Atonement," 315.

finity and culture shaping potential, conversion communities act as divine structuring causes of human transformation by providing the possibility for believers to act as agents of God's work in the world. In the following section, I will discuss an example of a conversion community. It should be noted that I do not seek to provide a specific method for facilitating religious conversion. To do so would be to participate in the very reductive systematization that I have argued against. Instead, this example is meant to demonstrate the type of communities where Christian religious conversion occurs.

Wesley's Methodism

The purpose of this section is to offer John Wesley's Methodist societies as an example of "conversion communities." Recall that the "axial theme" of Wesley's soteriology was the "renewal of the image of God." Humanity as the image of God is a mirror that reflects divine love to the world. As such the *imago Dei* is not a quality that a human being possesses; rather, it is a relational capacity. Thus salvation, for Wesley, was a renewal in the capacity to reflect the love, grace and justice of God to the world. The social component of Wesley's theology and practices cannot be overstated. In fact, Wesley asserted that "Christianity is essentially a social religion, and that to turn it into a solitary religion is indeed to destroy it. . . . When I say [Christianity] is essentially a social religion, I mean not only that it cannot subsist so well, but that it cannot subsist at all without society, without living and conversing with [others]."[29]

Wesley realized that Christian faith was initiated and flourished in a social context.[30] He also understood that faith itself required social expression in order to accomplish God's will for the world. This recognition gave birth to Wesley's distinctive emphasis on societies, classes, and bands. These groups provided the necessary social context for Christian faith to be developed.

This aspect of Wesley's Methodism was not the product of systematic theological contemplation; rather, it was born of practical observation. Because of the masses gathering for the revivals (1746–48), Wesley experimented with preaching while circumventing the formation of societies aimed at developing those responding to his message of salvation. The

29. Sermon 24, *Upon our Lord's Sermon on the Mount: Discourse the Fourth*, BE (1:533–34).

30. Wesley claimed that although "it is God only [who] changes hearts, yet he generally doth it by man." Ibid., 546.

results were disastrous. In his 1748 Conference Minutes, Wesley states
that without forming the societies

> "Almost all the seed has fallen by the wayside; there is scarcely any
> fruit remaining." The preacher had little opportunity for instruc-
> tions, the awakened souls could not "watch over one another in
> love," and the believers could not "build up one another and bear
> one another's burdens." [31]

The experiment had frayed the threads of connectionalism. [32]

As a result of these observations, Wesley invested a great deal of time
and energy toward developing a social organization that would nourish
believers toward sanctification. It is important to understand that the
transformative power of these early Methodist societies rested not in their
community of togetherness alone, but in the context of the actions in
which they engaged as a community.

It is crucial to the present argument to recognize that "the purposes
of God are only fulfilled as those who are reconciled with God serve as
'channels of grace' to other persons." [33] Individual religious conversion cannot be separated from the overall work that God is achieving through *new
creation*. Jesus initiated a new world (Kingdom of God) constituted not
by the salvation of individual souls, but by the renewal of the whole of
creation in love, mercy and justice. Conversion, as a component of new
creation, occurs in the overall context of God's action in the world.

Wesley recognized that God could indeed bring renewal to the world
by fiat; however, to do so would be to deny the very nature of God and
humankind.

> Only suppose the Almighty to act *irresistibly*, and the thing is done;
> yea, with just the same ease as when "God said, Let there be light;
> and there was light." But then man would be man no longer; his
> inmost nature would be changed. He would no longer be a moral
> agent, any more than the sun or the wind, as he would no longer
> be endued with liberty, a power of choosing or self-determination.

31. Quoted by Heitzenrater, *Wesley and the People called Methodists*, 165.

32. This emphasis on the importance of communal interaction is echoed in an empirical survey conducted by Thomas R. Albin. After surveying over five-hundred accounts of
involvement in early Methodism, Albin concludes that "Methodist spirituality could be
characterized as a positive process in which lay leadership and direction played a key role
along with that of the local community rather than sudden experiences related to a fear of
death and hell." See Albin, "An Empirical Study," 279.

33. Runyon, "Holiness," 83.

> Consequently he would no longer be capable of virtue, or vice, of reward or punishment.[34]

For Wesley, the transformation of individual persons is inextricably bound to the *telos* of new creation. Renewed humanity is the agent of God's grace to the world—"This is the great reason why the providence of God has so mingled you together with other men, that whatever grace you have received of God may through you be communicated to others."[35] Thus, humanity is in the "image of God" insofar as the benevolence of God is reflected in human action toward the rest of creation.[36]

Therefore, we must reflect on the social nature of Wesley's Methodism not only in relation to personal conversion or spiritual development, but also with serious consideration of what they accomplished in resonance with God's love and justice. Early Methodism was at the center of the eighteenth-century evangelical Movement in England. In a detailed historical review of the revival, John Wesley Bready notes that

> The movement was cradled and reared in an atmosphere of insolence, contempt and abuse. Yet the day was to dawn when the descendants of those who maligned it would acclaim it, "the moral salvation of England," and a mighty inspiration to all mankind. Few world movements, indeed, have ever emerged from the depths of slander to the heights of historical honour, with such consistent progress as did this remarkable revival of vital, practical religion.[37]

Methodism began as the "Holy Club" during Wesley's studies at Oxford. The group was made up of Wesley and fellow Christians who adopted a "practical program" of living the Christian life. They resolved to receive Holy Communion on a regular basis as well as to assist in the education of marginalized adults and children. In addition, they were committed to visiting and befriending prisoners in the Oxford jails and to "give freely, according to their means, to relieve necessity among the poor."[38]

Wesley's emphasis on moral righteousness was direct. In his treatise, *The Character of a Methodist* (1742), Wesley says "By *salvation* he means holiness of heart and life. . . . It is nonsense for a woman to fancy herself a *virtuous* woman only because she's not a prostitute; or [a man to] dream

---

34. Sermon 63, *The General Spread of the Gospel, BE* (2:488–89).

35. Wesley, Sermon 24, *Upon our Lord's Sermon on the Mount, BE* (1:537).

36. Runyon, "Holiness," 87.

37. Bready, *England*, 177.

38. Ibid., 187. It was in Oxford that they were scoffingly dubbed "Methodists."

he is an *honest* man merely because he does not rob or steal. May the Lord God of my fathers preserve me from such a poor, starved religion as this! Were this the mark of a Methodist I would sooner choose to be a *sincere* Jew, Turk, or pagan."[39]

Wesley insisted that the very foundations of Methodism were ethical, practical and experimental as opposed to doctrinal, theoretical or metaphysical. For Wesley the expression of true faith was found in works of service and love. In a *Letter to Mary Bishop* (1778) he writes

> I find more profit in sermons on either good tempers, or good works, than in what are vulgarly called Gospel sermons. That term has now become a mere cant word: I wish none of our society would use it. It has no determinate meaning. Let but a pert, self-sufficient animal, that has neither sense nor grace, bawl out something about Christ, or his blood, or justification by faith, and his hearers cry out, "What a fine Gospel sermon!" Surely Methodists have not so learned Christ! We know no Gospel without salvation from sin.[40]

At the core of this practical approach to Christian growth were the Methodist societies or class communities. It was here in these communities that early Methodists were "schooled" in the Christian way, not merely by mental assent, but by discussing "reverently and prayerfully their attitude to the social, ethical and religious problems of their daily life."[41] Even more important, these discussions moved them to *action*—the convert is always transformed for a social end.

Over the course of the revival, the Methodist communities played a vital role in the social reform of England.[42] Methodists were leaders in aspects of society ranging from education reform for the poor to the abolition of slavery. Jack Lawson, who served as a Member of Parliament in Durham City, wrote that "The first fighters and speakers for unions, C.-op. Societies, political freedom, and improved conditions, were Methodist preachers. That is beyond argument."[43]

It should not be assumed that the Methodists brought about this change without significant resistance. Even Epworth Church, where Wesley spent his youth, denied him the Sacrament claiming that he was

---

39. *BE* (9:35).
40. *BE* (6:213).
41. Bready, *England*, 217.
42. See Keefer, "John Wesley," 1–25.
43. Quoted by Bready. *England*, 379.

"not fit."[44] Methodist leaders regularly fell under violent attack by angry mobs and Methodists often found their homes burned or torn-down by protestors.

Eighteenth-century Methodism certainly possessed the counter-cultural quality characteristic of the pre-Constantinian church. Their relentless social engagement with the injustices (principalities and powers) of their day created a "space" in which Methodists could be transformed into a true Christian community. It is from within these "conversion communities" that individuals undergo the process of conversion. The fact that Wesley's Methodists were involved in the social concerns of their day is not a mere consequence of their conversion, but a contributor to it.

Conclusion

This book has primarily been about religious conversion. In chapter one, I offered an analysis of Christian spirituality with a particular focus on the American evangelical tradition. I suggested that this view of spirituality ultimately leads to a problematic doctrine of Christian religious conversion. From this diagnosis, I set out to formulate a new model of conversion that is not only faithful to long-held Christian convictions, but also takes seriously nuances in science and philosophy.

I constructed this model based on insights from two primary sources—a Wesleyan theology and a nonreductive physicalist view of human nature. Wesleyan theology is not only a key historical contributor to American evangelicalism, but the theological insights from John Wesley provide a vital language for Christian religious conversion. The practical nature of Wesley's work resonates with my own desire to articulate a theology that encourages holistic transformation and promotes sound Christian orthopraxis.

For Wesley, the "way of salvation" is marked by a transformation of the tempers. That is, Wesley understood conversion as an alteration in the underlying psychological motivators that lead to particular attitudes and behavior. Through both divine action and responsible human participation, human beings are transformed by the grace of God. This *process* is best represented by the notion of sanctification and possesses an inherent "telos" marked by Wesley's concept of "new creation."

In chapter three, I argued that one's view of human nature has significant repercussions for how he or she understands conversion. I suggested that the nonreductive physicalist view of human nature is the most viable

44. Ibid., 206.

option currently available. Nonreductive physicalism should not be seen as a philosophical thesis, but rather as a "research programme" that brings together data from multiple sources including historical and systematic theology as well as various scientific disciplines.

In this way, nonreductive physicalism offers a view of human nature that no single resource can offer (theology, anthropology, cognitive science, etc.). This view also allows a way of conceiving the distinctiveness of human nature as rooted in the human capacity for relatedness. This notion is not only compatible with scientific research, but is consistent with Wesley's concept of the *imago Dei*.

The multidimensional analysis presented in chapter four leads to a model of conversion that supports both scientific research consistent with a nonreductive physicalist view of human nature as well as theological insights from John Wesley. I have proposed a model of conversion which takes seriously the social dimension of human experience as well as our inextricably embodied nature.

The model that I have proposed is particularly Christian in that I have suggested that conversion is best understood as the acquisition of virtues intrinsic to Christian faith. This acquisition necessarily takes place within the context of the Christian community. Furthermore, transformation of the type that I have discussed necessarily involves divine action. This is true not only in the sense that God acts through *every* quantum event to sustain the physical laws that allow for human functionality; but, as I have suggested, the grace of God is ever-present and ever-moving creation to an ultimate end. In this way, general divine action can be understood to be equivalent to "prevenient grace."

In addition, I claimed that conversion requires a "structuring cause"—that is, God's activity in the world is constrained by the structures through which God can operate. I suggested that this structuring cause can be understood as the Christian community. In fact, it is through one's interaction with the community that neural assemblies are formed through which particular attitudes and behaviors can be realized.

This book has set out a new way of thinking about Christian conversion. Its uniqueness is found in the synthesis of existing work in the area of both theology and science. This model has serious implications for Christian community life. I have asserted above that the transformative power of the Christian community exists not in its affinity or "togetherness" alone, but in the reality which it seeks to achieve—the realization of the Kingdom of God.

The model of Christian conversion that I propose has some serious implications for Christian community life, not least of which includes the practices of evangelism and discipleship. Any model of Christian conversion will necessarily affect the "character" of these practices. The notion of evangelism is central to the "Great Commission." Here Christians are commanded to "make disciples of all nations, baptizing them in the name of the Father and of the Son and of the Holy Spirit, and teaching them to obey everything that [Jesus] commanded."[45] Although, there is little doubt that these words are an integral part of the Christian faith, the interesting question arises when we inquire into the *nature* of evangelism.

What is evangelism? Many would reply that it is the Christian call to "save souls." Religious conversion, as I have presented it in this book, requires no less than a conversion of evangelism—a transition from the "saving of souls" to the *transformation of whole persons*. If the goal of the Church becomes the latter, then methodologies built upon the view of Christian spirituality discussed in chapter one must significantly change. The goal of evangelism will transition from the climactic confession of the "sinner's prayer" to the *constant* and *consistent* encouragement of holistic transformation.

Practically, this means that the church will be involved in areas extending beyond "spiritual" concerns.[46] It means feeding the hungry, caring for the sick, supporting single parent families, providing therapy for victims of abuse; the list goes on indefinitely. A key feature of this type of care is that it is not to be viewed as "crisis management"; rather, the Christian community should seek out this type of human "dis-ease" and with the love and grace of God participate in the healing of wounded lives.

The social dimension of Wesley's practices is inescapable. A survey of Wesley's work will show minimal concern for evangelising methodology; rather, the Methodist movement was rich with concern to see God's love and justice expressed to the world. The early Methodist's involvement in the social realm rendered the movement a "presence" in eighteenth-century England.

According to James McClendon, this "presence" can be seen as a critical virtue to the practice of evangelism. Recall from MacIntyre, that a virtue is an acquired trait that allows access to goods internal to practices.

45. Mat 28:19–20, NRSV.

46. In fact, I claim that evangelism is an imperative "spiritual" concern (when understood as an inherently anthropological term); however, I place the term in scare quotes to emphasis that the majority view will consider "spiritual" concerns to imply an individual and private affair.

In the case of the practice of evangelism, where the "good" internal to the practice can be understood to be persons being brought into the community of believers, the virtue of "presence" is a critical trait.

McClendon defines "presence" as "*being there* for and with the other."[47] Presence is therefore a function of physical existence—the virtue is *embodied*. It is "being one's self for someone else; it is refusing the temptation to withdraw mentally and emotionally; but it is also on occasion putting our own body's weight and warmth alongside the neighbor, the friend, the lover in need."[48] In this sense, the possibility of embodying such a virtue is found only in the presence of an "other" whose need acts as the occasion of our ability to serve. It is through the other that we are able to overcome our self-absorption and be empowered by the gift of another's needs—"We are able to move from a self-centered narrative and enter into a service-oriented narrative which creates in us the character God has called us to be."[49]

Thus, Methodist "presence" within the social context of eighteenth-century England cannot be separated from their practice of evangelism. In this way, the model of religious conversion that I have proposed renders an understanding of evangelism that makes propositional solicitation unintelligible. Evangelism is first *being* God's community (Church, Body of Christ, visible Kingdom of God, etc.) in the midst of *need*. The counter-cultural character of such a community embodies the gospel that it seeks to propagate.

This new model of religious conversion makes evangelism not about getting people to "believe" this or that; rather, evangelism is characterized by graceful invitation to participate in a community where individuals are transformed together in a holistic fashion. Only then can beliefs and convictions have true meaning.

Likewise, discipleship should be no less interested in the development of the whole person. The rhetoric of "spiritual" development, when it characterizes the goal of Christian discipleship as abstract notions such as "bringing the flesh under the subjection of the spirit" or "tuning the soul to more effectively communicate with God," is deeply rooted in a body-soul dualism that I consider problematic for true Christian discipleship. A person should not be characterized by "interior" thoughts or beliefs, but should rather be understood as a holistic being whose values

---

47. McClendon, *Ethics*, 115.

48. Ibid., 116.

49. Loewen, "Rethinking Christian Ethics," 63.

are inseparably bound to his or her embodied life. Here, values are not only experienced as inner convictions, but expressed in a social context.

I have been asked on several occasions and in various ways how I feel that mainline evangelical churches in America have fallen short in the area of discipleship. It seems that rather than providing a clear *telos* (goal) within the context of a community that embodies the virtues of its goal, many mainline churches have opted to direct individuals toward various programs and "ministries" that aim at an abstract end such as "proper belief" or "spiritual maturity." Therein lies the shortcoming—that Christianity should be thought to consist of properly aligned beliefs that can exist apart from a community that embodies them.

Discipleship, the continued process of becoming Christian, should be concerned with the "means of grace." For Wesley, these means not only included practices such as prayer, fasting, and worship, but extended to all forms of social interaction between a convert and other members of the Christian community.

Given insights gained from a neuroscientific explanation of conversion, we understand discipleship to be a gradual process of change resulting from multidimensional experiences within the context of the Christian community. Such experiences include prayer, meditation, fasting, worship, participation in the Eucharist and any activity that acts to reinforce the Christian narrative in the life of the convert. The telling of the "story of Jesus" actively "rewrites" the personal narrative of every Christian—our lives and all of the experiences therein are interpreted through what God has done and is doing in the world.

A critical aspect of the type of discipleship (conversion) that I propose is that it must occur through active participation not just in the sacraments, but in the embodied content of those holy gestures. For example, in the case of the evangelical Protestant, the Lord's Supper is not simply about worship and remembrance. The act of participating in this holy sacrament is an active response to the call to *be* the Body of Christ in the world. Such a call can only be fulfilled within the context of the Christian community thus empowered by the Spirit of God to be the visible Kingdom of God in the world.

In conclusion, it is my hope that the present work will be viewed not as an isolated contribution to the academic discipline of philosophical theology, but as a sincere attempt to do philosophical theology in the therapeutic mode of those that have shaped me.

Bibliography

Aarts, Henk and A. Dijksterhuis. "Habits as Knowledge Structures: Automaticity in Goal-Directed Behavior," *Journal of Personality and Social Psychology* 78, no. 1 (2000) 53–63.

Abraham, Wickliffe C. "Memory Maintenance: The Changing Nature of Neural Mechanisms." *Current Directions in Psychological Science* 15, no. 1 (2006) 5–8.

Adolphs, Ralph. "Cognitive Neuroscience of Human Social Behavior, *Neuroscience* 4 (2003) 165–178.

———. "Social cognition and the human brain." *Trends in Cognitive Sciences* 3, no. 12 (1999) 469–79.

Albin, Thomas R. "An Empirical Study of Early Methodist Spirituality." In *Wesleyan Theology Today*, edited by Theodore Runyon, 275–80. Nashville, TN: Kingswood, 1985.

Allison, Truett. "Neuroscience and Morality." *Neuroscientist* 7, no. 5 (2001) 360–64.

Amso, Dima and B. J. Casey. "Beyond What Develops When: Neuroimaging May Inform How Cognition Changes With Development." *Current Directions in Psychological Science* 15, no. 1 (2006) 24–29.

Anderson, John R. *Cognitive Psychology and Its Implications.* New York: Worth, 2000.

Anderson, S. W., A. Bechara, H. Damasio, D. Tranel, and A. Damasio. "Impairment of social and moral behavior related to early damage in human prefrontal cortex." *Nature Neuroscience* 2, no. 11 (1999) 1032–37.

Aquinas, Thomas. "Commentary on Paul's First Epistle to the Corinthians." Translated by Matthew Rzeczkowski. In *Thomas Aquinas, The Gifts of the Spirit: Selected Spiritual Writings*, introduced and edited by Benedict M. Ashley, 21–78. Hyde Park, NY: New City, 1995.

———. *Summa Contra Gentiles.* Translated by Vernon J. Bourke. Notre Dame, IN: University of Notre Dame Press, 1992.

Aristotle, *De Anima.* Translated, with an introduction and notes, by Hugh Lawson-Tancred. New York: Penguin, 1987.

———. *Metaphysics.* Translated by Hugh Tredennick. 2 vols. Cambridge, MA: Harvard University Press, 1933.

———. *Nicomachean Ethics.* Translated and edited by Roger Crisp. Cambridge: Cambridge University Press, 2000.

Augustine, *Confessions.* Translated with an introduction and notes by Henry Chadwick. New York: Oxford University Press, 1998.

———. *Tractatus in Joannis evangelium* (23.10). In *Augustine on the Inner Life of the Mind* Translated by Robert Meagher. Indianapolis, IN: Hackett, 1998.

Aulén, Gustav. *Christus Victor.* New York: Macmillan, 1969. Reprint, Eugene, OR: Wipf and Stock, 2003.

Aune, Bruce A. *Rationalism, Empiricism, and Pragmatism: An Introduction*. New York: Random House, 1970.

Aune, David C. "Mastery of the Passions." In *Hellenization Revisited*, edited by Wendy Helleman, 125–58. Lanham, MD: University Press of America, 1994.

Ayala, Francisco J. "The Evolution of Life: An Overview." In *Evolutionary and Molecular Biology: Scientific Perspectives on Divine Action*, edited by Robert John Russell, William R. Stoeger, and Francisco J. Ayala, 21–58. Vatican City: Vatican Observatory, 1998.

———. "Human Nature: One Evolutionist's View." In *Whatever Happened to the Soul? Scientific and Theological Portraits of Human Nature*, edited by Warren S. Brown, Nancey Murphy, and H. Newton Malony, 31–48. Minneapolis, MN: Fortress, 1998.

———. "Introduction." In *Studies in the Philosophy of Biology: Reduction and Related Problems*, edited by Francisco J. Ayala and Theodosius Dobzhansky, vii–xvi. Berkeley, CA: University of California Press, 1974.

———. "So Human an Animal: Evolution and Ethics." In *Science and Theology: The New Consonance*, edited by Ted Peters, 121–35. Boulder, CO: Westview, 1998..

———. "Teleological Explanations *versus* Teleology." *History and Philosophy of the Life Sciences* 20 (1998) 41–50.

Badham, Paul. *Christian Beliefs about Life after Death*. London: Macmillan, 1976.

Baker, Frank, ed. *The Works of John Wesley*, multi-volume set. New York: Oxford University Press. Nashville, TN: Abingdon, 1984–.

Baker, Lynne Rudder. "Metaphysics and Mental Causation." In *Mental Causation*, edited by John Heil and Alfred Mele, 75–96. Oxford: Clarendon, 1993.

Baker, Mark D. *Religious No More: Building Communities of Grace and Freedom*. Downers Grove, IL: InterVarsity, 1999.

Barbour, Ian G. *Religion and Science: Historical and Contemporary Issues*. San Francisco: Harper San Francisco, 1998.

———. *Religion in an Age of Science*. San Francisco: Harper and Row, 1990.

———. *When Science Meets Religion: Enemies, Strangers, or Partners?* London: SPCK, 2000.

Bargh, John. "The Automaticity of Everyday Life." In *The Automaticity of Everyday Life*, edited by Robert S. Weyer, 1–62. Mahwah, NJ: Lawrence Erlbaum, 1997.

———. "Automaticity in Social Psychology." In *Social Psychology: Handbook of Basic Principles*, edited by E. Tory Higgins and Arie W. Kruglanski, 169–83. New York: Guilford, 1996.

———. "Goal ≠ Intent: Goal-Directed Thought and Behavior Are Often Unintentional." *Psychological Inquiry* 1, no. 3 (1990) 248–51.

———, and Kimberly Barndollar. "Automaticity in Action: The Unconscious as Repository of Chronic Goals and Motives." In *The Psychology of Action: Linking Cognition and Motivation to Behavior*, edited by Peter M. Gollwitzer and John Bargh, 457–81. New York: Guilford, 1996.

———, and Tanya L. Chartrand. "The Unbearable Automaticity of Being." *American Psychologist* 54, no. 7 (1999) 462–79.

———, and Melissa Ferguson. "Beyond Behaviorism: On the Automaticity of Higher Mental Processes." *Psychological Bulletin* 126, no. 6 (2000) 925–45.

———, Peter M. Gollwitzer, Annette Lee-Chai, Kimberly Barndollar, and Roman Trotschel. "The Automated Will: Nonconscious Activation and Pursuit of Behavioral Goals." *Journal of Personality and Social Psychology* 81, no. 6 (2001) 1014–27.

————, and Erin L. Williams. "The Automaticity of Social Life." *Current Directions in Psychological Science* 15, no. 1 (2006) 1–4.

Barker, F. G. "Phineas among the phrenologists: the American crowbar case and nineteenth-century theories of cerebral localization." *Journal of Neurosurgery* 82, no. 4 (1995) 672–82.

Baron-Cohen, Simon, Howard A. Ring, Sally Wheelwright, Edward T. Bullmore, Mick J. Brammer, Andrew Simmons, et al. "Social intelligence in the normal and austic brain: an fMRI study." *European Journal of Neuroscience* 11 (1999) 1891–98.

————, Helen Tager-Flusberg, and Donald J. Cohen, eds. *Understanding Other Minds: Perspectives from Developmental Cognitive Neuroscience.* 2nd ed. Oxford: Oxford University Press, 2000.

Barth, Karl, *Church Dogmatics.* Edited by G. W. Bromiley and T. F. Torrance. Translated by G. W. Bromiley. Edinburgh: T & T Clark, 1975–.

Batson, C. Daniel, Jim Fultz and Patricia Schoenrade. "Adults' Emotional Reactions to the Distress of Others." In *Empathy and Its Development*, edited by Nancy Eisenberg, and Janet Strayer, 163–84. Cambridge: Cambridge University Press, 1987.

Baumeister, Roy F. "How the Self Became a Problem: A Psychological Review of Historical Research." *Journal of Personality and Social Psychology* 52 no. 1 (1987) 163–176.

Beale, Greg K. "The Eschatological Conception of New Testament Theology." In *Eschatology in Bible and Theology*, edited by Kent E. Brower and Mark W. Elliott, 11–52. Downers Grove, IL: InterVarsity, 1997.

Bechara, Antoine. "The role of emotion in decision-making: Evidence from neurological patients with orbitofrontal damage." *Brain and Cognition* 55 (2004) 30–40.

————, Antonio Damasio, Hanna Damasio, and Steven W. Anderson. "Insensitivity to future consequences following damage to human prefrontal cortex." *Cognition* 50 (1994) 7–15.

————, Antonio Damasio, Hanna Damasio, and Gregory P. Lee. "Different Contributions of the Human Amygdala and Ventromedial Prefrontal Cortex to Decision-Making." *The Journal of Neuroscience* 19, no. 13 (1999) 5473–81.

————, Antonio Damasio, Daniel Tranel, and Hanna Damasio. "Deciding advantageously before knowing the advantageous strategy." *Science* 275 (1997) 1293–95.

————, Hanna Damasio, and Antonio Damasio. "Emotion, Decision Making and the Orbitofrontal Cortex." *Cerebral Cortex* 10 (2000) 295–307.

————, Daniel Tranel, and Hanna Damasio. "Characterization of the decision-making deficit of patients with ventromedial prefrontal cortex lesions." *Brain* 123 (2000) 2189–2202.

————, Daniel Tranel, Hanna Damasio, and Antonio Damasio. "Failure to respond autonomically to anticipated future outcomes following damage to prefrontal cortex." *Cerebral Cortex* 6 (1996) 215–25.

Bechtel, William, Pete Mandik, and Jennifer Mundale. "Philosophy Meets the Neurosciences." In *Philosophy and the Neurosciences: A Reader*, edited by William Bechtel, Pete Mandik, and Jennifer Mundale, 5–22. Oxford: Blackwell, 2001.

Bechtel, William, and Robert S. Stufflebeam. "Epistemic Issues in Procuring Evidence about the Brain: The Importance of Research Instruments and Techniques." In *Philosophy and the Neurosciences: A Reader*, and Robert S. Stufflebeam, 55–81. Oxford: Blackwell, 2001.

Bennett, M. R., and P. M. S. Hacker. *Philosophical Foundations of Neuroscience.* Oxford: Blackwell, 2003.

Berger, Peter L. *The Heretical Imperative: Contemporary Possibilities of Religious Affirmation.* Garden City, NY: Anchor, 1979.

Berkhof, Louis. *Systematic Theology.* Grand Rapids, MI: Eerdmans, 1941.

Berry, Dianne C., and Donald E. Broadbent. "On the relationship between task performance and associated verbalizable knowledge." *Quarterly Journal of Experimental Psychology* 36 (1984) 209–31.

Berry, Wendell. *Recollected Essays, 1965–1980.* San Francisco: North Point, 1981.

Bickle, John. "Empirical Evidence for a Narrative Concept of Self." In *Narrative and Consciousness: Literature, Psychology, and the Brain,* edited by Gary D. Fireman, Ted E. McVay, Jr., and Owen Flanagan, 195–208. New York: Oxford University Press, 2003.

Bjorklund, F. "Intuition and Ex-Post Facto Reasoning in Moral Judgments: Some Experimental Findings." *Lund Philosophy Reports* 2 (2004) 1–15.

Blasi, Augusto. "Emotions and Moral Motivation." *Journal for the Theory of Social Behaviour* 29, no. 1 (1999) 1–19.

Bohm, D. *Causality and Chance in Modern Physics.* Philadelphia: University of Pennsylvania Press, 1971.

Bolsinger, Tod E. *It Takes a Church to Raise a Christian: How the Community of God Transforms Lives.* Grand Rapids, MI: Brazos, 2004.

The Book of Discipline of the United Methodist Church. Nashville, TN: United Methodist Publishing House, 2004.

Bowie, G. Lee, Meredith W. Michaels, and Robert C. Solomon, eds. *Twenty Questions: An Introduction to Philosophy.* Orlando, FL: HBJ, 1992.

Boyd, Jeffrey H. "One's self-concept and Biblical theology." *Journal of the Evangelical Theological Society* 40, no. 2 (1997) 207–27.

———. *Reclaiming the Soul: The Search for Meaning in a Self-Centered Culture.* Cleveland, Ohio: Pilgrim, 1996.

Brantley, Richard E. *Locke, Wesley, and the Method of English Romanticism.* Gainesville, FL: University Press of Florida, 1984.

Bready, John Wesley. *England Before and After Wesley: The Evangelical Revival and Social Reform.* London: Hodder and Stoughton, 1938.

Bright, Bill, *Four Spiritual Laws.* San Bernardino, CA: Campus Crusade for Christ, 1965.

Brookes, Derek R. *Thomas Reid: An Inquiry into the Human Mind on the Principles of Common Sense.* University Park, PA: Pennsylvania State University Press, 2001.

Brothers, Leslie. "A Biological Perspective on Empathy." *American Journal of Psychiatry* 146, no. 1 (1989) 10–19.

———. *Friday's Footprint.* New York: Oxford University Press, 2001.

———. "The Social Brain: A Project for Integrating Primate Behaviour and Neurophysiological in a New Domain." *Concepts in Neuroscience* 1 (1990) 27–51.

———, and Brian Ring. "A Neurotheological Framework for the Representation of Minds." *Journal of Cognitive Neuroscience* 4, no. 2 (1992) 107–18.

Brown, Warren S. "Cognitive Contributions to Soul." In *Whatever Happened to the Soul? Scientific and Theological Portraits of Human Nature,* edited by Warren S. Brown, Nancey Murphy, and H. Newton Malony, 99–125. Minneapolis, MN: Fortress, 1998.

———. "Conclusion: Reconciling Scientific and Biblical Portraits of Human Nature." In *Whatever Happened to the Soul? Scientific and Theological Portraits of Human Nature,* edited by Warren S. Brown, Nancey Murphy, and H. Newton Malony, 213–28. Minneapolis, MN: Fortress, 1998.

————. "Evolution, Cognitive Neuroscience, and the Soul." In *Perspectives on an Evolving Creation*, edited by Keith B. Miller, 502–23. Grand Rapids, MI: Eerdmans, 2003.

————. "MacKay's View of Conscious Agents in Dialogue: Speculations on the Embodiment of Soul." *Journal of Philosophy and Psychology* 4 (1997) 497–505.

————. "Neurobiological Embodiment of Spirituality and Soul." In *From Cells to Souls— and Beyond: Changing Portraits of Human Nature*, edited by Malcolm A. Jeeves, 58–76. Grand Rapids, MI: Eerdmans, 2004.

————. "A Neurocognitive Perspective on Free WIL." *CTNS Bulletin* 19, no. 1 (1999) 22–29.

————. "Resonance: A Model for Relating Science, Psychology, and Faith." *Journal of Psychology and Christianity* 23, no. 2 (2004) 110–20.

————. "Nonreductive Physicalism and Soul: Finding Resonance Between Theology and Neuroscience." *American Behavioral Scientist* 45, no. 12 (2002) 1812–21.

————. *Science, Faith, and Human Nature: Reconciling Neuropsychology and Christian Theology*. 2005 Fuller Symposium on the Integration of Faith and Psychology, 16–18 February 2005, Pasadena, CA. Lectures available online at http://www.fuller.edu/sop/integration/Symposium/Symposium%202005/Symposium 2005.html

————, Nancey Murphy, and H. Newton Malony. *Whatever Happened to the Soul? Scientific and Theological Portraits of Human Nature*. Minneapolis, MN: Fortress, 1998.

Browne, Peter. *The Procedure, Extent, and Limits of Human Understanding*. London: Printed for W. Innys and R. Manby, 1737.

Browning, Gary. *Lyotard and the End of Grand Narratives*. Cardiff: University of Wales Press, 2000.

Bruner, Jerome. *Toward a Theory of Instruction*. Cambridge, MA: Harvard University Press, 1990.

Bryant, Barry. "John Wesley's Doctrine of Sin," PhD dissertation, Kings College, University of London, 1992.

Bultmann, Rudolf. "The Meaning of God as Acting." In *God's Activity in the World: The Contemporary Problem*, edited by Owen C. Thomas, 61–76. Chico, NY: Scholars Press, 1983.

————. *Theology of the New Testament*. Vol. 1. New York: Scribner, 1951.

Campbell, Donald T. "'Downward Causation' in Hierarchically Organised Biological Systems." In *Studies in the Philosophy of Biology: Reduction and Related Problems*, edited by Francisco J. Ayala and Theodosius Dobzhansky, 179–86. Berkeley, CA: University of California Press, 1974.

Cannon, William R. "John Wesley's Doctrine of Sanctification and Perfection." *Mennonite Quarterly Review* 35, no. 2 (1961) 91–95.

————. *The Theology of John Wesley, with Special Reference to the Doctrine of Justification*. New York: Abingdon, 1946.

Carter, Sid, and Marcia C. Smith Pasqualini. "Stronger autonomic response accompanies better learning: A test of Damasio's somatic marker hypothesis." *Cognition and Emotion* 18, no. 7 (2004) 901–11.

Carwardine, Richard. "The Second Great Awakening in the Urban Centers: An Examination of Methodism and the 'New Measures'." *Journal of American History* 59 (1972) 327–40.

Cary, Phillip. *Augustine's Invention of the Inner Self: The Legacy of a Christian Platonist*. New York: Oxford University Press, 2000.

Casebeer, William D. "Moral cognition and its neural constituents." *Neuroscience* 4 (2003) 841–46.

———. *Natural Ethical Facts: Evolution, Connectionism, and Moral Cognition* (Cambridge, MA: The MIT Press, 2003.

———, and Patricia Smith Churchland. "The Neural Mechanisms of Moral Cognition: A Multiple-Aspect Approach to Moral Judgment and Decision-Making." *Biology & Philosophy* 18 (2003) 169–94.

Catechism of the Catholic Church. Chicago: Loyola University Press, 1994.

Cato, M. A., D. C. Delis, T. J. Abildskov, and E. Bigler. "Assessing the elusive cognitive deficits associated with ventromedial prefrontal damage: a case of a modern-day Phineas Gage." *Journal for the International Neuropsychological Society* 10, no. 3 (2004) 453–65.

Chandler, Cynthia K., J. M. Holden, and C. A. Kolander. "Counselling for Spiritual Wellness: Theory and Practice." *Journal of Counselling & Development* 71 (1992) 168–75.

Chrestou, Panagiotos K. *Partakers of God* (Brookline, NY: Holy Cross Orthodox Press, 1994.

Christensen, Michael J. "Theosis and Sanctification: John Wesley's Reformulation of a Patristic Doctrine." *Wesleyan Theological Journal* 31, no. 2 (1996) 71–94.

Churchland, Patricia Smith. *Neurophilosophy: Toward a Unified Science of the Mind/Brain*. Cambridge, MA: The MIT Press, 1990.

———. "A Perspective on Mind-Brain Research." *Journal of Philosophy* 77 (1980) 185–207.

Churchland, Paul M. "Eliminative Materialism and Propositional Attitudes." *Journal of Philosophy* 78 (1981) 67–90.

———. *The Engine of Reason, the Seat of the Soul: A Philosophical Journey into the Brain*. Cambridge, MA: The MIT Press, 1995.

———. "Toward a Cognitive Neurobiology of the Moral Virtues." *Topoi* 17 (1998) 83–96.

Clapp, Rodney. *A Peculiar People: The Church as Culture in a Post-Christian Society* (Downers Grove, IL: InterVarsity, 1996.

Clapper, Gregory S. "Finding a Place for Emotions in Christian Theology." *Christian Century* 104, no. 14 (1987) 409–11.

———. *John Wesley on Religious Affections: His Views on Experience and Emotion and Their Role in the Christian Life and Theology*. Metuchen, NJ: Scarecrow, 1989.

———. "John Wesley's 'Heart Religion' and the Righteousness of Christ." *Methodist History* 35 (1997) 148–56.

———. "Orthokardia: The Practical Theology of John Wesley's Heart Religion." *Quarterly Review* 10 (1990) 49–66.

Clarke, Adam. *Christian Theology*, edited by Samuel Dunn. New York: Carlton and Porter, 1835.

———. *The Holy Bible, containing the Old and New Testaments: the Text carefully printed from the most correct copies of the present authorized translation, including the marginal readings and parallel texts; with a Commentary, and Critical Notes, designed as a help to a better understanding of the Sacred Writings*. 6 vols. New York: Ezra Sargent, 1811–25.

Clayton, Philip. *God and Contemporary Science*. Edinburgh: Edinburgh University Press, 1997.

Clendenin, Daniel B. *Eastern Orthodox Christianity: A Western Perspective*. Grand Rapids, MI: Baker, 1994.

Cohen, N. J. "Preserved learning capacity in amnesia: Evidence for multiple memory systems." In *Neuropsychology of Memory*, edited by Larry R. Squire and N. Butters, 83–103. New York: Guilford, 1984.

Collins, Kenneth J. *Exploring Christian Spirituality: An Ecumenical Reader.* Grand Rapids, MI: Baker, 2000.

———. *John Wesley: A Theological Journey.* Nashville, TN: Abingdon, 2003.

———. "A Reconfiguration of Power: The Basic Trajectory of John Wesley's Practical Theology." *Wesleyan Theological Journal* 33, no. 1 (1998) 164–84.

———, and John H. Tyson. *Conversion in the Wesleyan Tradition.* Nashville, TN: Abingdon, 2001.

Come, Arnold B. *Human Spirit and Holy Spirit.* Philadelphia, PA: Westminster, 1959.

Cook, C. M., and Michael A. Persinger. "Experimental induction of the 'sense of presence' in normal subjects and an exceptional subject." *Perceptual and Motor Skills* 85 (1997) 683–93.

Cooper, John W. *Body, Soul & Life Everlasting: Biblical Anthropology and the Monism-Dualism Debate.* Grand Rapids, MI: Eerdmans, 2000.

Coppedge, Allan. "How Wesleyans Do Theology." In *Doing Theology in Today's World*, edited by John Woodbridge and Thomas McComiskey, 267–89. Grand Rapids, MI: Zondervan, 1994.

———. *John Wesley in Theological Debate.* Wilmore, KY: Wesley Heritage, 1987.

Corcoran, Kevin. *Soul, Body and Survival: Essays on the Metaphysics of Human Persons.* Ithica, NY: Cornell University Press, 2001.

Crick, Francis. *The Astonishing Hypothesis: The Scientific Search For The Soul.* New York: Simon and Schuster, 1994.

Crisp, Roger, and Michael Slote. *Virtue Ethics.* Oxford: Oxford University Press, 1998.

Cronk, George. *The Message of the Bible: An Orthodox Christian Perspective.* Crestwood, NY: St. Vladimir's, 1982.

Crossley, Michele L. "Formulating Narrative Psychology: The Limitations of Contemporary Social Constructionism." *Narrative Inquiry* 13, no. 2 (2003) 287–300.

———. "Narrative Psychology, Trauma and the Study of Self/Identity." *Theory & Psychology* 10, no. 4 (2000) 527–46.

Cruikshank, S. J., and N. M. Weinberger. "Evidence for the Hebbian hypothesis in experience-dependent physiological plasticity of neocortex: A critical review." *Brain Research Reviews* 22 (1996) 191–228.

Cubie, David L. "Perfection in Wesley and Fletcher: Inaugural or Teleological?" *Wesleyan Theological Journal* 11 (1976) 22–37.

Cullmann, Oscar. "Immortality of the Soul or Resurrection of the Dead?" In *Immortality and Resurrection*, edited by Krister Stendahl, 9–53. New York: Macmillan, 1958.

Cushman, Robert E. *John Wesley's Experimental Divinity.* Nashville, TN: Kingswood, 1989.

Dalton, John. *A New System of Chemical Philosophy.* New York: Citadel, 1964.

Damasio, Antonio. *Descartes' Error: Emotion, Reason, and the Human Brain.* New York: Avon, 1994.

———. *The Feeling of What Happens: Body and Emotion in the Making of Consciousness.* San Diego, CA: Harcourt, 1999.

———. "How the Brain Creates the Mind." *Scientific American* (1999) 112–17.

———. *Looking for Spinoza: Joy, Sorrow, and the Feeling Brain.* London: Heinemann, 2003.

———. "Time-locked Multiregional Retroactivation." *Cognition* 33 (1989) 25–62.

Damasio, Hanna, Thomas J. Grabowski, R. Frank, A. M. Galaburda, and Antonio Damasio. "The return of Phineas Gage: clues about the brain from the skull of a famous patient." *Science* 264, no. 5162 (1994) 1102–5.

Damon, William. "The Lifelong Transformation of Moral Goals Through Social Influence." In *Interactive Minds: Life-Span Perspectives on the Social Foundation of Cognition*, edited by Paul B. Baltes and Ursula M. Staudinger, 198–220. Cambridge: Cambridge University Press, 1996.

———, and Anne Colby. "Social Influence and Moral Change." In *Moral Development Through Social Interaction*, edited by William Kurtines and Jacob L. Gewirtz, 3–19. New York: Wiley, 1987.

D'Aquili, Eugene and Andrew Newberg. "The Neuropsychological Basis of Religions, or Why God Won't Go Away." *Zygon* 33, no. 2 (1998) 187–201.

———. "The Neuropsychology of Aesthetic, Spiritual, and Mystical States." *Zygon* 35, no. 1 (2000) 39–51.

Darwall, Stephen. *Deontology*. Oxford: Blackwell, 2002.

Daugman, John G. "Brain Metaphor and Brain Theory." In *Philosophy and the Neurosciences: A Reader*, edited by William Bechtel, Pete Mandik, Jennifer Mundale, and Robert S. Stufflebeam, 23–36. Oxford: Blackwell, 2001.

Davidson, Donald. "Mental Events." In *Experience and Theory*, edited by L. Foster and J. Swanson, 79–101. Amherst, MA: University of Massachusetts Press, 1970.

Davidson, Richard J. and William Irwin. "The functional neuroanatomy of emotion and affective style." *Trends in Cognitive Sciences* 3, no. 1 (1999) 11–21.

Davidson, Richard J., Daren C. Jackson, and Ned H. Kalin. "Emotion, Plasticity, Context, and Regulation: Perspectives From Affective Neuroscience." *Psychological Bulletin* 126, no. 6 (2000) 890–909.

Davidson, Richard J. "Affective Style, Psychopathology, and Resilience: Brain Mechanisms and Plasticity." *American Psychologist* 55 (2000) 1196–214.

———. "Toward a Biology of Personality and Emotion." *Annals of the New York Academy of Sciences* 935 (2001) 191–207.

Davies, Rupert. *A History of the Methodist Church in Great Britain*. London: Epworth, 1965.

de Waal, Frans B. M. *Good Natured: The Origins of Right and Wrong in Humans and Other Animals*. Cambridge, MA: Harvard University Press, 1996.

Deacon, Terrence W. *The Symbolic Species: The Co-evolution of Language and the Brain*. New York: W. W. Norton, 1998.

Decety, Jean and Thierry Chaminade. "Neural Correlates of Feeling Sympathy." *Neuropsychologia* 41 (2003) 127–38.

Del Colle, Ralph. "John Wesley's Doctrine of Grace in Light of the Christian Tradition." *International Journal of Systematic Theology* 4 (2002) 172–89.

Dennett, Daniel C. *Consciousness Explained*. Boston: Back Bay, 1992.

Descartes, René. *Descartes: Philosophical Writings*. Translated by G. E. M. Anscombe and P. T. Geach. London: Thomas Nelson, 1970.

———. *The Philosophical Writings of Descartes*. Edited by John Cottingham, Robert Stoothoff, and Dugald Murdoch. Cambridge: Cambridge University Press, 1985.

———. *Selected Philosophical Writings*. Edited by John Cottingham, Robert Stoothoff, and Dugald Murdoch. Cambridge: Cambridge University Press, 1988.

Dobbs, David. "A Revealing Reflection." *Scientific American Mind* 17, no. 2 (2006) 22–27.

Downey, Michael. "Christian spirituality: Changing currents, perspectives, challenges." *America* 170, no. 11 (1994) 8–11.

———. *Understanding Christian Spirituality*. New York: Paulist, 1992.

Draganski, Bogdan, Christian Gaser, Volker Busch, Gerhard Schuierer, Ulrich Bogdahn, and Arne May. "Changes in grey matter induced by training: Newly honed juggling skills show up as a transient feature on a brain-imaging scan." *Nature* 427, no. 22 (2004) 311–12.

Dretske, Fred, "Mental Events as Structuring Causes of Behaviour." In *Mental Causation*, edited by John Heil and Alfred Mele, 121–36. Oxford: Clarendon, 1993.

Dreyer, Frederick. "Faith and Experience in the Thought of John Wesley." *American Historical Review* 88 (1983) 12–30.

Dunn, James D. G. *The Theology of the Apostle Paul*. Grand Rapids, MI: Eerdmans, 1998.

Dweck, Carol S. "Implicit Theories as Organizers of Goals and Behavior." In *The Psychology of Action: Linking Cognition and Motivation to Behavior* Gollwitzer, edited by Peter M. Gollwitzer and John A. Bargh, 69–90. New York: Guilford, 1996.

Eccles, John C. *How the Self Controls its Brain*. New York: Springer-Verlag, 1994.

Edelman, Gerald E. *Bright Air, Brilliant Fire: On the Matter of Mind*. New York: Harper Collins, 1992.

Eisenberg, L. "The Social Construction of the Human Brain." *American Journal of Psychiatry* 152 (1995) 1563–75.

Eisenberg, Nancy, Sandra Losoya and Tracy Spinrad. "Affect and Prosocial Responding." In *Handbook of Affective Sciences*, edited by Richard J. Davidson, Klaus R. Scherer, and H. Hill Goldsmith, 787–803. New York: Oxford University Press, 2003.

Eisenberg, Nancy, C. L. Shea, G. Carlo, and G. P. Knight. "Empathy-related responding and cognition: A 'chicken and the egg' dilemma." In *Handbook of moral behavior and development, Vol. 2: Research*, edited by William M. Kurtines, and Jacob L. Gewirtz, Jacob L., 63–88. New York: Erlbaum, 1991.

Emmons, Robert A. *The Psychology of Ultimate Concerns: Motivation and Spirituality in Personality*. New York: Guilford, 1999.

Eslinger, Paul J. "Neurological and Neuropsychological Bases of Empathy." *European Neurology* 39 (1998) 193–99.

———, Claire V. Flaherty-Craig, and Arthur L. Benton. "Developmental outcomes after early prefrontal cortex damage." *Brain and Cognition* 55 (2004) 84–103.

Farley, Edward. *Theologia: The Fragmentation and Unity of Theological Education*. Philadelphia, PA: Fortress, 1983.

Farrer, Austin. *Faith and Speculation*. London: A & C Black, 1967.

———. *The Freedom of the Will—The Gifford Lectures, 1957*. New York: Scribners, 1958.

Ferguson, Melissa and John Bargh. "How Social Perception Can Automatically Influence Behavior." *Trends in Cognitive Sciences* 8, no. 1 (2004) 33–39.

Ferngren, Gary B. *Science and Religion: A Historical Introduction* (Baltimore, MD: The Johns Hopkins University Press, 2002.

Fitzmeyer, Joseph A. "The Gospel According to Luke." In *The Anchor Bible Dictionary*, edited by David Noel Freedman, 1160–62. Garden City, NY: Double Day, 1985.

Flanagan, Owen. *The Science of Mind*. Cambridge, MA: MIT Press, 1991.

Fogelin, Robert J. *Wittgenstein*. London: Routledge and Kegan Paul, 1980.

Forgas, Joseph P. "Affective Influences on Attitudes and Judgments." In *Handbook of Affective Sciences*, edited by Richard J. Davidson, K. R. Scherer, and H. H. Goldsmith, 596–618. New York: Oxford University Press, 2003.

————. *Handbook of Affect and Social Cognition.* Mahwah, NJ: Lawrence Erlbaum Associates, Publishers, 2001.

Frith, Uta and Chris Frith. "The Biological Basis of Social Interaction." *Current Directions in Psychological Science* 10, no. 5 (2001) 151–55.

Frith, Chris D. and U. Frith. "Interacting Minds—A Biological Basis." *Science's Compass: Review: Cognitive Psychology* 286, no. 5445 (1999) 1692–95.

Galilei, Galileo. *Dialogues Concerning Two New Sciences.* New York: Prometheus, 1991.

Gallagher, Eugene V. *Expectation and Experience: Explaining Religious Conversion.* Atlanta, GA: Scholars Press, 1990.

Gallese, Vittorio. "The 'Shared Manifold' Hypothesis: From Mirror Neurons To Empathy." *Journal of Consciousness Studies* 8, no. 5–7 (2001) 33–50.

Gelpi, Donald L. *The Conversion Process: a reflective process for RCIA participants and others.* New York: Paulist, 1998.

Gillman, Neil. *The Death of Death: Resurrection and Immortality in Jewish Thought.* Woodstock, NY: Jewish Lights, 1997.

Gilson, Etienne. *The Spirit of Medieval Philosophy.* Translated by A. H. C. Downes. New York: Scribners, 1936.

Goodenough, Ursula. "Religious Naturalism and Naturalizing Morality." *Zygon* 38, no. 1 (2003) 101–9.

————, and Terrence W. Deacon. "From Biology to Consciousness to Morality." *Zygon* 38, no. 4 (2003) 801–19.

————, and Paul Woodruff. "Mindful Virtue, Mindful Reverence." *Zygon* 36 (2001) 585–95.

Graham, Billy. *The Collected Works of Billy Graham.* New York: Inspirational, 1993.

————. *How to Be Born Again.* Waco, TX: Work, 1977.

Granqvist, Pehr, M. Fredrikson, P. Unge, A. Hagenfeldt, S. Valid, D. Larhammer, et al. "Sensed presence and mystical experiences are predicted by suggestibility, not the application of transcranial weak complex magnetic fields." *Neuroscience Letters* 372, no. 3 (2004) 1–6.

Green, Joel B. *Beginning with Jesus: Christ in Scripture, the Church, and Discipleship.* Nashville, TN: Cokesbury, 2000.

————. "'Bodies—That Is, Human Lives': A Re-Examination of Human Nature in the Bible." In *Whatever Happened to the Soul? Scientific and Theological Portraits of Human Nature,* edited by Warren S. Brown, Nancey Murphy, and H. Newton Malony, 149–73. Minneapolis, MN: Fortress, 1998.

————. "Restoring the Human Person: New Testament Voices for a Wholistic and Social Anthropology." In *Neuroscience and the Person: Scientific Perspectives on Divine Action,* edited by Robert John Russell, Nancey Murphy, Theo C. Meyering, and Michael A. Arbib, 3–22. Vatican City: Vatican Observatory, 2000.

————. "Resurrection of the Body: New Testament voices concerning personal continuity and the afterlife." In *What about the Soul? Neuroscience and Christian Anthropology,* edited by Joel B. Green, 85–100. Nashville, TN: Abingdon, 2004.

————. *Salvation.* St. Louis, MO: Chalice, 2003.

————. *What About the Soul? Neuroscience and Christian Anthropology.* Nashville, TN: Abingdon, 2004.

————. "What Does It Mean to Be Human? Another Chapter in the Ongoing Interaction of Science and Scripture." In *From Cells To Souls—and Beyond: Changing Portraits of Human Nature,* edited by Malcolm A. Jeeves, 179–98. Grand Rapids, MI: Eerdmans, 2004.

Greene, Joshua D. "An fMRI Investigation of Emotional Engagement in Moral Judgment." *Science* 293, no. 5537 (2001) 2105–10.

———. "From Neural 'is' to Moral 'ought': What are the Moral Implications of Neuroscientific Moral Psychology?." *Neuroscience* 4 (2003) 847–50.

———, Leigh E. Nystrom, Andrew D. Engell, John M. Darley, and Jonathan D. Cohen. "The Neural Bases of Cognitive Conflict and Control in Moral Judgment." *Neuron* 44 (2004) 389–400.

———, and Jonathan Haidt. "How (and where) Does Moral judgment Work?." *Trends in Cognitive Sciences* 6, no. 12 (2002) 517–23.

Grenz, Stanley J. *The Social God and the Relational Self: A Trinitarian Theology of the Imago Dei.* Louisville, KY: Westminster John Knox, 2001.

Grigsby, Jim and David Stevens. *Neurodynamics of Personality.* New York: Guilford, 2000.

Guder, Darrell L. *The Continuing Conversion of the Church.* Grand Rapids, MI: Eerdmans, 2000.

Gundry, Robert H. *Soma in Biblical Theology with Emphasis on Pauline Anthropology* (Cambridge: Cambridge University Press, 1976.

Gunton, Colin E. "Salvation." In *The Cambridge Companion to Karl Barth*, edited by John Webster, 143–58. Cambridge: Cambridge University Press, 2000.

———. *The Promise of Trinitarian Theology.* Edinburgh: T&T Clark, 1999.

———. *The Triune Creator: A Historical and Systematic Study.* Grand Rapids, MI: Eerdmans, 1998.

Gustafson, James M. *Christian Ethics and the Community.* Philadelphia: Pilgrim, 1971.

Gustav, Jahoda. "Theodor Lipps and the shift from sympathy to empathy." *Journal of the History of the Behavioral Sciences* 41, no. 2 (2005) 151–63.

Haas, John W. "John Wesley's Vision of Science in the Service of Christ." *Perspectives on Science and Christian Faith* 47, no. D (1995) 234–43.

Haas, L. F. "Phineas Gage and the science of brain localisation." *Journal of Neurology, Neurosurgery and Psychiatry* 71, no. 6 (2001) 761.

Haidt, Jonathan. "'Dialogue Between My Head and My Heart': Affective Influences on Moral Judgment." *Psychological Inquiry* 13 (2002) 54–56.

———. "The Emotional Dog and Its Rational Tail: A Social Intuitionist Approach to Moral Judgment." *Psychological Review* 108, no. 4 (2001) 814–34.

———. "The Moral Emotions." In *Handbook of Affective Sciences*, edited by R. J. Davidson, K. R. Scherer, and H. H. Goldsmith, 852–70. Oxford: Oxford University Press, 2003.

———, and Craig Joseph. "Intuitive Ethics: How Innately Prepared Intuitions Generate Culturally Variable Virtues." *Daedalus* Special Issue on Human Nature (2004) 55–66.

———, S. Koller, and M. Dias. "Affect, Culture, and Morality, or is it Wrong to Eat Your Dog?" *Journal of Personality and Social Psychology* 65 (1993) 613–28.

Hall, John. "Neuroscience and Education." *Education Journal* 84 (2005) 27–29.

Halliwell, Stephen. *Aristotle's Poetics.* Chicago: University of Chicago Press, 1998.

Harak, G. Simon. *Virtuous Passions: The Formation of Christian Character.* New York: Paulist Press, 1993.

Hare, Richard M. *The Language of Morals.* Oxford: Clarendon, 1952.

Harrington, Daniel J. and James Keenan. *Jesus and Virtue Ethics: Building Bridges Between New Testament Studies and Moral Theology.* Lanham, MD: Rowman & Littlefield, 2002.

Harris, P. L. *Children and Emotion: The Development of Psychological Understanding.* Oxford: Blackwell, 1989.

Harrison, William P. "Wesley and Christian Perfection." *Methodist Quarterly Review* 36, no. 2 (1893) 396–405.

Hart, Stephen. "Privatization in American Religion and Society." *Sociological Analysis* 47 (1987) 319–34.

Hasker, William. *The Emergent Self.* Ithica, NY: Cornell University Press, 1999.

Hastings, James, ed. *A Dictionary of the Bible.* Edinburgh: T & T Clark, 1902.

Hatch, Nathan. "Democratization of Christianity and the Character of American Politics." In *Religion and American Politics: From the Colonial Period to the 1980's,* edited by Mark Noll, 92–120. New York: Oxford University Press, 1990.

Hauerwas, Stanley. *After Christendom: How the Church is to Behave if Freedom, Justice, and a Christian Nation are Bad Ideas* (Nashville, TN: Abingdon, 1999.

———. *Character and the Christian Life: A Study in Theological Ethics.* Notre Dame, IL: University of Notre Dame Press, 1994.

———. "Character, Narrative, and Growth in the Christian Life." In *The Hauerwas Reader,* edited by John Berkman and Michael Cartwright, 221–54. Durham, NC: Duke University Press, 2001.

———. *Christian Existence Today: Essays on Church, World and Living In Between* (Durham, NC: The Labyrinth Press, 1988; Reprint edition: Grand Rapids, MI: Brazos, 2001.

———. *In Good Company: The Church as Polis.* Notre Dame, IL: University of Notre Dame Press, 1995.

———. *The Peaceable Kingdom: A Primer in Christian Ethics.* Notre Dame, IL: University of Notre Dame Press, 1983.

———. "The Sanctified Body: Why Perfection Does Not Require a 'Self'." In *Embodied Holiness: Toward a Corporate Theology of Spiritual Growth,* edited by Samuel M. Powell and Michael E. Lodahl, Michael E., 19–38. Downers Grove, IL: InterVarsity, 1999.

———. *Sanctify Them in the Truth: Holiness Exemplified.* Nashville, TN: Abingdon, 1998.

———. "A Tale of Two Stories: On Being a Christian and a Texan." In *Christian Existence Today: Essays on Church, World and Living in Between,* 25–45.

———, and L. Gregory Jones, *Why Narrative? Readings in Narrative Theology.* Grand Rapids, MI: Eerdmans, 1989.

———, and Charles Pinches. "Virtue Christianly Considered." In *Christian Theism and Moral Philosophy,* edited by Michael Beaty, Carlton Fisher, and Mark Nelson, 287–304. Macon, GA: Mercer University Press, 1998.

———, and William H. Willimon, *Where Resident Aliens Live.* Nashville, TN: Abingdon, 1996.

Hays, Richard B. *The Moral Vision of the New Testament: Community, Cross, and New Creation.* San Francisco, CA: Harper Collins, 1996.

Hebb, Donald O. *The Organization of Behaviour: A Neuropsychological Theory.* New York: Wiley, 1949.

Hebblethwate B., and Henderson E., eds. *Divine Action: Studies Inspired by the Philosophical Theology of Austin Farrer.* Edinburgh: Clark, 1990.

Heekeren, H. R., Isabell Wartenburger, Helge Schmidt, Hans-Peter Schwintowski, and Arno Villringer. "An fMRI study of simple ethical decision-making." *NeuroReport* 14, no. 9 (2003) 1215–19.

Heim, Karl. *Die Wandlung im naturwissenschaftlichen Weltbild.* Wuppertal: Aussaat, 1975.

Heitzenrater, Richard P. *The Elusive Mr. Wesley.* Nashville, TN: Abingdon, 1984.

————. *Mirror and Memory: Reflections on Early Methodism*. Nashville, TN: Kingswood, 1989.

————. *Wesley and the People Called Methodists*. Nashville, TN: Abingdon, 1995.

Henderson, D. Michael. *John Wesley's Class Meeting: A Model for Making Disciples*. Nappanee, IN: Evangel, 1997.

Hick, John. *An Interpretation of Religion*. New Haven: Yale University Press, 1989.

Hobbes, Thomas. *Leviathan*. Edited by C. B. Macpherson. New York: Penguin, 1985.

Hoffman, Martin L. "The Contribution of Empathy to Justice and Moral Judgment." In *Readings in Philosophy and Cognitive Science*, edited by Alvin I. Goldman, 647–80. Cambridge, MA: The MIT Press, 1993.

————. "Developmental Synthesis of Affect and Cognition and Its Implications for Altruistic Motivation." *Developmental Psychology* 11 (1975) 607–22.

————. "Empathy and Prosocial Activism." In *Social and Moral Values: Individual and Societal Perspectives*, edited by Nancy Eisenberg, Janusz Reykowski, and Ervin Staub, 65–85. Hillsdale, NJ: Lawrence Erlbaum, 1989.

————. "Empathy, Social Cognition, and Moral Action." In *Handbook of Moral Behavior and Development: Volume 1: Theory*, edited by William M. Kurtines, and Jacob L. Gewirtz, 275–301. Hillsdale, NJ: Lawrence Erlbaum, 1991.

————. "Interaction of affect and cognition in empathy." In *Emotions, cognition, and behavior*, edited by Carroll E. Izard, Jerome Kagan, and Robert B. Zajonc, 103–31. Cambridge: Cambridge University Press, 1984.

————. "Toward a Theory of Empathic Arousal and Development." In *The Development of Affect*, edited by M. Lewis and L. Rosenblum, 227–56. New York: Plenum, 1978.

Hollinger, Dennis. *Individualism and Social Ethics: An Evangelical Syncretism*. Lanham, NJ: University Press of America, 1983.

Hooker, Brad. *Ideal Code, Real World: A Rule-Consequentialist Theory of Morality*. New York: Oxford University Press, 2000.

Horgan, Terrence E. "Supervenience." In *The Cambridge Dictionary of Philosophy*, edited by Robert Audi, 778–79. Cambridge: Cambridge University Press, 1995.

Horton-Parker, H. S. "John Wesley and the Roots of Contemporary Orthopathy: A Modest Proposal." *Journal of Renewal Studies* 1 (2005) 1–22.

Hume, David. *An Inquiry Concerning Human Understanding*. Indianapolis, IN: Bobbs-Merrill/Oxford University Press, 1955.

Hunter, James D. *American Evangelicalism: Conservative Religion and the Quandary of Modernity*. New Brunswick, NJ: Rutgers University Press, 1983.

Hurley, S., and N. Chater. *Perspectives on Imitation: From Neuroscience to Social Science—Volume 2: Imitation, Human Development, and Culture*. Cambridge, MA: The MIT Press, 2005.

Innes, Robert. *Discourses of the Self: Seeking Wholeness in Theology and Psychology*. Bern: Peter Lang, 1999.

Jackson, Philip L., Andrew Meltzoff, and Jean Decety. "How do we perceive the pain of others? A window into the neural processes involved in empathy." *NeuroImage* 24 (2005) 771–79.

James, William. *The Principles of Psychology*. London: Macmillan, 1890.

Jantzen, Grace. *God's World, God's Body*. Philadelphia, PA: Westminster, 1984.

Jeeves, Malcolm A. *From Cells to Souls—and Beyond*. Grand Rapids, MI: Eerdmans, 2004.

————. *Human Nature at the Millennium: Reflections on the Integration of Psychology and Christianity*. Grand Rapids, MI: Baker, 1997.

————, and R. J. Berry. *Science, Life, and Christian Belief.* Grand Rapids, MI: Baker, 1998.

Jeffreys, Derek S., "The Soul is Alive and Well: Non-reductive Physicalism and Emergent Mental Properties." *Theology and Science* 2 no. 2 (2004) 205–225.

Jennings, Theodore W. *Good News to the Poor: John Wesley's Evangelical Economics.* Nashville, TN: Abingdon, 1990.

Johnson, Paul. *A History of Christianity.* New York: Atheneum, 1976.

Johnson, W. Stanley. "Christian Perfection as Love for God." *Wesleyan Theological Journal* 18 (1983) 50–60.

Jones, L. Gregory. *Transformed Judgment: Toward a Trinitarian Account of the Moral Life.* Notre Dame, IL: University of Notre Dame Press, 1990.

Juarrero, Alicia. *Dynamics in Action: Intentional Behavior as a Complex System.* Cambridge, MA: The MIT Press, 2002.

Kallenberg, Brad J. "Conversion Converted: A Postmodern Formulation of the Doctrine of Conversion." *Evangelical Quarterly* 67, no. 4 (1995) 335–64.

————. *Ethics as Grammar: Changing the Postmodern Subject.* Notre Dame, IL: University of Notre Dame Press, 2001.

————. *Live to Tell: Evangelism in a Postmodern World* (Grand Rapids, MI: Brazos Press, 2002.

Kandel, E. R., and H. Schwartz, H. *Principles of Neural Science.* New York: Elsevier, 1992.

Kant, Immanuel. *Groundwork for the Metaphysics of Morals.* Edited by Thomas E. Hilland Arnulf Zweig. Oxford: Oxford University Press, 2002.

————. *Immanuel Kant's Critique of Pure Reason.* Edited by Norman Kemp Smith. New York: Bedford, 1969.

Kozorovitskiy, Y., C. G. Gross, C. Kopil, L. Battaglia, M. McBreen, A. M. Stranahan, and E. Gould. "Experience induces structural and biochemical changes in the adult primate brain." *Proceedings of the National Academy of Sciences of the United States of America* 102, no. 48 (2005) 17478–82.

Keefer, Luke L. "John Wesley, the Methodists, and Social Reform in England." *Wesleyan Theological Journal* 25, no. 1 (1990) 1–25.

Kelman, Herbert C. "The Role of Action in Attitude Change." In *Nebraska Symposium on Motivation, 1979: Attitudes, Values, and Beliefs,* edited by H. E. Howe and M. M. Page, 117–94. Lincoln, NB: University of Nebraska Press, 1980.

Kemp, Peter. "Mimesis in Educational Hermeneutics." *Educational Philosophy and Theory* 38, no. 2 (2006) 171–84.

Kerr, Fergus. *Theology After Wittgenstein.* London: SPCK, 1997.

Kim, Jaegwon. "Can Supervenience and "Non-Strict Laws" Save Anomalous Monism?" In *Mental Causation,* edited by John Heil, and Alfred Mele, 19–26. Oxford: Clarendon, 1993.

————. *Mind in a Physical World.* Cambridge, MA: The MIT Press, 2000.

————. "The Myth of Nonreductive Physicalism." In *Supervenience and Mind: Selected Philosophical Essays,* edited by Jaegwon Kim, 265–84. Cambridge: Cambridge University Press, 1993.

————. "The Non-Reductivist's Troubles with Mental Causation." In *Mental Causation,* edited by John Heil and Alfred Mele, 189–210. Oxford: Clarendon Press, 1993.

————. *Supervenience and Mind.* Cambridge: Cambridge University Press, 1993.

Klinger, Eric. "Emotional Influences on Cognitive Processing, with Implications for Theories of Both." In *The Psychology of Action: Linking Cognition and Motivation to Behavior* Gollwitzer, edited by M. Peter and John Bargh, 168–89. New York: Guilford, 1996.

Knight, Henry H. *The Presence of God in the Christian Life: John Wesley and the Means of Grace*. Metuchen, NJ: Scarecrow, 1992.

Koechlin, Etienne, Chrystele Ody, and Frederique Kouneiher. "The Architecture of Cognitive Control in the Human Prefrontal Cortex." *Science* 302, no. 14 (2003) 1181–85.

Kraus, C. Norman. *The Community of the Spirit*. Scottdale, NJ: Herald Press, 1993.

Kruschwitz, Robert B., and Robert C. Roberts. *The Virtues: Contemporary Essays on Moral Character*. Belmont, CA: Wadsworth, 1987.

Kuhn, Thomas. *The Structure of Scientific Revolutions*. Chicago: University of Chicago Press, 1962.

Kuyper, Abraham. *The Work of the Holy Spirit*. Grand Rapids, MI: Eerdmans, 1979.

LaCugna, Catherine Mowry. *God For Us: The Trinity & Christian Life*. San Francisco, CA: Harper San Francisco, 1991.

———. "The Relational God: Aquinas and Beyond." *Theological Studies* 46 (1985) 647–63.

Lakatos, Imre. "History of Science and Its Rational Reconstructions." In *Boston Studies in the Philosophy of Science, Vol. VIII*, edited by Roger C. Busch and Robert S. Cohen, 91–135. Dordrecht: Reidel, 1974.

———. *The Methodology of Scientific Research Programmes*. Edited by John Worrall and Gregory Currie. Cambridge: Cambridge University Press, 1978.

Langer, E. J., and L. G. Imber. "When practice makes imperfect: Debilitating effects of overlearning." *Journal of Personality and Social Psychology* 37 (1979) 2014–24.

Lee, Hoyoung. "Experiencing the Spirit in Wesley and Marcarius." In *Rethinking Wesley's Theology for Contemporary Methodism*, edited by Randy L. Maddox, 197–212. Nashville, TN: Kingswood, 1998.

Lee, Philip. *Against the Protestant Gnostics*. Oxford: Oxford University Press, 1987.

Leibniz, Gottfried W. *Discourse on Metaphysics and the Monadology*. Edited by George R. Montgomery. Amherst: Prometheus, 1992.

———. *New Essays on Human Understanding in Leibniz*. Edited by Mary Morris and G. H. R. Parkinson. London: Dent, 1973.

Leffel, G. Michael. "Prevenient Grace and the Re-Enchantment of Nature: Toward a Wesleyan Theology of Psychotherapy and Spiritual Formation." *Journal of Psychology and Christianity* 23, no. 2 (2004) 130–39.

Lieberman, Matthew D. "Intuition: A Social Cognitive Neuroscience Approach." *Psychological Bulletin* 126, no. 1 (2000) 109–36.

———, Kevin N. Ochsner, Daniel T. Gilbert, and Daniel L. Schacter. "Do Amnesics Exhibit Cognitive Dissonance Reduction? The Role of Explicit Memory and Attention in Attitude Change." *Psychological Science* 12, no. 2 (2001) 135–40.

Lindbeck, George A. *The Nature of Doctrine: Religion and Theology in a Postliberal Age*. Philadelphia, PA: Westminster, 1984.

Locke, John. *An Essay on Human Understanding*. Edited by Roger Woolhouse. London: Penguin, 1690.

Lodahl, Michael E. "The Cosmological Basis for Wesley's 'Gradualism'." *Wesleyan Theological Journal* 32 (1997) 17–32.

Loewen, Howard J. "Rethinking Christian Ethics: From Moral Decisions to Character Formation." *Directions* 18, no. 1 (1989) 55–66.

Lonergan, Bernard. *Method in Theology*. New York: Herder and Herder, 1972.

Long, D. Stephen. *John Wesley's Moral Theology: The Quest for God and Goodness.* Nashville, TN: Kingswood, 2005.

Lovejoy, Arthur O. *The Great Chain of Being: A Study of the History of an Idea.* New York: Harper and Row, 1960.

Lovin, Robin W. "The Physics of True Virtue." In *Wesleyan Theology Today*, edited by Theodore Runyon, 264–72. Nashville, TN: Kingswood, 1985.

Lyons, George. "Hermeneutical Bases for Theology: Higher Criticism and the Wesleyan Interpreter. *Wesleyan Theological Journal* 18 (1983) 63–78.

Lyotard, Jean-Francois. *The Postmodern Condition: A Report on Knowledge.* Manchester: Manchester University Press, 1984.

———. *Postmodern Fables.* Minneapolis, MN: University of Minnesota Press, 1997.

Macauley, Samuel. *The New Schaff-Herzog Encyclopedia of Religious Knowledge.* New York: Funk and Wagnalls, 1910.

MacIntyre, Alasdair. *After Virtue: A Study in Moral Theory.* Notre Dame, IL: University of Notre Dame Press, 1981.

———. "Epistemological Crises, Dramatic Narrative, and the Philosophy of Science." In *Why Narrative? Readings in Narrative Theology*, edited by Stanley Hauerwas and L. Gregory Jones, 138–57. Grand Rapids, MI: Eerdmans, 1997.

———. "The Intelligibility of Action." In *Rationality, Relativism, and the Human Sciences*, edited by J. Margolis, M. Krausz, and R. M. Burian, 63–80. Dordrecht: Martinus Nijhoff, 1986.

———. "The Virtues, the Unity of a Human Life, and the Concept of a Tradition." In *Why Narrative? Readings in Narrative Theology*, edited by Stanley Hauerwas and L. Gregory Jones, 89–110. Grand Rapids, MI: Eerdmans, 1997.

———. *Whose Justice? Which Rationality?* Notre Dame, IL: University of Notre Dame Press, 1988.

MacKay, Donald M. *Behind the Eye (Gifford Lectures, 1986).* Oxford: Blackwell, 1991.

———. *Human Science and Human Dignity.* Downers Grove, IL: InterVarsity, 1997.

Macmillan, Malcolm. "Inhibition and the control of behavior. From Gall to Freud via Phineas Gage and the frontal lobes." *Brain and Cognition* 19, no. 1 (1992) 72–104.

———. *An Odd Kind of Fame: Stories of Phineas Gage.* Cambridge, MA: The MIT Press, 2000.

Maddox, Randy L. "John Wesley—Practical Theologian?" *Wesleyan Theological Journal* 23, no. 1 (1988) 122–47.

———. "Nurturing the New Creation: Reflections on a Wesleyan Trajectory." In *Wesleyan Perspectives on the New Creation*, edited by Douglas M. Meeks, 21–52. Nashville, TN: Kingswood, 2004.

———. "Reading Wesley as a Theologian." *Wesleyan Theological Journal* 30 no. 1 (1995) 7–54.

———. "Reconnecting the Means to the End: A Wesleyan Prescription for the Holiness Movement." *Wesleyan Theological Journal* 33, no. 2 (1998) 29–66.

———. *Responsible Grace: John Wesley's Practical Theology.* Nashville, TN: Kingswood, 1994.

———. "Responsible Grace: The Systematic Nature of Wesley's Theology Reconsidered." *Quarterly Review* 6, no. 1 (1986) 24–34.

Maquire, Eleanor A., David G. Gadian, Ingrid S. Johnsrude, Catriona D. Good, John Ashburner, Richard S. Frackowiak, et al. "Navigation-related structural change in the hippocampi of taxi drivers." *Proceedings of the National Academy of Sciences* 97, no. 8 (2000) 4398–403.

Martin, Dale B. *The Corinthian Body*. New Haven: Yale University Press, 1995.

Martin, Troy W. "John Wesley's Exegetical Orientation: East or West?" *Wesleyan Theological Journal* 26, no. 1 (1991) 104–38.

McAdams, Dan P. "Can Personality Change? Levels of Stability and Growth in Personality Across the Life Span." In *Can Personality Change?*, edited by Todd F. Heatherton, and Joel L. Weinberger, 299–313. Washington D.C.: American Psychological Association, 1994.

―――. "The Psychology of Life Stories." *Review of General Psychology* 5, no. 2 (2001) 100–122.

McClendon, James Wm. *Ethics: Systematic Theology, Vol. 1*. Nashville, TN: Abingdon, 2002.

―――, and James Smith. *Convictions: Defusing Religious Relativism*. Valley Forge, VA: Trinity, 1994.

McKim, Donald K. *Westminster Dictionary of Theological Terms*. Louisville, KY: Westminster, 1996.

McFayden, Alistair I. *The Call to Personhood: A Christian Theory of the Individual in Social Relationships*. Cambridge: Cambridge University Press, 1990.

McGinn, Colin. "Consciousness and Content." In *The Nature of Consciousness: Philosophical Debates*, edited by Ned Block, Owen Flanagan, and Guven Guzeldere, 255–307. Cambridge: Cambridge University Press, 1997.

Mckinney, Laurence O. *Neurotheology: Virtual Religion in the 21st Century*. Arlington, MA: American Institute for Mindfulness, 1994.

McLoughlin, William G. *Modern Revivalism*. New York: Ronald, 1959.

Meagher, Robert. *Augustine on the Inner Life of the Mind*. Indianapolis, IN: Hackett, 1998.

Meeks, Wayne A. *The First Urban Christians: The Social World of the Apostle Paul*. New Haven: Yale University Press, 1984.

Meilaender, Gilbert C. *The Theory and Practice of Virtue*. Notre Dame, IL: University of Notre Dame Press, 1984.

Merritt, John G. "Dialogue Within a Tradition: John Wesley and Gregory of Nyssa Discuss Christian Perfection." *Wesleyan Theological Journal* 22, no. 2 (1987) 92–116.

Meyendorff, John. *Byzantine Theology: Historical Trends and Doctrinal Themes*. New York: Fordham University Press, 1979.

―――. *A Study of Gregory Palamas*. London: Faith, 1964.

Meyering, Theo C. *Historical Roots of Cognitive Science: The Rise of a Cognitive Theory of Perception from Antiquity to the Nineteenth Century*. Boston, MA: Kluwer, 1989.

Mill, John Stuart. *Utilitarianism*. Edited by George Sher. Indianapolis, IN: Hackett Publishing Company, 2002.

Miller, William R., and Janet C'de Baca. *Quantum Change: When Epiphanies and Sudden Insights Transform Ordinary Lives*. New York: Guilford, 2001.

Milner, B., M. Petrides, and E. R. Kandel. "Cognitive Neuroscience and the Study of Memory." *Neuron* 20 (1998) 445–68.

Mishkin, M., B. Malamut, and J. Bachevalier. "Memories and habits: Two neural systems." In *Neurobiology of Learning and Memory*, edited by G. Lynch, J. L. McGaugh, and N. M. Weinberger, 65–77. New York: Guilford, 1984.

Moll, Jorge, Ricardo de Oliveira-Souza, Ivanei E. Bramati, and Jordan Grafman. "Functional Networks in Emotional Moral and Nonmoral Social Judgments." *NeuroImage* 16 (2002) 696–703.

Moll, Jorge, Ricardo de Oliveira-Souza, Paul J. Eslinger, Ivanei E. Bramati, Janaina Mourao-Miranda, Pedro Angelo Andreiuolo, et al. "The Neural Correlates of Moral Sensitivity: A Functional Magnetic Resonance Imaging Investigation of Basic and Moral Emotions." *The Journal of Neuroscience* 22, no. 7 (2002) 2730–36.

Moll, Jorge, Ricardo de Oliveira-Souza, and Paul J. Eslinger. "Morals and the human brain: a working model." *NeuroReport* 14, no. 3 (2003) 299–305.

Moltmann, Jurgen. *The Trinity and the Kingdom*. Minneapolis, MN: Fortress, 1993.

Moore, G. E. *Philosophical Studies*. London: Routledge, 1922.

Moreland, J. P., and Scott B. Rae. *Body & Soul: Human Nature & the Crisis in Ethics*. Downers Grove, IL: InterVarsity, 2000.

Mundale, Jennifer. "Neuroanatomical Foundations of Cognition: Connecting the Neuronal Level with the Study of Higher Brain Areas." In *Philosophy and the Neurosciences: A Reader*, edited by William Bechtel, Pete Mandik, Jennifer Mundale, and Robert S. Stufflebeam, 37–54. Oxford: Blackwell, 2001.

Murphy, Nancey. *Anglo-American Postmodernity: Philosophical Perspectives on Science, Religion, and Ethics*. Boulder, CO: Westview Press, 1997.

———. *Beyond Liberalism & Fundamentalism: How Modern and Postmodern Philosophy Set the Theological Agenda*. Harrisburg, PA: Trinity, 1996.

———. *Bodies and Souls, or Spirited Bodies?* Cambridge: Cambridge University Press, 2006.

———. "Constructing a Radical-Reformation Research Program in Psychology." In *Why Psychology Needs Theology: A Radical Reformation Perspective*, edited by Al Dueck and Cameron Lee, chapter 3. Grand Rapids, MI: Eerdmans, 2005.

———. "Divine Action in the Natural Order: Buridan's Ass and Schrodinger's Cat." In *Chaos and Complexity: Scientific Perspectives on Divine Action*, edited by Robert John Russell, Nancey Murphy, and Arthur Peacocke, 325–57. Vatican City: Vatican Observatory, 1997.

———. "Downward Causation and Why the Mental Matters." *CTNS Bulletin* 19, no. 1 (1999) 13–21.

———. "God's Nonviolent Direct Action." In *Religion and Science: God, Evolution, and the Soul*, edited by Carl S. Helrich, 29–43. Kitchener, Ontario: Pandora, 2002.

———. "Human Nature: Historical, Scientific, and Religious Issues." In *Whatever Happened to the Soul? Scientific and Theological Portraits of Human Nature*, edited by Warren S. Brown, Nancey Murphy, and H. Newton Malony, 1–29. Minneapolis, MN: Fortress, 1998.

———. "Nonreductive Physicalism: Philosophical Issues." In *Whatever Happened to the Soul? Scientific and Theological Portraits of Human Nature*, edited by Warren S. Brown, Nancey Murphy, and H. Newton Malony, 127–48. Minneapolis, MN: Fortress, 1998.

———. "The Nonviolent Action of God." Unpublished lecture presented at Monmouth College, USA, March 24, 1998.

———. "On the Role of Philosophy in Theology-Science Dialogue." *Theology and Science* 1 no. 1 (2003) 79–93.

———. "Physicalism Without Reductionism: Toward a Scientifically, Philosophically, and Theologically Sound Portrait of Human Nature." *Zygon* 34, no. 4 (1999) 551–71.

———. "The Problem of Mental Causation: How Does Reason Get its Grip on the Brain?" *Science & Christian Belief* 14, no. 2 (2002) 143–58.

———. *Reconciling Theology and Science: A Radical Reformation Perspective*. Kitchener, Ontario: Pandora, 1997.

————. "Scientific Realism and Postmodern Philosophy." *The British Journal for the Philosophy of Science* 41, no. 3 (1990) 291–303.

————. "Supervenience and the Downward Efficacy of the Mental: A Nonreductive Physicalist Account of Human Action." In *Neuroscience and the Person: Scientific Perspectives on Divine Action*, edited by Robert John Russell, Nancey Murphy, Theo C. Meyering, Theo and Michael A. Arbib, 147–64. Vatican City: Vatican Observatory, 1999.

————. "Supervenience and the Nonreducibility of Ethics to Biology." In *Evolutionary and Molecular Biology: Scientific Perspectives on Divine Action*, edited by Robert John Russell, 463–90. Vatican City: Vatican Observatory, 1998.

————. "Theology and Science Within a Lakatosian Program." *Zygon* 34, no. 4 (1999) 629–42.

————. *Theology in the Age of Scientific Reasoning*. Ithaca, NY: Cornell University Press, 1990.

————. "Whatever Happened to the Soul? Theological Perspectives on Neuroscience and the Self." *New York Academy of Sciences* 1001 (2003) 51–64.

————, and Warren S. Brown. *Did My Neurons Make Me Do It? Philosophical and Neurobiological Perspectives on Moral Responsibility and Free Will*. Oxford: Oxford University Press, 2007.

————, and George F. R Ellis. *On the Moral Nature of the Universe*. Minneapolis, MN: Fortress, 1996.

————, and James Wm. McClendon. "Distinguishing Modern and Postmodern Theologies." *Modern Theology* 5 (1989) 191–214.

Myers, Bryant L. *Walking with the Poor: Principles and Practices of Transformational Development*. Mary Knoll, NY: Orbis, 1999.

Naito, H. and N. Matsui. "Temporal lobe epilepsy with ictal ecstatic state and interictal behavior of hypergraphia." *Journal of Nervous and Mental Disorders* 176 (1988) 123–24.

Nee, Watchman. *The Release of the Spirit*. Richmond, VA: Christian Fellowship, 2000.

Nelson, Paul. *Narrative and Morality: A Theological Inquiry*. University Park, PA: The Pennsylvania State University Press, 1987.

Newberg, Andrew. "Putting the Mystical Mind Together." *Zygon* 36, no. 3 (2001) 501–7.

————, and Eugene D'Aquili. "The Creative Brain/The Creative Mind." *Zygon* 35 no. 1 (2000) 53–68.

————. "The Neuropsychology of Religious and Spiritual Experience." *Journal of Consciousness Studies* 7, no. 11–12 (2000) 251–66.

Newberg, Andrew, Eugene D'Aquili, and Vince Rause. *Why God Won't Go Away*. New York: Ballantine, 2002.

Newbigin, Lesslie. *Signs Amid the Rubble: The Purposes of God in Human History*. Grand Rapids, MI: Eerdmans, 2003.

Newton, Isaac. *Isaac Newton: Philosophical Writings*. Cambridge: Cambridge University Press, 2004.

Noro, Yoshio. "Wesley's Theological Epistemology." *Iliffe Review* 28 (1971) 59–76.

Oatley, Keith, and Jennifer M. Jenkins. *Understanding Emotions*. Oxford: Blackwell, 1996.

Ochsner, Kevin N. and Liebermann, Matthew D. "The Emergence of Social Cognitive Neuroscience." *American Psychologist* 56 (2001) 717-34.

O'Connor, John D. "Are Virtue Ethics and Kantian Ethics Really so Very Different?" *New Blackfriars* 87 (2006) 238–52.

Oden, Thomas C. *John Wesley's Scriptural Christianity: A Plain Exposition of His Teaching on Christian Doctrine*. Grand Rapids, MI: Zondervan, 1994.

Ogata, A., and T. Miyakawa. "Religious experiences in epileptic patients with a focus on ictus-related episodes." *Psychiatry and Clinical Neurosciences* 52 (1998) 321–25.

Outler, Albert Cook. *John Wesley*. New York: Oxford University Press, 1964.

———. *Place of Wesley in the Christian Tradition*. Metuchen, NJ: Scarecrow, 1976.

———. "Towards a Re-appraisal of John Wesley as a Theologian." *The Perkins School of Theology Journal* 14 (1961) 5–14.

Palmer, Phoebe. *Faith and Its Effects*. Toronto: Sanderson, 1856.

———. *The Way of Holiness, with Notes by the Way*. New York: Lane and Tippett, 1845.

Pannenberg, Wolfhart. *Theology and the Philosophy of Science*. Edited by Francis McDonagh. Philadelphia, PA: Westminster, 1976.

Peacocke, Arthur. *God and the New Biology*. London: Dent, 1986. Vatican City: Vatican Observatory, 1995.

———. "God's Interaction with the World: The Implications of Deterministic 'Chaos' and of Interconnected and Interdependent Complexity." In *Chaos and Complexity: Scientific Perspectives on Divine Action*, edited by Robert John Russell, Nancey Murphy, and Arthur Peacocke, 263–88.

———. *Paths From Science Towards God: The End of All Our Exploring*. Oxford: One World, 2002.

———. *Theology for a Scientific Age: Being and Becoming—Natural, Divine and Human*. Minneapolis, MN: Fortress, 1993.

Pegis, Anton C. "The Separated Soul and Its Nature in St. Thomas." In *St. Thomas Aquinas, 1274–1974: Commemorative Studies – vol. I*, edited by Armand A. Maurer, 131–58. Toronto: Pontifical Institute of Mediaeval Studies, 1974.

Perkins, William. *A Golden Chain, or the Description of Theology; Containing the Order of the Causes of Salvation and Damnation*. London: Legatt, 1591.

Persinger, Michael A. "Experimental simulation of the god experience: Implications for religious beliefs and the future of the human species." In *Neurotheology: Brain, science, spirituality, religious experience*, edited by R. Joseph, 267–84. San Jose, CA: University Press, 2002.

———. "Neurobehavioral effects of brief exposures to weak intensity, complex magnetic fields within experimental and clinical settings." In *Magnetotherapy: Potential therapeutic benefits and adverse effects*, edited by M. J. Mclean, S. Engstrom, and R. R. Holocomb, 89–118. New York: TFG, 2003.

Peters, John Leland *Christian Perfection and American Methodism*. New York: Abingdon, 1956.

Peterson, Gregory R. *Minding God: Theology and the Cognitive Sciences*. Minneapolis, MN: Fortress, 2003.

Pinnock, Clark. *Most Moved Mover: A Theology of God's Openness*. Grand Rapids, MI: Baker, 2001.

———, Richard Rice, John, Sanders, William Hasker, and David Basinger. *The Openness of God: A Biblical Challenge to the Traditional Understanding of God*. Downers Grove, IL: InterVarsity, 1994.

Pizarro, David. "Nothing More Than Feelings? The Role of Emotions in Moral Judgment." *Journal for the Theory of Social Behaviour* 30, no. 4 (2000) 355–75.

Plato. *The Essential Plato*. Translated by Benjamin Jewett. New York: Quality Paperback Book Club, 1999.

———. *The Republic*. Translated by Desmond Lee. New York: Penguin, 1983.

Pojman, Louis P. *Who are We? Theories of Human Nature.* Oxford: Oxford University Press, 2005.

Polanyi, Michael. *The Tacit Dimension.* London: Routledge and Kegan Paul, 1967.

Polkinghorne, John. "The Metaphysics of Divine Action." In *Chaos and Complexity: Scientific Perspectives on Divine Action,* edited by Robert John Russell, Nancey Murphy, and Arthur Peacocke, 147–56. Vatican City: Vatican Observatory, 1997.

Pollard, William. *Chance and Providence: God's Action in a World Governed by Scientific Law.* New York: Scribner, 1958.

Popper, Karl. *The Logic of Scientific Discovery.* New York: Harper, 1965.

Post, Stephen G. "A Moral Case for Nonreductive Physicalism." In *Whatever Happened to the Soul? Scientific and Theological Portraits of Human Nature,* edited by Warren S. Brown, Warren S., Nancey Nancey, and H. Newton Malony, 195–212, Minneapolis, MN: Fortress, 1998.

Prigogine, I., and I. Stengers. *Order out of Chaos: Man's New Dialogue with Nature.* New York: Bantam, 1984.

Rack, Henry D. *Reasonable Enthusiast: John Wesley and the Rise of Methodism.* London: Epworth, 2002.

Ramachandran, V. S., and Sandra Blakeslee. *Phantoms in the Brain: Probing the Mysteries of the Human Mind.* New York: Quill, 1998.

Rambo, Lewis R. *Understanding Religious Conversion.* New Haven: Yale University Press, 1993.

Ramon y Cajal, Santiago. *Advice for a Young Investigator.* Edited by Neely Swanson and Larry W. Sanson. Cambridge, MA: The MIT Press, 1999.

Rause, Vince, Andrew Newberg, and Eugene D'Aquili. *Why God Won't Go Away.* New York: Ballantine, 2002.

Reis, Harry T., and W. Andrew Collins. "Relationships, Human Behavior, and Psychological Science." *Current Directions in Psychological Science* 13, no. 6 (2004) 233–37.

Richards, Larry. *Born to Grow.* Wheaton, IL: Scripture, 1977.

Ricoeur, Paul. *Time and Narrative: Volume 1.* Chicago: University of Chicago Press, 1990.

Roberts, R. E. *The Theology of Tertullian.* London: Epworth, 1924.

Robinson, H. Wheeler. *The Christian Doctrine of Man.* Edinburgh: T & T Clark, 1926.

Robinson, John A. T. *The Body: A Study in Pauline Theology.* London: SCM, 1952.

Rosenblatt, Allan. "Insight, Working Through, and Practice: The Role of Procedural Knowledge." *Journal of the American Psychoanalytic Association* 52, no. 1 (2004) 189–207.

Runyon, Theodore. "Holiness as the Renewal of the Image of God in the Individual and Society." In *Embodied Holiness: Toward A Corporate Theology of Spiritual Growth,* edited by Samuel M. Powell, and Michael E. Lodahl, 79–88. Downers Grove, IL: InterVarsity, 1999.

———. *The New Creation: John Wesley's Theology Today.* Nashville, TN: Abingdon, 1998.

———. "The New Creation: The Wesleyan Distinctive." *Wesleyan Theological Journal* 31 (1996) 5–19.

———. "What is Methodism's Theological Contribution Today?" In *Wesleyan Theology Today: A Bicentennial Theological Concentration,* edited by Theodore Runyon. Nashville, TN: United Methodist Publishing House, 1985.

Russell, Robert John. "Divine Action and Quantum Mechanics: A Fresh Assessment." In *Quantum Mechanics: Scientific Perspectives on Divine Action,* edited by Robert John Russell, Philip Clayton, Kirk Wegter-McNelly, and John Polkinghorne, 293–328. Vatican City: Vatican Observatory Publications, 2001.

————, Nancey Murphy, Theo C. Meyering, and Michael A. Arbib. *Neuroscience and the Person: Scientific Perspectives on Divine Action*. Notre Dame, IL: Vatican Observatory, 1999.

Ryan, Richard M., Kennon M. Sheldon, Tim Kasser, and Edward L. Deci. "All Goals Are Not Created Equal: An Organismic Perspective on the Nature of Goals and Their Regulation." In *The Psychology of Action: Linking Cognition and Motivation to Behavior*, edited by Peter M. Gollwitzer, and John Bargh, 7–26. New York: Guilford, 1996.

Ryle, Gilbert. *The Concept of Mind*. Chicago: University of Chicago Press, 2000.

————. *Dilemmas: The Tarner Lectures—1953*. Cambridge: Cambridge University Press, 1954.

Ryrie, Charles C. "What is Spirituality?" *Bibliotheca Sacra* 126 (1969) 204–13.

Saldanha, Chrys. *Divine Pedagogy: A Patristic View of Non-Christian Religions*. Rome: Editrice Libreria Ateneo Salesiano, 1984.

Sangster, W. E. *The Path to Perfection: An Examination of John Wesley's Doctrine of Christian Perfection*. Norwich: Epworth Press, 1984.

Sapir, Edward. cited in *Twenty Questions: An Introduction to Philosophy*, G. Lee Bowie, Meredith W. Michaels, and Robert C. Solomon (eds.), (Orlando, FL: Harcourt Brace Jovanovich, 1992).

Saunders, Nicholas. *Divine Action and Modern Science*. Cambridge: Cambridge University Press, 2002.

Schleiermacher, Friedrich. "Notes on Aristotle: Nicomachean Ethics 8–9." *Theology Today* 56, no. 2 (1999) 164–68.

————. *On Religion: Speeches to Its Cultured Despisers*. Translated by John Oman. New York: Harper Row, 1958.

Schmidt-Hieber, Christoph, Peter Jonas, and Josef Bischofberger. "Enhanced synaptic plasticity in newly generated granule cells of the adult hippocampus." *Nature* 429 (2004) 184–87.

Schneiders, Sandra M. "The Study of Christian Spirituality: The Contours and Dynamics of a Discipline." *Christian Spirituality Bulletin* 6 (1998) 3–12.

Schroeder, H. J. *Canons and Decrees of the Council of Trent*. Rockford, IL: Tan, 1978.

Schwartz, Jeffrey M. *Brain Lock: Free Yourself From Obsessive-Compulsive Behavior*. New York: Harper Collins, 1997.

————. "A Role for Volition and Attention in the Generation of New Brain Circuitry: Toward a Neurobiology of Mental Force." *Journal of Consciousness Studies* 6 no. 8–9 (1999) 115–142.

————, and Sharon Begley. *The Mind & The Brain: Neuroplasticity and the Power of Mental Force*. New York: Regan, 2003.

————, Henry P. Stapp, and Mario Beauregard. "The Volitional Influence of the Mind on the Brain, with Special Reference to Emotional Self-regulation." In *Consciousness, Emotional Self-Regulation and the Brain*, edited by Mario Beauregard, 195–238. Amsterdam: Benjamins, 2004.

Schwobel, Christoph, and Colin E. Gunton. *Persons Divine and Human*. Edinburgh: T & T Clark, 1991.

Searle, John R. *The Construction of Social Reality*. New York: Free, 1995.

————. *The Rediscovery of Mind*. Cambridge, MA: The MIT Press, 1992.

Sellars, Roy Wood. *The Philosophy of Physical Realism*. New York: Russell and Russell, 1966.

————. *Principals of Emergent Realism: The Philosophical Essays of Roy Wood Sellars*. Edited by W. Preston Warren. St. Louis, MO: Green, 1970.

Sereno, Martin I. "Plasticity and its Limits." *Nature* 435, no. 7040 (2005) 288–289.

Shamay-Tsoory, S. G., R. Tomer, B. D. Berger, and J. Aharon-Peretz. "Characterization of Empathy Deficits following Prefrontal Brain Damage: The Role of the Right Ventromedial Prefrontal Cortex." *Journal of Cognitive Neuroscience* 15, no. 3 (2003) 324–37.

Sheldrake, Philip. "What Is Spirituality?" In *Exploring Christian Spirituality: An Ecumenical Reader*, edited by Kenneth J. Collins, 21–42. Grand Rapids, MI: Baker, 2000.

Shelton, Charles M. *Morality of the Heart: A Psychology for the Christian Moral Life*. New York: Crossroad, 1990.

Sider, Ronald J. *The Scandal of the Evangelical Conscience: Why Are Christians Living Just Like the Rest of the World?* Grand Rapids, MI: Baker, 2005.

Siegel, Daniel J. *The Developing Mind: How Relationships and the Brain Interact to Shape Who We Are*. New York: Guilford, 1999.

Singer, Tania, Ben Seymour, John O'Doherty, Holger Kaube, Raymond J. Dolan, and Chris D. Frith. "Empathy for Pain Involves the Affective but not Sensory Components of Pain." *Science* 303, no. 20 (2004) 1157–62.

Skinner, B. F. *Beyond Freedom and Dignity*. New York: Knopf, 1972.

Snyder, Howard A. "John Wesley and Marcarius the Egyptian." *Asbury Theological Journal* 45 (1990) 55–60.

Sperry, Len. *Transforming Self and Community: Revisioning Pastoral Counseling and Spiritual Direction*. Collegeville, NY: Liturgical, 2002.

Spidlik, Thomas. *The Spirituality of the Christian East*. Kalamazoo, MI: Cistercian, 1986.

Spohn, William C. *Go and Do Likewise: Jesus and Ethics*. New York: Continuum, 2000.

———. "The Return of Virtue Ethics." *Theological Studies* 53 (1992) 60–75.

Squire, Larry R. *Memory and Brain*. New York: Oxford University Press, 1987.

———, and Daniel L. Schacter. *The Neuropsychology of Memory*. New York: Guilford, 2002.

Stanford, Miles. *Principles of Spiritual Growth*. Lincoln: Back to the Bible, 1976.

Stassen, Glen H., and David P. Gushee. *Kingdom Ethics: Following Jesus in Contemporary Context*. Downers Grove, IL: InterVarsity, 2003.

Stevenson, Leslie. *Ten Theories of Human Nature*. New York: Oxford University Press, 1998.

Stone, Valerie E., Simon Baron-Cohen, and Robert T. Knight. "Frontal Lobe Contributions to Theory of Mind." *Journal of Cognitive Neuroscience* 10, no. 5 (1998) 640–56.

Strauss, David Friedrich. *The Life of Jesus Critically Examined*. Edited with an introduction by Peter C. Hodgson. Translated from the 4th German edition by George Elliot. Minneapolis: Fortress, 1973; Reprint edition: Ramsey, NJ: Sigler, 1994.

Strawn, Brad D., and Warren S. Brown. "Wesleyan Holiness through the Eyes of Cognitive Science and Psychotherapy." *Journal of Psychology and Christianity* 23, no. 2 (2004) 121–29.

Strawn, Brad D., and G. Michael Leffel. "John Wesley's orthokardia and Harry Guntrip's 'heart of the personal': convergent aims and complementary practices in psychotherapy and spiritual formation." *Journal of Psychology and Christianity* 20, no. 4 (2001) 351–59.

Stromberg, Peter G. *Language and Self-Transformation: A study of the Christian conversion narrative*. Cambridge: Cambridge University Press, 1993.

Sutherland, Stewart. "Providence and the Narrative Life." In *Philosophical Assessment of Theology*, edited by Gerard J. Hughes, 171–85. Tunbridge Wells: Search, 1987.

Sweet, William Warren. *The American Churches: An Interpretation*. New York: Abingdon-Cokesbury Press, 1947.

Taber, Charles R. "The Gospel as Authentic Meta-Narrative Source." In *Scandalous Prophet: The Way of Mission After Newbigin*, edited by Thomas F. Foust, George R. Hunsberger, J. Andrew Kirk, and Werner Ustorf, 182–94. Grand Rapids, MI: Eerdmans, 2002.

Taliaferro, Charles. *Consciousness and the Mind of God*. Cambridge: Cambridge University Press, 2005.

Taylor, Charles. *Sources of the Self: The Making of the Modern Identity*. Cambridge, MA: Harvard University Press, 1989.

Telford, John, ed. *The Letters of the Rev. John Wesley*. London: Epworth, 1931.

Temple, William. *Christianity and Social Order*. New York: Seabury, 1977.

————. *Nature, Man and God*. London: Macmillan, 1934.

————. *Christus Veritas: An Essay*. London: Macmillan, 1924.

Teresa of Avila. "Interior Castle." In *The Collected Works of St. Teresa of Avila: Vol. 2*, edited by Otilio Rodriguez, and Kieran Kavanaugh. Washington DC: Institute of Carmelite Studies, 1980.

Teske, John A. "The Social Construction of the Human Spirit." In *The Human Person in Science and Theology*, edited by Niels Henrik Gregersen, Willem B. Drees, and Ulf Görman, 189–211. Grand Rapids, MI: Eerdmans, 2000.

Thelen, E. "Self-organization in developmental processes: Can systems approaches work?" In *Minnesota Symposium on Child Psychology: Systems and Development – vol 22*, edited by M. Gunnar, and E. Thelen, E., 77–117. Hillsdale, NJ: Erlbaum, 1989.

————, and L. B. Smith. *A Dynamic Systems Approach to the Development of Cognition and Action*. Cambridge, MA: The MIT Press, 1994.

Thomas, Owen C. *God's Activity in the World: The Contemporary Problem*. Chico, NY: Scholars Press, 1983.

————. "Interiority and Christian Spirituality." *The Journal of Religion* 80, no. 1 (2000) 41–60.

————. "Some Problems in Contemporary Christian Spirituality." *Anglican Theological Review* 82, no. 2 (2000) 267–281.

Thompson, E. P. *The Making of the English Working Class*. New York: Vintage, 1966.

Tillich, Paul. *Christianity and the Encounter of World Religions*. New York: Columbia University Press, 1963.

Torrance, Thomas F. *The Christian Doctrine of God, One Being Three Persons*. Edinburgh: T&T Clark, 1997.

Tranel, Daniel. "Emotion, Decision Making, and the Ventromedial Prefrontal Cortex." In *Principles of Frontal Lobe Function*, edited by Donald T. Stuss, and Robert T. Knight, 338–53. New York: Oxford University Press, 2002.

Tripolitis, A. *The Doctrine of the Soul in the Thought of Plotinus and Origen*. New York: Libra, 1978.

Turner, Denys. *The Darkness of God: Negativity in Christian Mysticism*. Cambridge: Cambridge University Press, 1995.

Tuttle, Robert G. *John Wesley: His Life and Theology*. Grand Rapids, MI: Zondervan, 1978.

Urry, H. L., J. B. Nitschke, I. Dolski, D. C. Jackson, K. M. Dalton, C. J. Mueller, et al. "Making a Life Worth Living: Neural Correlates of Well-Being." *Psychological Science* 15 (2004) 367–72.

van Gulick, Robert. "Who's in Charge Here? And Who's Doing All the Work?" In *Mental Causation*, edited by John Heil and Alfred Mele, 233–51. Oxford: Clarendon, 1993.

———. "Three Bad Arguments for Intentional Property Epiphenomenalism." *Erkenntnis* 36, no. 3 (1992) 311–32.

Volf, Miroslav. *After Our Likeness: The Church as the Image of the Trinity.* Grand Rapids, MI: Eerdmans, 1998.

Vollmer, Fred. "The Narrative Self." *Journal for the Theory of Social Behaviour* 35, no. 2 (2005) 189–205.

von Neumann, John. "Measurement and Reversibility." In *Mathmatical Foundations of Quantum Mechanics*, 347–57. Translated from the German edition by Robert T. Beyer. Investigations in Physics 2. Princeton: Princeton University Press, 1955.

———. "The Measuring Process." In *Mathmatical Foundations of Quantum Mechanics*, 417–37. Translated from the German edition by Robert T. Beyer. Investigations in Physics 2. Princeton: Princeton University Press, 1955.

Wagar, B. M., and P. Thagard. "Spiking Phineas Gage: a neurocomputational theory of cognitive-affective integration in decision making." *Psychological Review* 111, no. 1 (2004) 67–79.

Wallace, C. *Susanna Wesley: The Complete Writings.* New York: Oxford University Press, 1997.

Walters, Orville S. "Concept of Attainment in John Wesley's Christian Perfection." *Methodist History* 10 (1972) 12–29.

Ward, Keith. *Defending the Soul.* Oxford: One World, 1992.

Watson, David L. *The Early Methodist Class Meeting: Its Origins and Significance.* Nashville, TN: Discipleship Resources, 1985.

Weaver, J. Denny. "Atonement for the Nonconstantinian Church." *Modern Theology* 6, no. 4 (1990) 307–23.

Welker, Michael "'We Live Deeper Than We Think': The Genius of Schleiermacher"s Earliest Ethics." *Theology Today* 56, no. 2 (1999) 169–79.

Wesley, John. "A Collection of Forms of Prayers, 'Prayer for Families'." In *The Works of the Rev. John Wesley, M.A.*, edited by Thomas Jackson. London: Wesleyan Methodist Book Room, 1872.

———. *The Works of John Wesley—Volume 1.* Kansas City, MO: Nazarene, 1958.

Westphal, Merold. "Postmodernism in Philosophy of Religion and Theology." *Perspectives* 15, no. 4 (2000) 6–10.

Wetzel, James. *Augustine and the Limits of Virtue.* New York: Cambridge University Press, 1992.

Whittaker, Edmund. *Space and Spirit: Theories of the Universe and Arguments for the Existence of God.* London: Nelson, 1946.

Wildman, Wesley J. "The Divine Action Project, 1988–2003." *Theology and Science* 2, no. 1 (2004) 32–75.

Wiles, Maurice. *God's Action in the World.* London: SCM, 1986.

Wilkinson, David, "The Activity of God in Methodist Perspective." In Marsh, Clive, Shier-Jones, Angela, & Wareing, Helen (eds.) *Unmasking Methodist Theology.* New York: Continuum, 2004) 142–54.

Willard, Dallas. "Spiritual Formation in Christ: A Perspective on What it is and How it Might be Done." Address delivered on 22 October 1993 at Fuller Theological Seminary in honour of the inauguration of seminary president Richard Mouw.

Wink, Walter, *Naming the Powers: The Language of Power in the New Testament.* Philadelphia, PA: Fortress, 1984.

Wispé, Lauren. "History of the Concept of Empathy." In *Empathy and It's Development*, edited by Nancy Eisenberg and Janet Strayer, 17–37. New York: Cambridge University Press, 1987.

Wood, Jacqueline N., "Social Cognition and the Prefrontal Cortex." *Behavioral and Cognitive Neuroscience Reviews* 2 no. 2 (2003) 97–114.

Wood, John A., *Christian Perfection as Taught by John Wesley*. Boston, Mass.: McDonald & Gill, 1885.

Wood, Laurence *The Challenge of Jesus: Rediscovering Who Jesus Was and Is*. Downers Grove, IL: InterVarsity, 1999.

Wright, N. T., *The Resurrection of the Son of God*. London: Society for Promoting Christian Knowledge, 2003.

———. "Wesley's Epistemology." *Wesleyan Theological Journal* 10 (1975) 48–59.

Yoder, John Howard, *The Politics of Jesus*. Grand Rapids, MI: Eerdmans, 1994.

———. *The Priestly Kingdom: Social Ethics as Gospel*. Notre Dame, IL: University of Notre Dame Press, 1985.

Zeleny, M., *Autopoiesis, Dissipative Structures, and Spontaneous Social Orders*. Boulder, Co.: Westview, 1980.

Zigler, Ronald Lee, "The Formation and Transformation of Moral Impulse." *Journal of Moral Education* 28 no. 4 (1999) 445–57.

Zinnbauer, Brian J., Pargament, Kenneth I., and Scott, Allie B. "The Emerging Meanings of Religiousness and Spirituality: Problems and Prospects." *Journal of Personality* 67 no. 6 (1999) 889–919.

Zizioulas, John D., *Being as Communion: Studies in Personhood and the Church*. Crestwood, NY: St. Vladimir's Seminary Press, 1997.

Index